# FICTION AND THE LAW

*Legal Discourse in Victorian
and Modernist Literature*

Law and literature have been two of the most powerful discourses in the construction of social reality. The relationship between the two has emerged as a vital new area of study, as literary representation has proved immensely influential in framing popular understanding of law. In *Fiction and the Law: Legal Discourse in Victorian and Modernist Literature*, Kieran Dolin examines the dialectical interplay between legal discourse and the novel in the century between Walter Scott and E. M. Forster, the period when the institution of the law was undergoing radical reform and the novel was at the peak of its cultural power. Dolin's comprehensive study argues that this cultural power is attributable in part to the novel's critical engagement with the law. His study draws on legal and literary theory to trace this important convergence of disciplines in a series of canonical Victorian and Modernist texts.

Kieran Dolin lectures in the Department of English, University of Western Australia. He has published articles in *Texas Studies in Literature and Language, Journal of Commonwealth Literature, and Law/Text/Culture*.

# FICTION AND THE LAW

*Legal Discourse in Victorian
and Modernist Literature*

KIERAN DOLIN

CAMBRIDGE
UNIVERSITY PRESS

PUBLISHED BY THE PRESS SYNDICATE OF THE UNIVERSITY OF CAMBRIDGE
The Pitt Building, Trumpington Street, Cambridge CB2 1RP, United Kingdom

CAMBRIDGE UNIVERSITY PRESS
The Edinburgh Building, Cambridge, CB2 2RU, UK http://www.cup.cam.ac.uk
40 West 20th Street, New York, NY 10011–4211, USA http://www.cup.org
10 Stamford Road, Oakleigh, Melbourne 3166, Australia

First published 1999

Printed in the United Kingdom at the University Press, Cambridge

Typeset in 11/12½pt Baskerville   [GC]

*A catalogue record for this book is available from the British Library*

*Library of Congress Cataloguing in Publication data*
Dolin, Kieran.
Fiction and the law : legal discourse in Victorian and modernist
literature / Kieran Dolin.
p.   cm.
Includes bibliographical references and index.
ISBN 0 521 62332 4 (alk. paper)
1. Legal stories, English—History and criticism.   2. English
fiction—19th century—History and criticism.   3. English
fiction—20th century—History and criticism.   4. Law and
literature—History—19th century.   5. Law and literature—
History—20th century.   6. Modernism (Literature)—Great Britain.
I. Title.
PR878.L43D65   1999
823′.809355—dc21   98–38602 CIP

ISBN 0 521 62332 4

# Contents

v

# Acknowledgments

The subject of this book reflects a personal decision to quit law for literary studies. In making that transition I have been helped by many people. I am deeply grateful to my mother and father for their unfailing encouragement. Tim Dolin has been brother, colleague and friend, and I have benefited immeasurably from his expertise, generosity and insight. In recent years Patrick, Michael and Anna Dolin have shown me new aspects of the pleasures of reading. My deepest debt is to my wife, Jane Courtney, whose love has sustained and inspirited me throughout.

The Department of English at the University of Western Australia has provided financial and administrative support as well as intellectual sustenance. I especially thank Hilary Fraser, Richard Freadman (now in Melbourne) and Bob White, who read earlier drafts and helped focus the argument as thesis supervisors, and whose continued advice and support has been vital. Daniel Brown, Ray Forsyth, Judith Johnston, Gail Jones, Andrew Lynch and Ken Rowley have made welcome suggestions. The staff of the University of Western Australia Library have been always efficient.

I record with pleasure the hospitality and helpfulness of Simon Petch, who offered constructive criticism on the thesis and shared his own work, and Richard Weisberg, who supplied resources from his archive. I have also profited from the comments of Rowland McMaster and Alexander Welsh, and the two anonymous readers for Cambridge University Press. I would like to thank my editor, Ray Ryan, for his support and professionalism.

Parts of this book draw on the following publications: "*Bleak House*: Chancery versus Equity," in *The Happy Couple: Law and Literature*, J. Neville Turner and Pamela Williams (eds) (Leichardt: Federation Press,

1994), pp. 71–80; "Sanctioned Irregularities: Martial Law in *Billy Budd, Sailor,*" *Law/Text/Culture,* 1 (1994), pp. 129–37; "Freedom, Uncertainty and Diversity: *A Passage to India* as a Critique of Imperialist Law," *Texas Studies in Literature and Language,* 36 (1994), pp. 328–52.

## CHAPTER ONE

# Narrative forms and normative worlds

Wilkie Collins's *The Woman in White* relates, at least according to its Preamble, a story of events that "might have claimed their share of the public attention in a Court of Justice," but which "is left to be told for the first time in this place." The pages of the novel are constructed as an alternative forum for an inquiry into a crime and a proclamation of right that cannot be pursued through the courts. The novel represents itself as an intervention in the public sphere, more particularly as a supplement to the law, going where it cannot go, but performing a similar function. Justice is the story's end, in both senses of that word; and it is a justice that restores the heroine to her rightful position in society, a justice that fulfils the law. Thus, while the Preamble acknowledges the limitations of the law, it also invokes the standards of legal proof in order to tell, and indeed to validate, its story:

the story here presented will be told by more than one pen, as the story of an offence against the laws is told in Court by more than one witness – with the same object, in both cases, to present the truth always in its most direct and most intelligible aspect; and to trace the course of one complete series of events, by making the persons who have been most closely connected with them, at each successive stage, relate their own experience word for word.[1]

The analogy between the process of the legal trial and the techniques and concerns of the English novel has often been remarked upon, most notably perhaps by Ian Watt in *The Rise of the Novel*: "The novel's mode of imitating reality may therefore be equally well summarized in terms of the procedures of another group of specialists in epistemology, the jury in a court of law. Their expectations and those of the novel reader coincide in many ways: both want to know 'all the particulars' of a given case . . . and they also expect the witnesses to tell the story 'in his own words.'"[2] For Watt, however, the analogy helps to ground the "formal realism" of the English novel, and Collins's deployment of an evidential model derived from the fiction of Defoe,

Richardson and Fielding, Watt's exemplars, only highlights the "sensational" story he has to unfold. The self-conscious legal framework seems
to function by conferring an effect of reality upon this romance.

The opening of *The Woman in White* introduces and exemplifies the
complex strands which connect the novel and the law during the nineteenth and early twentieth centuries, strands including an evidentiary
model of narration, a plot concerned with the commission and recti-
fication of crime and civil wrong, and the adoption of a critical tone
with respect to official agencies of law. The object of this study is to
explore such connections between fiction and law from Sir Walter
Scott to E. M. Forster.

Collins's Preamble is a particularly direct articulation of a widespread phenomenon, one certainly wider than the realist novel. As
M. M. Bakhtin observes in his discussion of the Greek Romance: "In
the subsequent history of the novel, the *criminal trial* – in its direct and
oblique forms – and legal-criminal categories in general have an enorm-
ous organizational significance."[3] In addition to noting that the law
has been a structural resource for the novel, Bakhtin proceeds, as part
of his quest for a "historical poetics,"[4] to posit a social function for
these formal incorporations: "The significance of legal-criminal categories in the novel, and the various ways they are used – as specific
forms for uncovering and making private life public – is an interesting
and important problem in the history of the novel." I approach the
exploration of this topic as a "problem" that involves socio-legal history as well as literary history: *The Woman in White* inherits and extends
a novelistic tradition, but its form and discourse can be further illu-
minated by a study of post-Romantic legal culture. How is it that
the canons of legal evidence come to govern the practice of fictional
storytelling? What is the cultural status of the law in Victorian England
that enables this conjunction? And what are the beliefs concerning
story and imaginative literature that inspire this ambition to follow
the law?

I

Historical studies of the relationship between law and literature in
earlier epochs of Western culture commonly begin by stressing the
modern separation of the two discourses. R. Howard Bloch introduces
his study, *Medieval French Literature and the Law*, as follows. The language
of literature:

has since the Renaissance become increasingly synonymous with a discourse emanating from and belonging to a personalized self: the product variously of inspiration, imagination, desire, neurosis, dream. The [language of the law] has, since the age of Montesquieu and Rousseau, come to represent the collective discourse governing relations between individuals or between individuals and the state. Where one stands as a vehicle for the expression of the private and the particular, the other serves as a mechanism for their regulation.[5]

For some cultural historians this separatism is a matter for implicit or explicit regret. Historians of the Scottish Enlightenment note with pride that a "republic of letters" existed in eighteenth-century Edinburgh, in which lawyers contributed through their writings to emerging theories of societal development.[6] This tradition is visible in Sir Walter Scott, the lawyer-novelist whose work begins the detailed studies of this book.

Another eighteenth-century society in which lawyers dominated the republic of letters and the general political culture was early Republican America. Robert A. Ferguson describes this "configuration of law and letters" and offers it as an example of an integrated culture: "To study this legacy is to retain the example for a modern culture in which the stark separation of intellect, art and politics should give every citizen pause."[7] Ferguson argues that this configuration declined under the influences of democracy and romantic individualism in the nineteenth century. However, Brook Thomas, in his study of the subsequent generation of American writers, argues that this paradigm-shift effected a different relationship between literature and law, rather than annulling it. Despite the separation of the professions, the law continued to contribute to the intellectual and political formation of writers, and, perhaps less affirmatively, to their imaginative and aesthetic concerns.[8] Thomas studies the ideology of law through the narrative constructions of cases and novels. Under this methodology, fictional narrative functions in the public sphere, contesting or supporting the dominant legal ideology.[9] Central to his methodology, and mine, is a dialectical understanding that novels can represent legal and alternative world-views and that the law itself can structure those literary representations. Both Ferguson and Thomas (whose differences are further explored in my reading of *Billy Budd*) situate literary texts in a cultural milieu dominated by law.

Hitherto obscured links between literature and law in the post-Enlightenment period are also revealed in Theodore Ziolkowski's *German Romanticism and its Institutions*. Noting that the major German Romantic writers were legal "insiders," – lawyers, court officials, legal scholars

– Ziolkowski shows how the great legal controversy over codification
and traditional law "embraced nearly every important theme of the
Romantic period,"[10] including nationalism, vernacularism and the conflict between aristocracy and bourgeoisie. Many of these themes are
taken up in my chapter on Scott, including his legal career. Many of
the writers here studied had juridical "connections," as legal journalists, law students, or bureaucrats. The course of the codification controversy in England can be viewed through the novels of Dickens,
Trollope and Forster. The historical studies by Thomas and Ziolkowski
alert us to the danger of reading the present discursive separatism back
on to nineteenth-century culture, and of adopting a critical methodology predicated on literary isolation.

It seems clear then, despite the apparent opposition of the discourses
of literature and law fostered by professional specialization, that a
contextualized study of the fictional representations and appropri-
ations of law, and of the institutions of writing and legal practice will
materially enhance our understanding of the nineteenth-century culture and its dominant genre, the novel. A significant sociological index
of the law-novel connection in Victorian England is an empirical study
by John Sutherland, which shows that in a sample of 676 Victorian
novelists, one in five was a lawyer. Of these, the largest number were
failed barristers. According to Sutherland's researches, writing appealed
as an alternative career, with journalism as a transitional stage between
law and fiction.[11] In this period the dual practice of literature and law
in the manner of Scott wanes, but lawyers turn to writing and writers
to law. Sutherland concludes that, "although it is a hard link to discern,
there is probably an affinity between the mentalities of jurisprudence
and Victorian fiction, shaped as both were by the study of individual
cases and the canons of (poetic) justice."[12] This suggestion, though
tentatively proposed, provides a succinct and defined point of entry for
this essay in integrated legal and literary history. In the next chapter I
shall attempt to provide an account of the developing "mentality" of
English law from the late eighteenth to the early twentieth centuries,
and thereafter demonstrate its many links with literary history through
the detailed readings of individual novels in subsequent chapters. For
the moment, *The Woman in White* may once again be adduced as an
exemplary text. Collins, who was himself called to the bar but never
practised law, concludes the novel with the return of Laura, Lady
Glyde, to her family home, and the public reiteration of the "case"
established by Walter Hartwright that her "death" was the fraudulent
conspiracy of her husband and Count Fosco. The sanction of legal

proof is given to his narrative by the family solicitor, "that my case was proved by the plainest evidence" (p. 638). The novel underwrites Laura and Walter's struggle for justice by dispensing death to Fosco and Sir Percival Glyde, and securing the inheritance of Limmeridge House to the Hartrights' infant son. Thus "the good end happily and the bad unhappily," in an epitome of the poetic justice mocked by Oscar Wilde in the 1890s. Wilde's insistence in *The Importance of Being Earnest* that such endings are definitive of "Fiction" alerts us to the diminishing confidence in the fulfilment of desires for justice, and to changing narrative forms and conventions late in Collins's century, which are traceable in certain contrasts between earlier writers, such as Scott and Dickens on the one hand, and later works by Conrad and Melville on the other.

II

The representation of the individual case and the emplotment of the operation of poetic justice are but two of the many possible points of convergence between law and novel. Sutherland's work prompts further investigations in intellectual history with an implied recommendation that these be linked to a study of the material conditions and institutions of literary production and legal practice. Accordingly, this book considers the circumstances of first publication, the writer as litigant, the lawyer as reviewer as well as novelist, and the journalism of novelists. Another line of enquiry is to explore modes of representation in law and fictional narrative. In an important work of intellectual history, Alexander Welsh's *Strong Representations: Narrative and Circumstantial Evidence in England* explores how changing notions of proof can be traced in the fields of theology, philosophy, literature and law resulting in an acceptance that "circumstances" possess evidential value superior or equal to personal testimony. While *The Woman in White* reminds us of novelists' enduring interest in testimonial narration, Welsh compellingly connects the development of a legal category of circumstantial evidence with that of third-person narrative point of view. In this way he extends and consolidates Ian Watt's perception (quoted on page 1) that the novel, like the jury, demands a "circumstantial view of life."[13]

It is notable that several recent studies locate eighteenth-century fiction in various juridical contexts. Lennard Davis revisits the "rise of the novel," situating the beginnings of the novel in the history of printing in the seventeenth century, especially its attempted regulation by law and its genres of prose narrative. Among these is a hybridized "news/novels discourse," popular crime narratives mingling factual and fictional elements. This is the field from which the novel emerges, with its claims to being "true history" and its fascination with criminal biography.[14] John Bender posits that the emergence of the penitentiary is imaginatively projected in novels by Fielding and Gay, and paintings by Hogarth, that ostensibly treat the old prison and punishment regime. These texts, he argues, are constructive: changes in forms of representation expose "the precariousness of the old prisons," and thereby serve as "a medium for culture emergence."[15] John P. Zomchick sees law and novels as part of the "collective consciousness" of eighteenth-century English society. He studies the "construction of the juridical subject within the eighteenth-century novel" and identifies a dialectical relationship between the private sphere of the family and the public domain of civil society. The ideological value of the domesticated space is asserted through endings of "secure and dignified retirement" from a "competitive and hostile public sphere" into a "family idyll." However, "in retreating . . . the protagonists do not simply leave the public sphere behind; rather they carry with them the principles that have enabled both survival and profit in that sphere."[16]

Taken together, these studies justify the thesis of David Punter's synoptic overview, that "Eighteenth-century fiction is obsessed with the law."[17] After examining the representation of lawyers, of legal language, of trials, and of prisons throughout the century, Punter concludes that, "In the later part of the eighteenth century the emphasis of the fiction moves substantially into the realm of private experience, and more specifically into the area of confrontation between private experience and the 'outside world,' often perceived as a single oppressive system."[18] (It is noteworthy that for both Punter and Zomchick, novelistic representations of law put the public/legal and private/literary discourses, which for Bloch are separate, into dialogue with each other.) Punter places this plot in the context of both the emergence of Gothic fiction and of the contemporary legal system's incapacity to adapt to social change. Thus, he proposes

a dialectical interchange between developments in legal and social history, and developments in forms of literary representation – both, of course, presumably referable back to the massive set of social and intellectual changes which we now think of in terms of the onset of romanticism.[19]

The most fertile source of studies of the dialectic between law and fiction in the post-Romantic era has been Michel Foucault's *Discipline and Punish*, due in large measure to its ground-breaking argument about the extent to which disciplinary techniques associated with the criminal law have ramified throughout modern society. The role of literature in this "policing" process has been investigated in D. A. Miller's *The Novel and the Police* and in Marie-Christine Leps' *Apprehending the Criminal*. Leps and others focus on connections between the development of criminology in the nineteenth century and the rise of the detective as a fictional hero in popular culture.[20] The rise of the prison and the eclipse of torture were accompanied by new theories of punishment, the circulation of which in literary, educational, religious and other discourses has been studied by John R. Reed and Alexander Pettit.[21] Practitioners of New Historicism have begun to trace the many ways in which nineteenth-century legal developments, especially in commercial law, have impinged on fictional representation. For example, Walter Benn Michaels demonstrates the embeddedness of Hawthorne's *The House of Seven Gables* in debates about title to land; and Brook Thomas studies the invention of privacy in James's *The Bostonians* and contemporary tort law, in an essay with broad implications for the understanding of subjectivity in capitalist society.[22] Thomas's work in *Cross-Examinations* and since shows that the relations between law and literature in America during this period are complex and mutually illuminating. That the situation in England is comparably rich is suggested by the work on criminality mentioned above, and in the studies of circumstantial evidence by Welsh and Roslyn Jolly.[23] Connections between legal and generic formations are posited by Franco Moretti in respect of the English *Bildungsroman*.[24] Moretti distinguishes the English and European *Bildungsromane* on the basis of plot, the former being characterized by a restitutive rather than revolutionary development for the hero. He contextualizes this difference by reference to the particularities of English constitutional history, especially its early bourgeois revolution and rule-of-law ideology, which create a "culture of justice." Welsh and Moretti examine continuities as well as changes across the Romantic divide, through eighteenth- and nineteenth-century texts. Already numerous, these studies underline the formative importance of law in nineteenth-century culture. They are all, in various ways, products of the "return to history" in literary criticism.[25] By following and drawing on the methodologies and insights of the critics here surveyed, I continue the critical project of reassessing the apparent discursive autonomy of law and literature in the modern West.

Such an interdisciplinary study could not take place without an existing disposition among both literary and legal scholars to look beyond the ramparts of their various formalisms, and contextualize their production of knowledge within wider social and political frameworks. Within literary studies, the significance of the legal context has been closely studied by feminist and postcolonial as well as new historicist critics.[26] The value of such approaches for this study of fictional representations of law is that they produce a sharpened awareness of the dialectical relationship between novelistic and other signifying practices, or in the words of the new historicist Stephen Greenblatt, of "the forms of power and the power of forms," and a methodological imperative to reconnect the political and the aesthetic realms.

Within the study of law, particularly in America, the Law and Literature movement has, since the 1970s, sought to reconnect its theoretical base and teaching practices with the humanities. This "movement" began with the recognition of a fundamental homology: "Law is associated with Literature from its inception as a formalized attempt to structure reality through language."[27] From this premise, language becomes an object of legal study, and legal constructions a source and analogue for literary ones. This rationale originally sponsored the study of legal representations in canonical literary texts and the stylistic and ethical analysis of judicial opinions, but the introduction of literary-critical concepts from a discipline that was itself undergoing the paradigm shift of post-structuralist and feminist critiques has inevitably broadened the field of convergence. The Law and Literature umbrella now covers a variety of projects, in which linguistic analysis is put to the service of a number of more politically-charged studies, including feminist jurisprudence, Critical Race Studies, Critical Legal Studies, and the theorization of legal interpretation. For many of its proponents, the integrated study is a cultural necessity, an attempt to overcome the professional isolation of legal education and, more ambitiously, to reconstitute the eighteenth-century ideal of a unified public culture. One of the movement's pioneers, James Boyd White, has argued through a series of books that law is primarily a language, an interpretative and rhetorical enterprise like literature. Through the rhetorical analysis of literary, legal, historical and philosophic texts, he aims to demonstrate that the writing and reading inherent in the law in a democracy constitutes a "culture of argument," a community open to the voice of the "other" as well as its powerful.[28] Similarly, Richard H. Weisberg argues that the Law and Literature movement generates a fusion of poetics and ethics, – a "poethics" – a new sensitivity to form and figurative language, and to the values inscribed therein, by legal writers and readers, enabling legal arguments and decisions that are rhetorically more powerful and attuned to the achievement of substantive justice.[29] A second consequence is the demand for a literary criticism that is reconnected to the exploration of social values. In Weisberg's critical practice, literary texts offer unique insights into the relation between law and justice, the self-understandings of lawyers and the position of minorities under the legal system.

Gary Minda correctly observes the "distinctively humanistic aspirations" of White and Weisberg, their concern with ethics, their ideal of an enriched humanity in contrast to the denuded functionalism of rational-scientific legal discourse, and their commitment to the Enlightenment project of emancipation through dialogue.[30] Ian Ward praises the primacy of the "educative" over the "political" ambition in Law and Literature in his lucid and wide-ranging review of this field. He believes that the "naked politicisation" of Critical Legal Studies shortened its use-by date within law schools, and that one of the merits of Law and Literature is that political analysis arises out of the interpretation of language.[31] Such suspicion of politics is not universally shared, even within the movement. The inscription of ideas about race, ethnicity or gender in legal texts binds questions of power to questions of meaning.[32] Indeed, the advocates of "narrative jurisprudence" argue that this literary form is specially suited to the articulation of minority positions within legal forums.[33] Simon Petch has also contrasted Law and Literature and CLS, but succinctly recognizes the politics of the original proponents of Law and Literature as "liberal rather than radical, . . . strictly non-subversive of legal institutions[,] . . . plea[ding] for compassion, sympathy, pluralism, and for the humanism of 'great fiction,' rather than a demand that social or legal structures be changed."[34] With the increasing diversity of the methodologies and topics in the field, the political implications have tended both to move to the surface and to spread across the spectrum from left to right. Although my study takes as its object the representation of law in novels, it is also alert to the interaction between law and other discourses and thereby attentive to the position of marginalized subjects within the literary texts.

No summary can comprehensively report on all the scholarly intersections between law and literature. I can only note in passing the linguistic and semiotic studies of legal language undertaken by Peter Goodrich and others. Goodrich's critiques of judicial rhetoric and of the "monological" mode of legal discourse have brought a welcome political inflection to the poetics of the law.[35] In Goodrich the neo-classical dream of a unified culture is replaced by a utopian projection of a dialogical society derived from the work of M. M. Bakhtin. A consistent omission from most commentaries on Law and Literature, owing perhaps to their legal provenance, is discussion of the cultural histories of the interrelation of the two disciplines in specific societies, as practised by Ferguson and Thomas, or Weisberg in his studies of legal rhetoric in Vichy France.[36] Though this seems to be the province of literary scholars (and I have treated it thus myself in this chapter), Weisberg's work shows that it is equally at home here. While institutional boundaries are capable of being crossed, some are still approached with respect in the interdisciplinary study of Law and Literature.

In the midst of this interdisciplinary endeavour, one irreducible difference between law and literature has often been reasserted: that legal interpretation cannot be assimilated to literary interpretation, because the production and reception of texts within the law takes place within a context of the systemic application of state-sanctioned force. Legal judgment has consequences in the world that are immediate and non-textual. In Robert M. Cover's stark phrasing:

We begin, then, not with what the judges say, but with what they do.
    The judges deal pain and death.
    That is not all they do. Perhaps that is not what they usually do. But they *do* deal death, and pain. From John Winthrop to Warren Burger, they have sat atop a pyramid of violence, dealing . . .[37]

Though strongly expressed, these words do not invalidate the law and literature enterprise, so much as mark the limit of a law-as-language perspective. This forceful, aphoristic prose unsettles the reader used to the abstractions of academic legal discourse and to the modern separation of the juridical and penal realms.[38] It is literally and metaphorically sensational. In breaking what Foucault calls "the seal of secrecy," it enacts a kind of discursive violence itself. It is a liminal text, poised between the two terms of its title, and its sensitization to physical pain is sharpened by Cover's negotiation with his earlier argument for the constructive power of language and literary form in law, in "*Nomos* and Narrative." The latter article, which integrates legal history and cultural theory, offers a powerful framework for studying the imbrication of fictional narrative and the law.

In "*Nomos* and Narrative" Cover postulates a profound dependence of law on narrative: "No set of legal institutions or prescriptions exists apart from the narratives that locate it and give it meaning. For every constitution there is an epic, for every decalogue a scripture."[39] Here he draws on the proposition advanced by Louis O. Mink, Hayden White and others that narrative is a fundamental way of making sense of reality, one employed in many disciplines' construction of knowledge.[40] He is also contextualizing law within a more general social function of world-making: law as "a distinctive way of imagining the real," as Clifford Geertz has put it; or law as "the quintessential form of the symbolic power of naming, that creates the things named, and creates social groups in particular," in Pierre Bourdieu's later sociological formulation. In drawing on Geertz's interpretative anthropology, Cover rejoins law "to the other great cultural formations of human life – morals, art, technology, science, religion" in the construction of social life.[41] Taken together, laws and their governing narratives constitute for Cover "a *nomos* – a normative universe . . . a world of right and wrong, of lawful and unlawful, of valid and void." Law as *nomos* encodes a society's meanings and values, ideals and norms in what Donald R. Kelley calls its "legal mythology."[42] Kelley and Cover both recognize that such worlds are "products of the juristic imagination."[43] Cover images the process of world-making as "a system of tension or bridge linking a concept of reality to an imagined alternative."[44]

Narrative is the means of embodying and apprehending the *nomos*:

the codes that relate our normative system to our social constructions of reality and to our visions of what the world might be are narrative. The very imposition of a normative force upon a state of affairs, real or imagined, is the act of creating narrative.

This argument rests on a recognition of various capacities of narrative form: to link abstract ideas to concrete circumstances; to represent or objectify in language both current and possible worlds; and to enable the representation of time and change. The narratologist Gerald Prince summarizes the metamorphic capacity of narrative in terms which echo Cover's notion of law as a bridge between reality and alternity:

through providing its own brand of order and coherence to (a possible) reality, it furnishes examples for its transformation or redefinition, and effects a mediation between the law of what is and the desire for what may be.[45]

In answer to the question, what are these narratives, Cover admits the "diffuse and unprivileged character of narrative in a modern world,"[46] and its corollary, the absence of a single universe of meaning in modern societies. He contrasts this with the ancient Hebrew legal society, whose legal precepts, narrative history and mythology were collated in the Bible. How does this thesis about the constitutive function of narrative apply in a world where the *nomos* is secular and pluralistic, where there is no comparable sacred narrative, and law is conceived primarily in terms of social control?

Cover addresses this problem by historical analysis, distinguishing between two aspects of *nomos*, the "paideic" or world-creating and the "imperial" or world-maintaining. The former predominated in ancient Israel while the Temple stood, he argues, the latter after its destruction. Together they co-exist in all normative worlds. One immediate benefit of this analysis is that it helps to identify the meaning components of contemporary society. This in turn may enable us to retrieve for narrative a function in the modern *nomos*. Cover's notion of *paideia* is derived from Werner Jaeger's account of the Greek educational ideal of inculcating and transmitting the whole culture. The concept of *imperium* derives from the Roman magistrate's writ, which conferred authority throughout an empire composed of numerous different cultures. A. M. Honoré offers a similar bipartite analysis, describing law as an arch combining violence (e.g. coercion and punishment) and education (e.g. socialization and the formation of consciousness).[47] If anything, the discourse of norms in Cover's use of "imperial" tends to undervalue the sense of political domination encoded in this word's current usage. Rather it emphasizes the ability to administer justice, assuming the perspective of the imperial centre rather than that of its subject peoples. Cover's *imperium* descends from Virgil's admonition to Rome:

> *tu regere imperio populos, Romane, memento,*
> *hae tibi erunt artes, pacique imponere morem,*
> *parcere subiectis et debellare superbos*

and its orientation is well captured in Robert Fitzgerald's translation,

> Roman, remember by your strength to rule
> Earth's peoples – for your arts are to be these:
> To pacify, to impose the rule of law,
> To spare the conquered, battle down the proud.[48]

Where the "paideic" experience is characterized by strong demands and "culture-specific designs" such as a common narrative and a strong sense of community, the "imperial" is characterized by liberal values that enable the co-existence of worlds in a civil society. It relies less on interpersonal commitments and common meanings than on the impartial application of norms. Yet it must possess enough "commonalities of meaning to make continued normative activity possible."[49] Although Cover insists that this is an analytic distinction and not a taxonomic description of types of community, it will be argued in the next chapter that the "imperial" values are historically dominant in the post-Enlightenment legal culture. Meanwhile, several questions remain. Does any narrative form dominate the secular and pluralistic imperium, or is explicit narrative the province of a predominantly paideic culture? And does Cover's conceptual apparatus commit him to the exclusive study of dominant narratives and hegemonic norms? As this last question affects the identities of possible storytellers and the range of narratives, I address it first.

Introducing a *Michigan Law Review* symposium on "legal narrative and its 'counterhegemonic' power," Kim Lane Scheppele analyses the use and effects of "we/they" discourse in the law. Her principal argument is that in legal processes and rhetoric "we" designates any group that consents to the law and whose self-believed stories about the world are invested with judicial approval, in consequence of which other groups with other versions of reality are constructed as outsiders, and their stories excluded.[50] One of her many examples is the opening of "*Nomos* and Narrative": "We inhabit a *nomos* . . ." Cover's magisterial tone, his use of the plural subject combined with a singular object, and the valuation of cultural authority implicit in his concept of *nomos*, all suggest that reverence for tradition rather than ideological critique is the goal of his narrative jurisprudence. Cover's "we" grounds legal meanings and commitments on a communitarian and not an individualist footing, distancing him from mainstream liberal theories of law.[51] Moreover, whilst drawing his concept and vocabulary from classical and Judaic sources, Cover proceeds to examine the "*nomos* and narrative" of a minority group, the brief of a Mennonite community which intervened in a Supreme Court case challenging the refusal of tax-exempt status to a denominational university.[52] The Mennonites invoked the constitutional guarantee of religious freedom, not in simply discursive or preceptual terms, but by locating that provision in a narrative of the community's history and ideals. Cover argues that through their intervention the Mennonites sought to maintain their own insular *nomos*, and, in a radically pluralist claim, that within the realm of meaning, "the Mennonite community creates law as fully as does the judge."[53] Normative communities are numerous in contemporary America, and all have their own law. To reserve this appellation for the state alone "confuses the status of interpretation with the status of political domination."[54]

Like Scheppele, Cover recognizes that courts act to limit this communal law-making, to suppress the multiplicity of voices claiming the sanction of the state for their visions. In this context, he understands civil disobedience as commitment to an alternative vision of *nomos*, which depends not only on meaning but on action. Thus he acknowledges the likelihood of political and social conflict, the experience of minorities that all voices are not listened to, and hence the limitations of a conversational model of law. Cover's model brings into focus the shifting relations between centre and margins in modern legal culture, through what Michael Ryan identifies as his "sense of how power is exercised through narrative and of how alternative narrative can disrupt that power either by undermining narrative itself or by generating new visions and alternate world constructions."[55] Thus, he opens up the space for the studies of counter-hegemonic narrative that Scheppele and others have pursued.

The Mennonite intervention was not fruitful, for the religious university was still denied tax-exemption, because it discriminated on racial grounds. Cover argues that the judgment does not adequately address the competing claims of the excluded race and the autonomous community: "the force of the Court's interpretation is very weak," adding little to the development of the *nomos*.[56] The finding in this case represents, it may be thought, the normal practice of courts, the institutional tendency to narrow the range of inquiry and restrict the grounds of decision as a means of "neutraliz[ing] the stakes" in the conflict.[57] Judges need not adopt this approach, as Cover's reference to the schools' desegregation case, *Brown v. Board of Education* (1954), or as the native title case in Australia, *Mabo v. Queensland (No. 2)* (1992), indicate. This conclusion highlights the idealist element in Cover's project, the overemphasis on meaning from which he retreated in "Violence and the Word." It also reveals an ambiguity in "the *nomos*," which shifts between the official legal system and the various normative worlds circulating in society. (This shift in effect creates the space for the conflict between hegemonic and dissenting voices, between tradition and innovation.) In this, as perhaps in most cases, the minority narrative is rejected from any normative conversation. To find such expressions of "alternity" or to realize his idea of a "radical relativization of law," Cover directs our attention to the "general domain of sacred texts" rather than to the law reports. In a subsequent article, "The Folktales of Justice: Tales of Jurisdiction," he identifies some of the narratives through which the tradition of judicial independence has emerged and preserved itself. He there argues that "the claim to a 'law' is a claim as well to an understanding of a literature and a tradition."[58] The contents of the canon vary with each interpretive community, and the "sacred stories" may, it seems, be secular ones: "the text might be two tablets, or the infinity of Borges' library of Babel."

Cover's insights into the social constructivism of law and the working therein of narrative and power provide a framework for understanding the interfusion of law and novel in the nineteenth and early twentieth centuries. Brook Thomas draws on the general linkage of "*nomos* and narrative" to begin his "cross-examinations" of the legal and literary stories of ante-bellum America. The canon of literary fictions inscribes aspects of the *nomos*, "in a much more obvious way than law, reveal[ing] the stories a culture tells about itself."[59] Whilst the range of sources for these narratives is potentially vast, it is significant that Thomas bases his interpretation of this legal culture on novels and novellas, because the novel emerged as the pre-eminent narrative form during the period covered by his study and mine.

The inter-relation between the modern *nomos* as conceived by Cover and the rise of the novel is not accidental. Bakhtin argues in "Epic and Novel" that there is a structural affinity between this genre and the modern world:

The novel has become the leading hero in the drama of literary development of our time because it best of all reflects the tendencies of a new world still in the making; it is after all the only genre born of this world and in total affinity with it.[60]

Bakhtin identifies this common tendency as "polyglossia." The novel has a "multi-languaged consciousness" and structures its images in a "zone of maximal contact with the present ... in all its open-endedness."[61] These formal attributes depend on:

a very specific rupture in the history of European civilization: its emergence from a socially isolated and culturally deaf semi-patriarchal society, and its entrance into international and interlingual contacts and relationships . . . The world becomes polyglot once and for all and irreversibly. The period of national languages, coexisting but closed and deaf to each other, comes to an end. Languages throw light on each other: one language can after all see itself only in light of another language. . . . [T]here is no more peaceful co-existence between territorial dialects, social dialects and jargons, literary language, generic languages within literary language, epochs in language, and so forth.

Although this epoch is not precisely dated, the novel is historically related to the emergence of the nation-state and international trade in Europe since the Renaissance.[62] While this account seriously undervalues the extent and persistence of patriarchal power, its central recognition of the "inter-illumination" of various, contending languages and dialects within modern society and its analysis of the novel's openness to and registration of the polyglot world are persuasive. Bakhtin's vision of "heteroglossia" or "the social diversity of speech types" within a language, and of the dialogic relation between them, is itself a construct which bridges linguistic observation and an ideological commitment to plurality. With its blend of description and evaluation, it is readily translatable into normative terms: for example, Cates Baldridge in *The Dialogics of Dissent in the English Novel*, applies Bakhtin's term to modern democracy: "the liberal state is characterized by its 'heteroglossia'."[63] Baldridge's Bakhtinian reading of Victorian (and earlier) novels emphasizes that this linguistic analysis is politically charged: "This task necessarily throws [the novel] into the midst of political conflict, for the various discourses thus depicted are never *merely* private or personal . . . Rather, they are always the individual embodiments of ideological differences and political disputes."[64] Thus, the novel's dialogism forces a recognition of the diversity of, and more importantly, the conflict between various discourses, and undermines the authoritative claims of any one of them. Bakhtin's theory provides a means whereby contemporary readers may identify and recover subordinate voices and marginalized discourses in canonical texts. Accordingly, Cover's "radical relativization of law" may be nowhere more clearly observed than in novels.

Moreover, Bakhtin's contrastive account of the worlds of epic and novel is more pointedly commensurate with Cover's distinction between paideic and imperial tendencies in *nomos*. The epic world, that of "the national heroic past," with its source in the national tradition parallels the *paideia*, while the novel, with its core in "personal experience and free creative imagination," accords with the plurality of the *imperial*.[65]

The novel, then, is the modern descendant of Cover's "sacred narratives," or, structurally speaking, the equivalent among symbolic forms to the epic in ancient societies. This is stressed by Lukács in *The Theory of the Novel*: "The novel is the epic of an age in which the extensive totality of life is no longer given, in which the immanence of meaning in life is no longer given, yet which still thinks in terms of totality."[66] With its implicit contrast between totality and multiplicity, immanence and constructedness, the given and the desired, this formulation also offers an articulation of meaningful forms of social life and narrative fiction in a context of historical change.

## IV

My aim in this study is to particularize this synthesis of novelistic form and normative world, to trace in detail the relations between fiction and law in Anglophone societies in the nineteenth and early twentieth centuries. Many of the novels here studied evidence an awareness that the world has expanded: writing in the aftermath of the Act of Union, Scott seeks to mediate Scottish customs for the English; Dickens employs heteroglossia in order to propose connections between the many classes and groups in Victorian London; Melville writes the hidden life of a sailor in the Year of Mutinies, juxtaposing order and revolution; and both Conrad and Forster submit their protagonists to confrontations with otherness in Asia.

Contemporary writers on the novel recognized that the genre developed with the society, becoming, in the words of an anonymous critic in the *Prospective Review*, "the modern Epos," the new narrative form of cultural self-understanding:

We accordingly find that as society expands to a consideration of its vital interests the province of fiction expands; it becomes the chosen medium for the discussion of the vexed and difficult questions, moral, religious, social and political, which agitate the minds of men; and the various theories adopted for their solution endeavour to obtain a hearing, by assuming an imaginative expression and embodying themselves in a concrete form.[67]

For this critic writing in 1853, the novel has become a symbolic *agora* or marketplace where "the various theories . . . endeavour to obtain a hearing." The latter phrase implies that competition in the economic sphere carries over into the ideological and especially into the fictional zones. This recasting of the novel in terms of the dominant discourses of the nineteenth century highlights its openness to the present and represents an investment in its growing cultural significance, a consignment of social concern to the imaginary shores of fictional worlds. It was this forum, as Harry Levin observed, that extended the "literary franchise" to the middle classes and then the proletariat.[68] More recent criticism, written from an oppositional stance, has taught us an alertness to the voices that remain excluded from this fictive democracy, to groups that are spoken about, rather than speaking themselves. The Bakhtinian overtones of the *Prospective Review* article, while considerable, are limited by its liberal vision of equality in the marketplace of public debate. In representing law, nineteenth-century novels often foreground its social inequity: Wilkie Collins, for example, calls it "the pre-engaged servant of the long purse" in opening *The Woman in White*. Consequently, in the novels to be studied here, legal discourse is represented among many other language strata, and placed in dialogue with other public and private, authoritative and alternative discourses. The effect of this incorporation and juxtaposition is not only to enable critiques of the law, but also to embody in narrative form the competing visions of *nomos*.

Implicit in the trope of the novel as a marketplace of ideas is the necessity of buyers as well as sellers. As Janice Carlisle has demonstrated, by the middle of the nineteenth century novelists were peculiarly conscious of a responsibility to their audience. The treatment of controversial social concerns is undertaken with a dialogical sensitivity to the expectations and needs of readers. Carlisle views "the bonds of reading" less as a constraint than as a moral and aesthetic challenge to find the rhetorical means of enlarging the sympathies. Accordingly, the development of omniscient narration, the use of analogy, the awareness of focalization are formal experiments in the creation of consensus. Not only is community "the predominant subject of Victorian fiction," Carlisle argues, but its end and means as well.[69] By virtue of its readerly orientation as well as its heteroglossia, the novel is adapted to the formation of normative worlds. Carlisle's thesis is of particular interest to the study of novelistic representations of law, as the latter's power to punish through exclusion and confinement can be viewed both as maintaining the identity of moral community and as conflicting with any formal commitment to inclusiveness. This tension is visible in a wide range of novels studied by Alexander Pettit, where the various claims of "community," and changing attitudes to punishment, issue in a socially challenging notion of "sympathetic criminality."[70]

The material conditions of novel-reading in the nineteenth century – especially the dominance of serial publication – kept the plural and contradictory social world before readers. Linda Hughes and Michael Lund describe the culture of serialization as one of worldly rather than textual immersion. "It was not possible to enter into an imaginary world and remain there until the story's end; instead, readers repeatedly were forced to set aside a continuing story and resume everyday life." When they did read, "signs of the outer world were a part of a reader's text. Novels issued in separate monthly parts were framed by advertisements . . . [I]n addition they were surrounded by other stories – political, historical, scientific – on neighbouring pages."[71] In this mode of production, novels representing the law were intervening in current controversies and were working to ground the "imaginary world" of justice in "everyday life."

My study of the fictional production of *nomos* focuses especially on the legal trial, in which the "endeavour to obtain a hearing" is formally undertaken, and in which some resolution to the conflicting visions of reality represented by different characters and their actions and languages is attempted. The trial is, as W. Wolfgang Holdheim has argued, a "hermeneutic mode," and the "dialectic of this process of understanding and interpretation is effectively dramatized by the conflict between a prosecutor and a defender."[72] Moreover, the framing of a legal trial within a larger narrative operates to highlight the special interpretive assumptions and processes of the law. The common "interpretive urge" of law and novel is revealed, but so too is the possibility of variation between legal and other interpretations. On this basis, novelistic structure and discourse become the means of critiquing the law. A recurrent feature of the fictional trial, as I shall demonstrate, is the paradox of legal injustice: the presumption of child murder in *The Heart of Midlothian*; the waste and death engendered by Chancery in *Bleak House*; the acquittal of the guilty Lady Mason in *Orley Farm*; and the execution of the innocent Billy Budd. In this respect, the authority of the law is undermined. However, this conclusion is by no means necessary or complete. Legal procedure provides such an influential model of reality-construction in the modern West that fictional critiques of the law are often unable to escape its forms and its rhetoric: among other examples to be discussed, *The Heart of Midlothian* reconstitutes the notion of witnessing, *Bleak House* draws on the tradition of equity to critique the Court of Chancery, and *Orley*

*Farm* criticizes the ethics of common law advocacy, but its narrator pleads to his readers on behalf of the heroine.

To read canonical fiction through this critical conjunction of narrative form and normative world, then, is to encounter a dialectic of social affirmation and critique in the literary text. This structure derives, I shall argue, from the compromise between tradition and innovation introduced into the Anglo-American *nomos* by the reform movement, and is visible in all the texts to be studied. While its repetition is significant, as evidence of the imaginative pressure exerted by legal and alternative values on novelists, the manifestations of the structure are even more interesting. The "interanimation" of juridical and literary discourses has effects on the representation of subjectivity, on the inscription of space and on plot. The extent to which the interaction of fiction and the law from Scott to Forster can be composed into a single movement from affirmation to critique is the ultimate question for this book. We can begin to answer it by exploring the leading developments in nineteenth-century Anglo-American legal history. Accordingly, chapter two presents an outline of the modern *nomos*.

# *The modern Western* nomos

The study of fictional representations of law demands a contextual criticism. In this chapter I attempt to establish this context for the subsequent analysis of my chosen novels by presenting a short account of the intellectual and social history of European law since the eighteenth century. The ultimate aim is not to supply a mere background for critical analysis, but to enable the novels themselves to be read as texts in the cultural history of the modern *nomos*. For Cover, every normative world is specific to the culture which gives birth to it. The "thickness of legal meaning" in every society must be comprehended before its juridical practices can be properly understood.[1] In the following essay in the "thick description" of modern, Western law I aim to establish what Dominick LaCapra calls a "viable interaction between the forms of literature and forms of life" in the post-Enlightenment era and to establish some specific connections between these developments and formal and thematic changes in the novel's treatment of law.[2]

I

*The "noble pile" under attack*

There is no more paideic paragraph in English legal writing than the conclusion to Sir William Blackstone's *Commentaries on the Laws of England* (1765–9). Here Blackstone articulates a "Whig interpretation" of the development of English law, in which its "fundamental maxims and rules . . . have been and are everyday improving, and are now fraught with the accumulated wisdom of the ages."[3] This normative perfection emerges from an historical narrative which plots a double movement of evolving improvement and gradual reclamation of the ancient freedoms of "our British and Saxon ancestors." Daniel J. Boorstin's argument that in Blackstone's hands the law becomes "at once a conservative and a mysterious science" is borne out by this complex progress towards past glory.[4] Diachrony is suspended as the author conceives of the law as a single structure, as "a constitution so wisely contrived, so strongly raised, and so highly finished, it is hard to speak with that praise which is justly and severely it's [sic] due." The troping of space and site is an important resource of normative language in both literature and history, a means of symbolizing the right and might of the *nomos* which will be traced throughout the following chapters of this study. Blackstone exploits this trope, constructing the law as a "noble pile" whilst purporting "to examine it's solid foundation, to mark out it's extensive plan, . . . to demonstrate the elegant proportion of the whole." The common law is thereby presented not as a set of rules, but as a normative tradition, a crystallization of custom, combining "the noble monuments of ancient simplicity and the curious refinements of modern art." Blackstone finally exhorts his students and readers to share his commitment to this *nomos*, to see themselves as having their being in the mythic time-scheme of the common law:

The protection of THE LIBERTY OF BRITAIN is a duty which they owe to themselves, who enjoy it; to their ancestors, who transmitted it down; and to their posterity, who will claim at their hands this, the best birthright, and noblest inheritance of mankind.

The power of Blackstone's rhetoric, and of the ideology of English law and liberty, is attested to by the speed with which his *Commentaries* came to be accepted as the classic exposition of its subject. Michael Meehan points to its place in the English social imagination when he calls the work "one of the great pre-Romantic texts."[5] What I have called Blackstone's plot of the reclamation of right finds literary expression in the English *Bildungsroman*, which, Franco Moretti argues, is a symbolic form generated by what he calls England's "culture of justice." Moretti contrasts the characteristic plots of English and Continental *Bildungsromane*, finding that the latter are plots of transformation while the former are conservative, ending with the restitution of right.[6] Moretti's phrase, "the culture of justice," provides a usefully compendious characterization of the English *nomos*, within which homologous legal and novelistic forms were generated.

This vision of the English *nomos* was about to be challenged, however, by various manifestations of what Northrop Frye has called the "myth of freedom," most notably by the democratic inspiration of the French Revolution with its rhetoric of natural human rights, and by philosophical critiques based in rationalism and utilitarianism.[7] I shall examine these developments in more detail during the course of this chapter. At this point, I shall exemplify the challenge by reference to one of Blackstone's students, Jeremy Bentham.

Bentham not only heard Blackstone's Oxford lectures, but read and re-read them in published form. Two of his own works, *Comment on the Commentaries* and *A Fragment on Government*, offer fundamental and detailed criticisms of Blackstone's conservative approach to law. Legal historians have recently revised our understanding of Bentham's relationship with Blackstone's text, noting his deep engagement with it. Michael Lobban points to an underlying similarity: "Bentham's Pannomion was a natural successor to Blackstone, and . . . the conception of law as a unity that both men held stood outside the common law view."[8] Whilst Blackstone's search for common law principles enabled Bentham's project, it did so by negation. The narrative presented by Blackstone was to Bentham "the Romance of our Jurisprudence, rather than the History," and its effect was to "varnish," rather than to pull off "the mask of the law."[9] This iconoclastic attitude to both the common law and its most famous living exponent attracted some interest when the *Fragment* was published in 1776, but not enough to warrant a second edition until 1823. By that time, Bentham's views on the inadequacy of the law and the need for reform had influential support in Parliament. In a Preface intended for the second edition he recapitulated his opposition to the *Commentaries*, using the same figure as Blackstone. His object is,

the pointing attention to the imperfections which even at that time of day [1776] were seen swarming in the frame of government, and to the rickettiness of its only foundations, in which, on the ground of argument it had ever found support. No such imperfection having place but what brought profit, in some shape or other, to those among whom power was shared, – their interest of course was, that the same imperfections should, in their whole mass, remain forever unremoved, and therefore be, at all times, as little as possible in view.[10]

Bentham presents himself as the enemy of mystification and reaction in the law, the positivistic analyst of "imperfections" in the law. His own jurisprudence was based on a single, but far-reaching, premise, the "principle of utility," which becomes the basis for evaluation of laws, procedures, moral problems, and systems of government:

the Fragment . . . may be seen setting up . . . the greatest happiness of the greatest number in the character of the proper, and only proper and defensible, end of government; as the only standard, by which any apt judgment could be formed, on the propriety of any measure, or the conduct of any person, occupied in making opposition or giving support to it.

Bentham's rhetoric eschews the formal eloquence of Blackstone in favour of a plain style in which repetition is the sign not of decoration, but of insistence ("only proper . . . end," "only standard;" "any judgment," "any measure," "any person"). If there is an effect of dogmatism in this assertive, crowded prose, it is qualified by an underlying sense that the constitution of the *nomos* is open to debate and to question. These possibilities are virtually closed off in Blackstone's schema. Equally, Bentham's project is as potentially creative as destructive, for it is sustained by a faith in the power of reason not only to detect the flaws in traditional arrangements, but to build a good society from sound first principles.

With what may be called their contrasting "traditionalism" and "modernism," Blackstone and Bentham stand as representative figures at the head of this historical survey of developments in the modern European *nomos*. They embody the English equivalent of the conflict between customary law and codification traced in Germany by Ziolkowski.[11] The interaction between these two impulses, fidelity to an inherited culture and the desire for radical change, had various effects in the philosophy and the practice of law, and in the normative response to such economic and political developments as industrialism and imperialism, which will be explored in this chapter.

II

*Cultural particularism and natural law*

The notion that human societies develop highly distinctive cultures and that such societies with their diverse cultures are susceptible of systematic study first emerged in the eighteenth century. An important intellectual tradition, which places law in a wider and less dogmatic cultural frame than Blackstone, may be traced from Montesquieu's *The Spirit of the Laws* through such writers of the Scottish Enlightenment as Hutcheson, Kames and Adam Smith to Sir Walter Scott. This school sought to explain variations in law and other social phenomena by reference to the complex of geographic, economic, religious and political systems of the society in question. Law was *nomos*: culturally specific and historically evolving. Further it compared societies and sought to formulate principles of social evolution. Scott's development of the historical novel is directly related to his education in this tradition. The interaction between it and the romance plots dominant in his fiction will be studied in detail in the chapter on *The Heart of Midlothian*. Scott is also the inheritor of a tradition of the lawyer as *littérateur*: many of the eighteenth-century Scottish writers were lawyers. As in England and France a "republic of letters" existed,

a society in which the historians, both of the Enlightenment and of the early Romantic period . . . had mingled freely and shared common experiences and aspirations with novelists, poets, philosophers, political thinkers, economists, scientists and statesmen.[12]

Bentham affords an example of this intermingling through his correspondence with Voltaire, and his translation of the latter's tale, "The White Bull."[13]

In "Narrative Form as a Cognitive Instrument" Louis O. Mink investigates a paradigm shift in conceptions of history often attributed to the rise of sociology, but which he argues derives from Romanticism.

Universal History did not deny the great diversity of human events, customs and institutions; but did regard this variety as the permutation of a single and unchanging set of human capacities and possibilities.[14]

Mink argues that Romanticism provided the initial, implicit revaluation of Universal History through its emphasis on the "uniqueness, vividness and intrinsic value of individuals, whether of individual persons, individual culture or individual epochs." Romanticism enabled the upsurge of a new historical consciousness, which is reflected in the championing of folk culture, in a fascination with the lives of great men, and the rewriting of national histories. It will readily be seen that the folk and nationalistic interests are central to the literary achievement of Sir Walter Scott. Conrad, too, demonstrates this inheritance in his emphasis on the storytelling and the solidarity of "men of the sea." However, this communal element co-exists with Romanticism's underlying individualism, which will be shown to have a longer-lasting effect on later novelists.

Universal History depended on a belief in the uniformity of human nature. Its equivalent in jurisprudence – in preconception as in declining influence – was "natural law." This theory of law is essentially aprioristic: law is either the divine order and accessible to reason, or, in the rationalistic theories of Grotius and Pufendorf, it is the order of nature, "the necessary relations arising from the nature of things." The latter is a quote from Montesquieu, but he dispenses with natural law in one page and focuses the rest of his study on actual laws in actual societies.[15] Natural law jurisprudence had always acknowledged the existence of "positive law" or the law promulgated and in force in society, but had distinguished this from its deductions about the law of nature, which was universal and unchanging. As the study of society increased, positive law and juridical practice became the basis for a more scientific approach to theorizing about law. Not only did actual laws become primary objects of study, but it became difficult to reconcile universalism with the emerging evidence of cultural diversity. Two approaches to the philosophy of law emerged in response to this difficulty: "legal positivism," the theory that law consists only in the command of a sovereign authority; and the German school of historical jurisprudence, which saw in the history of a nation's laws the operation of the *Volksgeist* or spirit of the people. Their rivalry dominated jurisprudence in the nineteenth century, but even then, remnants of natural law thinking survived. During the previous century it had been the most important theory, providing the philosophical underpinning for Blackstone's account of the accumulating perfection of the common law. Bentham's criticisms, by contrast, were derived from positivist premises. However, natural law thinking led not only to the justification of the *status quo*. Its continental adherents included Voltaire and Diderot. As Cassirer argues, it was central to Enlightenment thought and ultimately provided the philosophical basis for political change.[16] Speculation as to the content of law in the state of nature led political thinkers to a belief in the existence of inalienable human rights. If the positive law of the state denied these rights, it had no claim to obedience. The American and French Revolutions, with their resounding declarations of liberty and equality, are lasting political monuments to this jurisprudence. In England a blend of naturalist and positivist theories was successfully invoked by those charged in the Treason Trials of 1794.[17]

III

*Law and romantic individualism*

In a significant complication in cultural history the Romantic movement, which scorned rationalism in general, found in natural law an instrument of social critique. This applies not only to such supporters of the French Revolution as Godwin, Wordsworth, and Shelley, but also to the American Romantics of the mid-nineteenth century. Robert A. Ferguson has argued that Emerson, Thoreau, and Melville deployed natural law thinking against the social order sanctioned by the newer, positivistic jurisprudence.[18] As will be outlined in chapter six, Melville's *Billy Budd* has been read as an allegory of the clash between the two systems of jurisprudence. For Robert M. Cover, and Charles Reich, the execution of Billy represents the tragic outcome of a strict application of the Code and the exclusion of any consideration of personal justice. Cover sees Melville's novella as a commentary on the inadequacy of legal positivism, especially on the judicial formalism to which it gave rise in the nineteenth century.[19] These interpretations of *Billy Budd* are imbued with an exalted respect for the individual will and a radical commitment to social reform characteristic of their era of production, the late 1960s. In their sympathy for the "criminal" and critique of the system of law, they are latter-day Romantics, celebrating the Handsome Sailor for his uniqueness, and lamenting the inadequacy of the law's categories of judgment to deal justly with him. During this century literary texts repeatedly construct an opposition between individuality and a legal philosophy which stresses the letter at the expense of the spirit of the law, which excludes questions of moral value from its enquiry and which makes no exception on individual grounds for persons covered by the terms of the law. The legal historian John T. Noonan examines the effects of "depersonalization" in several American cases from the latter nineteenth and earlier twentieth centuries. He attributes this trend to the ideal of a scientific praxis developed by legal positivism and its successor, legal realism. Noonan concludes that by systematically abstracting the individual litigant into a "slave" or "contractor" or other anonymous legal entity, these schools promoted the legalization of such immoral practices as slavery and the corrupt monopolization of industry through trusts.[20] Cover presents *Billy Budd* as a literary exploration of the course taken by nineteenth-century American judges who overrode their personal antislavery opinions and returned runaway slaves to their owners pursuant to the Fugitive Slave Act.

Post-Romantic novelists, with their enduring interest in individual psychology and moral development, have remained largely unsympathetic to law, to its enforcement of public standards, its empiricism, its rationality and categorization. In chapter four I demonstrate

how Dickens seeks to reinstate the individual person in *Bleak House*
by invoking the ancient notion of equity, itself the product of
classical natural-law thinking, as an alternative to legalism. In the
following chapter the contradictions between a conservative attachment to the traditions of English law and an aesthetic centred upon
fully-rounded individual characters is explored through Trollope's
*Orley Farm*.

Yet, as Foucault and others have noted, the notion of justice dominant in the modern "episteme" incorporates such Enlightenment ideals
as fixed and known laws, as impartiality and universal application, as
rational systems of evidence, and penalties graduated according to the
gravity of offences. These ideals are homologous to Cover's "imperial"
virtues. Co-existing in modern society with the Romantic mistrust of
legalism, therefore, is an endorsement of part of the normative basis of
law. Such pluralism is for Cover definitive of the modern *nomos*. While
the Romantic movement may have originated in a reaction against
Enlightenment rationalism, it is possible to trace in the nineteenth-
and twentieth-century history of the West the lasting effects of both
movements. The consequent interaction between literary and legal
cultures is therefore a complex of compatible and contradictory influences: the Romantic endorsement of the self meets the liberal concept
of the autonomous legal subject, rational, responsible, and bearer of
rights; the emergence of an existential morality meets an inherited
system of normative categories, known rules and general sanctions.
No simple binary opposition between literary culture and law can be
sustained. Legal discourse, despite its privileged social location and
relative autonomy, could not avoid contact with the developing discourses of the individual. Franco Moretti, following Weber, notes that
"Modern law is directed against the agent, not against the action. It
enquires into subjective 'guilt.'"[21] Moreover, as Martin Wiener and
others have shown, the individual criminal becomes subject to new
quasi-legal knowledges.[22] It has been postulated that Romanticism's
major effect on criminal justice was in the recognition of a criminal defence of insanity, traceable to the acceptance that some individuals may not be responsible for their actions.[23] Some sense of the
gradual acceptance of this view during the nineteenth century will be
gleaned by contrasting the centrality and sympathy accorded to characters in mental extremity by the narrators of *Heart of Midlothian* and
*Billy Budd*.

IV

## The reform movement

One of the major expressions of the Enlightenment in the field of law is the reform movement usually associated with the name of Bentham. In this movement philosophical critique sought translation into political and social action. Bentham's Utilitarian principle, "the greatest happiness of the greatest number," was of continental origin, deriving from Beccaria's *Of Crimes and Punishments* (1764). The major aim of the reformers, as I have anticipated, was to sweep away traditional, usually Roman or customary, legal systems and replace them with modern, rational, comprehensive codes. The two *exempla* with which Foucault begins *Discipline and Punish*, the narrative of the public execution of Damiens, the regicide, in 1757 and the timetable of the young offenders' prison in 1837, demonstrate the difference between the old and the new systems most graphically. Although Foucault's interest is in punishment, he recognizes that this eighty-year period saw "a new theory of law and crime, a new moral or political justification of the right to punish; old laws were abolished, old customs died out."[24] The French *Code Napoléon* is perhaps the best-known of the "modern" codes, but the movement refashioned the European legal landscape in the late eighteenth and early nineteenth centuries, achieving codification in Prussia (1780), Tuscany (1786), and Austria (1788), as well as France.

Bentham and his followers failed to attain this goal in England, such was the hegemony of the common law. While Bentham wished for a code of the entire law, draft codes for the criminal law were placed before Parliament after exhaustive enquiries into the operation of the criminal justice system, but were rejected upon lobbying by the judges and senior members of the profession. Nevertheless, the inadequacy of the "evolved" law was manifest from the first decades of the century. Reform was pursued through a variety of related strategies: following Beccarian principles, conformity to the law was sought not through the "severity" of punishment, but through its "certainty," and hanging was accordingly replaced by imprisonment; a new professional Police Force was established first in London by the Metropolitan Police Act (1827), and then throughout the country with a view to protecting property and maintaining order in a time of political turbulence; and, finally, laws to consolidate and amend the criminal law, rather than to begin afresh with a code, were passed.[25]

Another area of law in need of reform was the organization and procedure of the civil courts. Once again, enquiries and legislation attempted to reduce the delays, cost, and formal technicality of the inherited common law and equity systems. As I shall demonstrate in chapter four, Dickens actively intervened in the reform of Chancery, not only through his journalism, but through the satire and symbolism of *Bleak House*. His novel was begun in the same year as one of the Chancery Procedure Acts (1851). Simon Petch has shown that the reform of equity, culminating in its "fusion" with common law under the Judicature Acts of 1873 and 1875, entailed philosophical as well as practical considerations. Chancery, with its origins in the conscience of the monarch, depended on natural law theory in a predominantly positivistic age. The "law of nature" was a site of intense debate ramifying beyond legal controversy into the writings of Tennyson, Darwin, George Eliot and F. D. Maurice.[26]

Changing social and economic conditions were another source of legal change. Industrial production and the resulting urban agglomeration created crises in public health, in work safety, in the exploitation of children, and in the relief of poverty. New laws were needed, and new administrative measures proposed to deal with these problems, among them the New Poor Law of 1834 and the Factories Acts of 1833, 1844 and 1847. It is worth noting here that the impulse for reform came not only from the Benthamites, but from Evangelical Christianity, as in the case of the factories campaign led by Shaftesbury.

The history of reform is a history of contention, of campaigns for and against, of protest at injustice and resistance by vested interests. The refashioning of the *nomos* was an intensely political process. This was nowhere more visible than in respect of the legal status of women, which for many legislators was of minor importance. Laws for the reform of custody, divorce and property were enacted piecemeal and slowly. A major step on this long road, the Married Women's Property Act (1882), established the right of married women to acquire and sell property in their own right. Enactment of substantially new, as well as reformist, legislation became the dominant mode of law-making and has remained so. In a convulsive series of Acts, Parliament itself was reformed by the gradual extension of the franchise in 1832, 1867 and 1884. Female suffrage was finally granted in 1918 to women over 30, a qualification abolished in 1930. Democracy based on universal adult voting was therefore slowly achieved, but its replacement of an oligarchical polity in England and elsewhere is perhaps the most distinctive feature and fundamental principle of the modern Western *nomos*.

While the reform movement has not completely renovated the legal system or cured all its inherited defects of cost and delay, it has enhanced both the sovereignty of Parliament as the ultimate legislative authority and the appeal of positivist theories of law. An active and representative legislature has come to seem the most legitimate mode of law-making in modern Western political culture. One effect of this legislative creativity has been the invention of new juristic entities, whether fictional (companies) or social (pensioner, student, worker). David Sugarman argues that because of the law's power in the formation of consciousness, these legal categories have been important in the development of social identity.[27] It is worth noting here that much of this legislative activity has itself been subject to change, either to remedy defects which become apparent or because the original enactment is perceived by its opponents as partisan and is repealed when they gain political office. Law has, that is to say, become "instrumental," a means of consciously achieving particular social goals.[28] Underlying the changing landscape of legal controversy, Brian Simpson argues, a fundamental shift has occurred in the function of law: "Law has come to be regarded as an instrument of social improvement and not simply the expression of a just regulation of life within a society whose leading characteristics are given."[29]

I have thus far focused on Parliamentary legislation as the chief vehicle of legal and social reform. The justification for treating this aspect of modern normative transformation in such detail is that social injustice became a major source of and motivation for fictional plotting in the nineteenth century. As Patrick Brantlinger and others have shown, numerous Victorian novelists used the form to bring social abuses to light and convince readers of the need for reform.[30] Such writers both imbibed and helped to spread the "spirit of reform," creating a wider audience for reformist ideas and adding an affective dimension to the intellectual and religious mainsprings of social improvement. Many fictional representations of the law in this age of review were actuated by reformist sentiment. In this respect they, like the various Acts of Parliament, exemplify the governing narrative of this *nomos* in process. The "Newgate novels" of Bulwer-Lytton, Ainsworth, and others, and the attacks on matrimonial and lunacy laws in Charles Reade's *Griffith Gaunt* and *Hard Cash* some thirty years later evidence the longevity of the reformist impulse in fiction. The

career of Dickens virtually spans the period, and as the most committed and subtle novelist working in the field, his work is dealt with in
the first of two chapters on this interaction.

While these writers are often credited with inspiring legal reform,
they were also subject to criticism by conservatives, especially on the
grounds of their failure to conform to canons of realism. Literary
conflicts, such as those between barrister-critics like Fitzjames Stephen
and reform-minded novelists, and between radical and conservative
writers of fiction like Dickens and Trollope are aesthetic versions of
larger political conflicts. As Brantlinger has argued, a commitment
to realism entailed for Trollope a commitment to the English Constitution.[31] To represent the conservative side in this debate I have
chosen to examine Anthony Trollope's *Orley Farm*, which attacks reformism as being prone to idealistic fantasy, and places the movement in
the context of a long, realistic, but not uncritical, account of a trial.
Trollope's Blackstonian views are put into the mouth of a character in
*The Eustace Diamonds*, who suggests that the common law is wiser than
those who would improve her. This novel generates its plot from the
question of whether common law principles are capable of adaptation
to new, problematic situations. The traditional law showed itself will-
ing in some areas to develop doctrines that would support changes
taking place in society. To one of these I now turn.

v

*Law and economy: freedom of contract*

Dickens's paternalistic interest in the protection of the weak, his highlighting of systemic inequalities in *Bleak House* and elsewhere, was at
odds with an important current of English legal development, namely
the rise of freedom of contract. His attack in *Hard Times* on Utilitarianism and *laissez-faire* economics is well known. The equitable values
he espouses in *Bleak House* had, from Lord Eldon's Chancellorship
onwards, been progressively retracted from the Chancery jurisdiction,
and equity's influence on contract law weakened. In particular, Chancery's doctrine that a contract not based on a "fair exchange" would
be set aside was replaced by the non-interventionist "freedom of contract."[32] In the nineteenth-century common law courts, *laissez-faire* economics enabled the law of contract to be modelled on the rule of the
marketplace, which was believed to be a "natural" system.

There is, as Walter E. Houghton and P. S. Atiyah have noted, a significant strain in Victorian attitudes which bases dogmatism in social thought on the postulation of quasi-scientific "laws."[33] Social Darwinism is the best example of this process, wherein biological evolution is applied to human societies and used to justify numerous political policies from the colonization of Africa to different education systems for different social classes. Theories of the evolution of law became popular in the later nineteenth century, the most influential text being Sir Henry Maine's *Ancient Law* (1861). One of the laws proposed by Maine from his research on ancient societies was the gradual replacement of the legal recognition of relationships and obligations based on "status" by legal recognition of "contract," of relationships created by the will of individuals. Freedom of contract could thus be justified as an inevitable part of social progress.[34]

The doctrine assumed the equality of the bargaining parties and the sanctity of their bargain: they were said to contract "at arms' length" and without responsibility for each other; they were free to set their own terms and the court would not interfere other than to interpret and order its performance. This was an area of rapid growth in legal doctrine, for the contract was "instrumental" in consolidating and supporting the emerging industrial capitalism.[35] However, Atiyah argues that the dominance of this doctrine declined in England after the 1870s, when the 1867 Reform Bill set the stage for a democratic polity in which political attention began to be paid to such social needs as housing, sanitation and transport created by the urban overcrowding of people attracted to work and live in the new industrial centres and to underlying social and economic inequality. Atiyah, following the somewhat simplistic formulation of the Victorian jurist A. V. Dicey, calls the resultant movement "collectivism" because it saw the establishment of public welfare programmes like old-age pensions and universal education, the (not uncontested) rise of trade unionism, and an increased government involvement in economic and other social fields.

If the common law courts gave general support to the needs of the emerging capitalist economy, the prevailing literary response was sympathetic to the collectivist reaction. From *Past and Present* (1843) to *Little Dorrit* (1855) to *The Way We Live Now* (1874), novelists and historians looked darkly on the "Gospel of Mammonism" and questioned how the new wealth benefited the community. In their objection to economic individualism they sought redemption through community, constructing narratives which looked back to medieval practices, or forged

networks of friendship and charity in the impersonal city, or valorized
rural society. Perhaps the most haunting fictional commentary on the
theme of contract and other social bonds is Melville's *Bartleby*. Set in a
Wall Street law office, it defamiliarizes labour in a market economy
through its protagonist's baffling double refusal of work and the sack.
Bartleby's "'I would prefer not to,'" has been interpreted by Brook
Thomas and Walter Benn Michaels as, respectively, a sign of resistance to and participation in this contractarian ideology.[36]

Accordingly, stories of agreement and breach were derived mainly
from the contractual relations of marriage and to a lesser extent employment. In general, contract between entrepreneurs plays a remark-
ably small part in English narrative fiction of the period, especially
when contrasted with the omnipresent theme of inheritance. The persistence of inheritance plots in an era of industrial and urban expansion is indicative not only of the political strength of the landed classes,
but of their ideological power.[37] The latter is strongly evident in the
desire of successful middle-class professional, commercial and industrial families to acquire land and its social prestige. Such is the history
of the Mason family in *Orley Farm*. Both this novel and *Bleak House* are
concerned with wills and the disputed succession to property, but both
incorporate industrial or commercial elements in ways suggestive of
either hegemonic contest or hegemonic anxiety. The introduction
of "iron" into the country serves to expose tensions in both novels:
Mr. Rouncewell the Ironmaster offers an energetic contrast to the lan-
guid Sir Leicester in a local version of bourgeois accession to power;
while the bargaining over Kantwise's iron furniture is a bitter Ruskinian
comedy of modern debasement. The introduction of this subplot by
Trollope in a story of the problematics of primogeniture suggests that
the new forms of economic life were impinging on the old in ways that
could not be ignored by a "professional" novelist who valued the landed
tradition. The Victorian novel both expresses and explores these contradictions in contemporary visions of the *nomos*.

VI

*The rule of law*

It has been suggested that the dominant discourse of the seventeenth
century was religion, that of the eighteenth century was law, and that
of the nineteenth economics.[38] While this view is an extremely long

one, it is of interest here because of the central place occupied by law. Replacing this model of univocal progression with a heteroglossic one, the voice of law may be also traced in the religious and economic eras. The concept of "the rule of law" emerges in the seventeenth century and achieves one of its most influential formulations in the nineteenth century, as well as being a characteristic and highly significant doctrine in eighteenth-century England. This continuity alone ensures its importance for a history of legal culture. Indeed, it is arguable that the history of the emerging idea of the supremacy of law becomes the fundamental narrative of the modern *nomos*, underlying all the developments so far discussed in this chapter.

As E. P. Thompson shows in his famous conclusion to *Whigs and Hunters*, "the rule of law" was formulated in support of the Parliament's campaign against monarchical absolutism.[39] It began life as a partisan idea and became an entrenched constitutional doctrine with the Civil War and Restoration. Thompson and the authors of *Albion's Fatal Tree* argue that during the following century Walpole and the ruling Whig aristocrats began to use legislation systematically to implement and maintain their own sectional interests. Together with a flood of statutes – including the "Bloody Code" of over two hundred capital offences – they promoted the rule of law as an ideology system, to consolidate and mask their own ascendancy. Three aspects, identified by Douglas Hay as majesty, justice and mercy, were emphasized, by deploying ritualized displays of judicial power, rhetorical assertions of the impartiality and universal application of the laws, and widespread use of the royal prerogative of mercy.[40] While Hay views law as a virtually invincible hegemony, Thompson shows how Whig ideology and political actions faced organized resistance – both violence and appeals to older common law rights – from the "Blacks."[41] He concludes that the rule of law cannot be regarded as a merely ideological concept, that the Whigs did not fill a vacant conceptual space with their enactments, but entered a field already cultivated with customary rights, with "common" land, and with judicial traditions of impartiality and independence from government, and of the strict interpretation of statutes abrogating common law rights. The political will had to contend with the autonomous, inherited standards of the common law, which Blackstone had so recently and so magisterially expounded. Judges to whom the rule of law was a vocational commitment and not a political mask freed persons charged on insufficient evidence or defective indictments and even, occasionally, hanged aristocratic criminals. The rule of law, then, did not merely pretend to govern the rulers as well as the ruled; it sometimes succeeded! Had it not done so, Thompson points out crucially, it would have failed as ideology. The result was that the ideology acquired a life of its own, entering the English political consciousness and creating what Moretti calls a "culture of justice."

The mythology of the rule of law, by which I mean the belief system, has had a long life. It first migrated to America along with the common law. Robert A. Ferguson argues that Blackstone's interpretation of the Glorious Revolution as a victory of law over tyranny and of the recovery of lost liberties provided the *legal* justification for the American Revolution. Ferguson crystallizes the American reception of the rule of law through Tom Paine's 1776 statement, "In America the law is king."[42] Brook Thomas continues the American genealogy of this mythology in his discussion of *Billy Budd*. He argues that Melville puts into question the rule of law (Thomas calls it "rule by law," presumably to signal his own questioning of it) through the dubious legalism of Captain Vere.[43] This important argument will be examined in chapter six, along with Melville's more direct and less ambivalent advertisement for law against power in *White-Jacket*.

Shortly before Melville began *Billy Budd*, one of Blackstone's successors as Vinerian Professor of English Law at Oxford, A. V. Dicey, presented the rule of law as a fundamental principle of the English Constitution. He argued for its tripartite meaning:

in the first place, the absolute and fundamental supremacy . . . of regular law as opposed to the influence of arbitrary power, and exclud[ing] the existence of arbitrariness, of prerogative, or even of wide discretionary authority on the part of the government . . .
It means, again, equality before the law, or the equal subjection of all classes to the ordinary law of the land administered by the ordinary courts; the "rule of law" in this sense excludes the idea of any exemption of officials from the duty of obedience to the law which governs other citizens or from the jurisdiction of the ordinary tribunals; there can with us be nothing corresponding to the "administrative law" (*droit administratif*) . . . of France . . .
The "rule of law," lastly, may be used as a formula for expressing the fact that with us the law of the constitution . . . [is] not the source, but the consequence of the rights of individuals . . .[44]

Dicey's ideas, though controversial, had great influence both educationally and politically,[45] and they remain the best-known nineteenth-century articulation of the subject. Even when originally delivered, however, they did not comprehend the amount of legislative and bureaucratic activity generated in the modern state and their unqualified terms provided a distorted picture of its legal and administrative practice, particularly with reference to the discretionary power of administrators and administrative law generally. This legislative expansion has been called "rule through law," rather than "rule of law."[46] In addition, other European legal systems did develop similar doctrines, especially *la prééminence du droit* in France and the *Rechtsstaat* (or Law-State) in Germany.[47] Nonetheless, Foucault's genealogy of the regime of the norm in *Discipline and Punish* helps us to establish the crucial ideological importance of Dicey's ideas in a liberal democracy. Indeed, David Sugarman has argued that in the period 1850–1907 jurists like Dicey and Maine, whose *Ancient Law* was a best-seller, were "conceptive ideologists," elevating the profile of legal ideas in the culture: "juristic categories were a vital ingredient of the educated person's conception of state, society and politics."[48] At the end of this period, two of Galsworthy's plays, *The Silver Box* (1906) and *Justice* (1910), invoke the Diceyan principle of equality before the law, and their popular and critical success attests to the truth of Sugarman's claim. The rule of law is a fundamental concept in the history of this *nomos*, and together with the other developments discussed here justifies Oliver MacDonagh's description of the Victorians as "a people of the Law."[49]

E. P. Thompson argues that the expansion of power in the twentieth century means that the rule of law remains an ideal worth upholding. He suggests that notions of the regulation of power by law and the reconciliation of conflict through law represent a substantial cultural achievement, the influence of which can be traced in such modern movements as the campaigns for Indian independence led by Gandhi and Nehru. The failure of the British to uphold the requirements of the rule of law during the Amritsar massacre and its aftermath was a crucial factor in Gandhi's decision to advocate and practise civil disobedience, but his campaign rested as much on "homespun" Indian norms as on imported British ones. The problematic relationship between English law and Indian culture is explored in *A Passage to India*. In chapter eight I examine Forster's attempts to imagine a dialogue between these two normative worlds. Forster is highly critical of the British abandonment of the liberal conception of the rule of law and the resort to authoritarian power in India. His novel had a measurable effect on the British perception of India and its demand for independence.

The importance of narrative to the rule of law is demonstrable not only in particular novels, but in the mythic and historical accounts of actual cases. One of the "folk-tales of justice" retold by Robert Cover is of Lord Chief Justice Coke in *Fuller's Case* asserting his jurisdiction against the wishes of King James I. Cover points out that Coke's self-serving report of this encounter in *Proclamations del Roy* is idealized, but that later generations of readers found the principle of judicial independence which he articulated through this story to be a compelling norm: the myth became the law.[50]

From the late eighteenth century anthologies of legal trials became a popular literary genre. The most famous example was the French *Causes Célèbres* begun in 1773 by Nicholas-Toussaint Lemoyne Desessarts, which eventually numbered 180 volumes. It was reprinted throughout the succeeding century, and its example inspired the English to imitation. The telling of the stories of the Porteous Riots and of the Deans sisters in Scott's *Heart of Midlothian* emerges from a proposal for a *Causes Célèbres of Caledonia*.[51] An English anthology, *Celebrated Trials*, was edited in 1825 by George Borrow, his first major literary project after abandoning his solicitor's training. His epigraph from Edmund Burke shows that a combination of psychological and paideic considerations underlay the collection.

The annals of criminal jurisprudence exhibit human nature in a variety of positions, at once the most striking, interesting, and affecting. They represent the tragedies of real life, often heightened in their effect by the grossness of the injustice and the malignity of the prejudices which accompanied them. At the same time, real culprits, as original characters, stand forward on the canvas of humanity as prominent objects for our special study. [52]

The study of criminal psychology was a special interest of Joseph Conrad as well as of the Newgate novelists. That this could easily degenerate into prurience is illustrated by the collections of Peter Burke published a generation later: his *Celebrated Trials connected with the Aristocracy in their Private Relations* (1849) draws on his own knowledge gained as a divorce barrister, while his *Romance of the Forum* (1852) follows Scott in asserting the imaginative pleasures of the *cause célèbre*. If the narrative motivation here seems illicit, the tragedy of injustice and prejudice endows some of the anthologies with a normative function. Moreover, all such stories bring law into juxtaposition with its other, whether viewed as crime, scandal, madness, or rebellion, and thereby test the boundaries of the *nomos*. Certain such collections seem intended to entrench the authority of the law in the public memory. Lord Birkenhead, the former

Lord Chancellor, wrote two popular books which were soon reissued in an omnibus volume, *Famous Trials* in 1926. Its anonymous preface complacently fuses legal and literary forms in the representation of authorized norms of subjectivity: "As lawyer, as craftsman in words and as student of human nature, Lord Birkenhead is equally master of his materials."[53] The "celebrated trial" has continued to attract writers such as Truman Capote, Diana Trilling and John Bryson to new reflections on the quest for justice through law in modern society.[54]

The struggle between law and power finds its most significant expression in a sub-genre of modern narrative, running from Koestler's *Darkness at Noon* to the novels of Primo Levi and the prison memoirs of Timmerman, Breytenbach and others. These are predicated on the hope uttered by Godwin's Caleb Williams in the formative era of the rule of law: "I will tell a tale -! The justice of the country shall hear me."[55] In this context the imprisonment of Godwin and his fellow eighteenth-century radicals reminds us that throughout the period under review legal ideals have been opposed by what Foucault has called "the will to power," freedom of expression has been opposed by censorship, and heteroglossic dialogue by state-sponsored monologue. It is important to recognize the material and political constraints upon narration, including the existence of categories of forbidden utterance within the supreme law, namely libel, sedition and blasphemy. The decline of the last two categories and the more recent relaxation of systems of censorship suggest an equally important, if hard won, expansion of freedom of expression, the predominance of what Cover would call an "imperial" *nomos*.

If the literary effect of this reformation of the "justice of the country" is an increased and more varied repertoire of stories, has there been a homologous positive effect on the law? No comprehensive analysis of changes in substantive law is possible here, but the history of a single principle offers evidence of a correspondence between legal and literary narrative practice. I refer to the *audi alteram partem* rule, literally translatable as "hear the other side," but often rendered as "the right to be heard." One of the two principles of "natural justice" known to English law, it can be traced to Roman law through Seneca. According to its modern usage, no-one may be deprived of any right without being offered the opportunity to address the court or tribunal making the decision. During the nineteenth century this rule was firmly established and extended beyond courts proper to "every body of persons invested with authority to adjudicate upon matters involving civil

consequences to individuals."[56] What is primarily expanded here is the
number of "bodies" required to listen to both sides, but the corollary is
an increase in the range and number of citizens having a right to tell
their stories in the legal forum. A corresponding development in the
law of evidence was the gradual repeal of the rule that parties to a case
were not competent to testify in their own cause.[57]

We cannot uncritically infer from these developments that the
stories of all socially subordinate groups were thereby "heard" at law.
For example, Victorian fiction and memoirs show the material and
ideological barriers to communication faced by female witnesses in the
public space of the courtroom.[58] The adversary system and the rules of
*locus standi* favoured the individual over the class claimant, and limited
the types of injury or interest that could claim protection. In this
context the novel continued to tell stories that the law deemed inadmissible. Nonetheless, these extensions of the "right to speak" fit into
the changing constitutional configuration of Victorian England, with
its gradual enlargement of the franchise, its policy of reform through
legislation, and its anxiety that such legislation should not undermine
the rule of law. In this context Harry Levin's metaphor of the literary
"enfranchisement" of the middle and working classes is particularly
apt, for it connects literary and legal representation, and suggests that
any dialogical form in the fiction of the period has a nomic, a legal-
cultural, as well as a linguistic basis.

VII

*Twentieth-century challenges*

Thompson's argument that the rule of law remains a valuable ideal in
this century of the expansion of power implicitly acknowledges that
law's "supremacy" is under threat. That Dicey's values should appeal
so strongly to a socialist historian is in itself noteworthy, for Dicey
regarded socialism, or (to use his preferred term) "collectivism" as
inimical to the rule of law. In his *Lectures on the Relation of Law and Public
Opinion in England in the Nineteenth Century* collectivism is the dominant
principle in "legislative opinion" after 1865, succeeding Blackstonian
"old Toryism" and "Benthamism or Individualism." Its influence is
redoubled in the period 1900–1912, which Dicey surveys in the long
"Introduction to the Second Edition" of 1913. Here, what purports to
be a neutral description of a movement in law and society is on close

reading a catalogue of sober warnings about the expanding role of government and the potential transformation of society. In this analysis individualism is not just one historical movement, but the fundamental constant in "the course of English history."[59]

Dicey's attempt to trace parallels between law and other sites of opinion, such as theology and literature, makes his work a valuable text in the *nomos* which I have been attempting to sketch. More recent historians have, however, presented the developments he notes in broader, and cooler, terms. I have already foreshadowed how the vastly increased volume of legislative and executive activity is, according to A. W. B. Simpson, indicative of a changed conception of law, in which it functions as an "instrument of social improvement":

a conception of law according to which its function was thought to be the achievement of individual justice – giving to each man his due – has come to seem quite inadequate in a society which employs law to pursue a more extended list of social and individual values. Today we value rule through law rather than the essentially static conception of the rule of law.[60]

In an analogous argument drawing on sociological theory Kamenka and Tay connect the rule of law to nineteenth-century individualism and to the emergence of a *Gesellschaft* type of social organization. The latter entails "not an organic merger or fusion, but a rational coming together for ends that remain individual."[61] Its common sphere is exemplified by the commercial contract. The Diceyan rule of law was predicated on a horizontal or egalitarian relationship between individuals with a small, defined role for the state. The twentieth-century phenomenon of central planning and rationalist development of policy for the economy and society cannot be adequately understood through the *Gesellschaft* model, so Kamenka and Tay draw on Weber's "bureaucratic-administrative" ideal type to describe the socially instrumental conception of law. It draws attention to "the socio-technical norm . . . the regulations required to alter consciously a society and its ways of living."[62] Though their origin is different, these terms are strongly reminiscent of Foucault's analysis of the modern approach to social control that he calls "discipline." Perhaps because of its legal genealogy, Kamenka and Tay's argument retains a humanistic concern within its recognition of an impersonal discourse of power: the bureaucratic-administrative model's "presupposition and concern is neither an organic human community nor an atomic individual [but] a non-human ruling interest, public policy, or ongoing activity of which

human beings are subordinates, functionaries or carriers." In suggesting that this development is an altered condition of law rather than a
"breaking-free" into an altogether new formation of power, this analysis departs from Foucault's.[63] Racial discrimination legislation, and
administrative rulings thereon, such as were challenged in the *Bob
Jones University* case discussed by Cover, are a good example of this
legal ideal type.

Of equal interest to this study of *nomos* is the sociologists' representation of community, their location of distinct legal systems in particular
types of social organization. Cover's "paideic" normative world has
much in common with the *Gemeinschaft* and with Durkheim's notion
of "social solidarity."[64] The pioneer sociologists – Durkheim, Marx,
Tonnies, Weber – wrote out of their own historical experience of industrial change, and the concepts they developed, especially "alienation"
and "anomie," are instinct with loss and longing. It is not surprising
that their analyses often led them into political polemic and action: just
as English critics from Carlyle to Ruskin built a conservative politics
out of medievalist ideals, so socialism beckoned Marx, Morris, and
Tonnies as the way of reintegration; and even the Weimar democracy
found its sociologist-supporter in Weber.

As Donald R. Kelley has shown, these theorists took many of their
basic concepts from jurisprudence, but they moved steadily away from
the exposition of the law towards social-scientific forms of analysis such
as sociology and political economy. A critical spirit was nurtured in
these disciplines which aimed to demystify rather than to transmit the
legal heritage, and came to view law, in Kelley's words, as "the locus
classicus of 'ideology' and juridical false consciousness."[65] Such critiques, which aim not only for enlightenment, but for emancipation,
appeared in a number of disciplines in the late nineteenth century, and
their common approach to interpretation has been elucidated by Paul
Ricoeur as a "hermeneutic of suspicion." Ricoeur unites Marx, Freud
and Nietzsche under this umbrella, emphasizing their rigorous questioning of authority. Nietzsche offers an image of this attitude to the
legal tradition: Zarathustra sitting on the mountain, "surrounded by
broken old tablets and new tablets half covered with writing."[66] In a
well-known metaphor the rejection of the old norms (and faith) is
compared to sailing the high seas. Nietzsche revels in "the great fight,
the great looking-around, the great sickness, the great nausea," urging
courage: "stormier than the great sea, storms our great longing" to
discover the new world, "our children's land," the new values.

Whilst the Mosaic tablets remain a potent visual symbol of law, their significance in the English context may be doubted owing to the severing of law from divine justice in positivistic legal theory. James Fitzjames Stephen, however, invokes this symbolism in his *History of the Criminal Law in England* (1883). Here he describes his projected Criminal Code as "an expansion of the second table of the Ten Commandments."[67] Its moral force remains unaffected by the prevalence of "doubt" and the multiplication of belief systems in contemporary society: the criminal law "represents nothing less than the deliberate measured judgement of the English nation" on crimes and punishments. Stephen responds to the breakdown of the English Christian *nomos* by an authoritarian overriding of free thought and epistemological crisis, by asserting law as force, when he urges resort to "unquestionable, indisputable sanction as clear, and strong, and emphatic, as words and acts can make it."[68] Stephen's code never passed into law, and although criminal sanctions remained in the common law and statute books, the gaps he tried to foreclose – between individual and society, between young and old, between word and act – began increasingly to be recognized. In the writings of his niece, Virginia Woolf, and of her contemporaries, doubts about the Victorian normative order are radical and irrepressible. D. H. Lawrence exemplifies the Nietzschean quest for transvaluation in his desire to go beyond law through vitalism: "If man would but *keep* whole, integral, everything could be left at that. There would be no need for laws and governments; agreement would be spontaneous."[69] For Bertrand Russell, anarchism and socialism provide the way forward:

[g]overnment and law will still exist in our community, but both will be reduced to a minimum. There will still be acts which will be forbidden, for example, murder. But very nearly the whole of that part of the criminal law which deals with property will have become obsolete.... Those who nevertheless still do commit crimes will not be blamed or regarded as wicked: they will be regarded as unfortunate and kept in some kind of mental hospital until it is thought they are no longer a danger. By education and freedom and the abolition of private capital the number of crimes can be made extremely small.[70]

In Russell's innocent and idealistic replacement of the court by the hospital, and moral discourse by social-scientific discourse, may be traced the outline of an emerging bureaucratic regime of the norm.

Richard Weisberg argues that the earliest mediation of Nietzsche's ideas on "legality" was in the novel. He points not to the breaking of the old tablets of the law, but to its virtual opposite, Nietzsche's high valuation of the Jewish belief in justice through written law. He quotes from *The Genealogy of Morals* Nietzsche's argument that the establishment of a code is an assertion of the righteousness of the strong against the *"ressentiment"* of the weak, and the further claim that during the nineteenth century the ressentient many had begun to undermine the law, to *"mime* justice" in the service of their own vindictiveness.[71] No historical instance is given in support of this thesis, and in the light of the present survey of nineteenth-century changes in law, especially of the felt needs addressed by "reform" and "collectivism," it is hard to avoid the conclusion that it is authoritarian and anti-democratic. Nonetheless, Weisberg's exploration of a "structure of negativity" in novels by Dostoevski, Melville and Camus, wherein a "creative verbalizer" (who is usually a lawyer) manipulates the legal system to deny justice to a spontaneous, integrated "man of action," provides ample literary evidence of this *ressentiment* through law. Nietzsche's writings can be read, it would seem, in two quite contradictory ways, one celebrating the normative confidence of the codifiers and the other intimating the collapse of traditional values. These antithetical propositions are symptomatic of the commitment to irreconcilable dualities of freedom and order, critique and faith, in modernity. The dramatic potential of the resultant crisis in the modern Western *nomos* is highlighted when legal values are imposed on non-Western peoples through the "civilizing mission" of imperialism. In *Lord Jim* and *A Passage to India* the Orient becomes a stage on which the shallow ideals and fragile certitudes of the West are played out with pessimistic clarity. In these texts the value of the rule of law is asserted while its efficacy is doubted.

The achievement of justice through traditional legal processes has remained an embattled ideal in twentieth-century Western culture. Its paideic resilience was unexpectedly, and perhaps even ironically, illustrated when the aged Bertrand Russell, together with Jean-Paul Sartre, sought to reconvene the International War Crimes Tribunal during the Vietnam War, to invoke the forms of legality to condemn the American conduct of the war. His attempt to control power through law was not successful.[72]

## CHAPTER THREE

# *True testimony and the foundation of* nomos – The Heart of Midlothian

Sir Walter Scott combined writing with a career in the law, as an Advocate of the Scottish Bar, as Sheriff-Depute of Selkirkshire and as a Clerk of the Court of Session. His dual career arose out of the culture of eighteenth- and nineteenth-century Edinburgh, a dominant aspect of which was the interrelated practice of the discourses of law and literature. An account of this interdiscourse will serve as the context for a reading of the representation of law in *The Heart of Midlothian* (1818). Significantly, as the first in this sequence of studies, it is a novel of the foundation of *nomos*, one in which the establishment of a single family in peace and prosperity functions as a figure for the expulsion of disorder and the creation of a state of supremacy of law in Scotland. The advent of a recognizably modern normative world is announced by the critique of an archaic, punitive and formalistic law relating to child murder. The "rule of law" is represented as emerging from the experience of rebellion, madness and crime. *The Heart of Midlothian* therefore offers a complex narrative of the law in history and the law as ideal.

I

In his *Life of Lord Jeffrey* (1852), Henry Cockburn wrote that the Scottish legal profession's "higher practice has always been combined with literature, which indeed is the hereditary fashion of the profession. Its cultivation is encouraged by the best and most accessible library in this country, which belongs to the bar."[1] Cockburn was a younger contemporary and political opponent of Scott, a judge and a contributor to *The Edinburgh Review*, of which Jeffrey was the founding editor from 1802 to 1829. The motto of the journal was distinctly judicial: *Judex damnatur, cum nocens absolvitur* (the judge is damned when the guilty is absolved). As Ina Ferris points out, the success of the *Review* entailed a reconfiguration of the relation between criticism and society, the former coming to occupy "less the space of conversation and exchange between equals . . . than a judicial space of judgment and discipline."[2] Another lawyer associated with the founding of the *Review* was the reformer, Henry Brougham.[3] Scott contributed to its early numbers until political differences became apparent. Despite these, Tories and Whigs alike inherited and extended a tradition of combining legal and literary pursuits. The judge and philosopher Lord Kames may be taken as the exemplary figure for this tradition in the eighteenth century. In addition to *Elements of Criticism* (1762) he published *Essays upon . . . British Antiquities* (1747), *Essays on the History of Property and of the Criminal Law* (1760) and various compilations of decisions of the Court of Session. These writings place him at the centre of the Scottish Enlightenment, but he was only one of several lawyers who contributed to its study of human society. The methodology of this movement was historicist. As Donald R. Kelley notes, "Kames nourished the hope of tracing the 'progress of manners, of laws, of arts from their birth,' . . . perhaps with the help of 'hints from the poets and historians.'"[4] In consequence, law came to be understood not as a self-sufficient collection of rules, but "as the product of particular political, cultural and social forces existing and developing over time" in society.[5] In its turn, literature embraced essays, history and biography as well as poetry, drama and romance. Closely allied with rhetoric, literature was conceived as instructing the individual and contributing to the understanding and therefore the development of society. In Hugh Blair's *Lectures on Rhetoric and Belles Lettres* (1783), history is treated first among the genres.

The historical novel emerged from Scott's education in this tradition. Duncan Forbes argues that the Waverley novels depend on the Enlightenment belief in historical progress. Their characters are "dominated and led into tragic conflicts by historical forces beyond their control." In consequence, their "real hero is usually the particular 'state of society'."[6] Kames' biographer suggests that Scott "worked over" the same material as Kames' *Essays upon . . . British Antiquities.*[7] The avowed hope of the *Essays* was:

to raise a Spirit among his Countrymen of Searching into their Antiquities, those especially which regard the law and the Constitution, being seriously convinced that nothing will more contribute than this Study to eradicate a Set of Opinions, which by Intervals, have disquieted this Island for a Century and a half.[8]

Scott certainly drew on Scottish and other antiquities, making "a creative and symbolic use of what he knew." Ross explicitly connects *Waverley* and Kames' beliefs: "Rose Bradwardine voices the hope for the kind of Scotland [Kames] desired: free of family feuding, where every man was equal before law." However, he acknowledges the complexity of Scott's response to history:

> he is at once emotionally committed to an old order of things dominated by personal relationships, and vitally interested in progress, meaning the development of national understanding, rule of law, and economic growth.[9]

Recent critics have suggested that the first half of this formulation has not received its due emphasis, that Scott's imaginative engagement with his evocations of the past undermines his expressed belief in the present. For example, Daniel Cottom asks: "If the laws of nature and narrative, like civil and religious laws, are to repress violence and institute orderly events, how can an interest in the violent and disorderly events of these novels be understood as anything but a release of that repression?"[10] Cottom therefore suggests that Scott's novels "betray" a lack of faith in law and a Romantic belief in transparent personal relations. A more fluid sense of Scott's dual interest is conveyed by Alexander Welsh: "The emotional values of the Highland world intrigued Scott: in his romance he constructed a fable by which these values could be enjoyed in the very act of reaffirming the claims of society."[11] Nevertheless, Cottom's Romantic emphasis is supported by certain formal features of the novels: the conscious sensibility of characters such as Edward Waverley and the adoption of romance conventions. This second context, the history of the novel, is connected with the Enlightenment background for Scott through Henry MacKenzie, another Scottish lawyer and author of *The Man of Feeling*, a link between the generation of Kames and that of Scott, and dedicatee of *Waverley*.

The co-presence of Enlightenment and Romantic influences on Scott raises the question, to what extent do the novels support legal discourse and thereby make "social affirmations," and to what extent do they postulate a conflict between society and individual experience?[12] Ferguson relates the decline of the American "configuration of law and letters" to the rise of Romantic individualism in the nineteenth century. If Scott is part of a similar configuration in Scotland – and Ferguson proposes an analogy between the two societies in this respect – then his treatment of relations between individuals and various social

groups, between the powerful and the marginalized, and between conceptions of right and the deployment of force will be crucial areas for
study. The very existence of the configuration places the literary lawyer in a privileged position. As Ferguson suggests, "law in Scottish
and American society represented both the primary means of public
advancement and a vital source of national definition for countering
the cultural hegemony of England."[13] The interaction of these two
aspects of law suggests a complex of conservatism and creativity: a
commitment to an ordered society which is, at the same time, in a
state of change.

The second of the aspects noted by Ferguson is particularly important. The Treaty of Union of 1707 abolished the Scottish Parliament,
but permitted the Scots to retain their independent legal system. The
law became, with the Church, an important expression of national
identity. Scott recognized this and spoke passionately against reforms
promoted by Jeffrey and the Whigs in 1806. Lockhart records a much-
quoted incident in which Scott tearfully cried out to Jeffrey,

"you will destroy and undermine until nothing of what makes Scotland Scotland shall remain."[14]

Lockhart is also the source of the argument that Scott's literary work
has a nationalist focus. He argues that Scott sought to reanimate and
ennoble Scottish history, customs, feeling and language by incorpor-
ating them in his poetry and novels.[15] Cockburn's recollection of the
reception of *Waverley* highlights these aspects:

The unexpected newness of the thing, the profusion of original characters, the
Scotch language, Scotch scenery, Scotch men and women, the simplicity of
the writing and the graphic force of the descriptions, all struck us with an
electric shock of delight.[16]

His insistence on the novelty and approbation of the project suggests
that Scott extended the society's definition of prose literature through
his interest in national identification.

There is, however, a creative and not just a referential element in
Lockhart's "reanimate and ennoble" formulation, which implies that
"Scotland" as a cultural and perhaps normative entity is not fixed but
in process, being formed through Scott's selection and organization of
its stories and words in his own fictional narratives. Two such stories
from Scotland's "antiquities" form the basis for *The Heart of Midlothian*,
the publicly-known Porteous affair and that of the personal heroism of

Helen Walker, a previously obscure Scottish peasant who walked to London to obtain a pardon for a sister condemned for child murder, which was told to Scott privately. The creative element is apparent in Scott's conjunction of the two stories which, except for the common involvement of the Duke of Argyle, were not related.[17] The significance of this creative conjunction will be discussed below. Here it may be noted that both stories are drawn from the legal archive and involve relations between Scotland and England. Law and narrative may be nationalist projects, but it cannot be assumed that they work with a common function – the representation of Scotland – or towards the same goal. Audience identity is an essential element of any nationalist thesis: Cockburn's response stresses the pleasure of communal self-recognition, but Scott wrote for a wider audience. In the "General Preface" to the Waverley novels he writes that he hoped through his fiction to introduce the Scots to the English, "to procure sympathy for their virtues and indulgence for their foibles." In doing so, he wished to emulate Maria Edgeworth whose Irish novels,

have done more towards completing the Union, than perhaps all the legislative enactments by which it has been followed up.[18]

The question of whether Scott favoured the Union has been much debated. It seems fair to infer from these remarks that he was a nationalist but not a separatist, that he was concerned both to represent Scottish history and manners and to use these representations to ensure understanding and peace between the Scottish and English. The legal as well as the aesthetic meaning of representation is involved here: Scott is an advocate for his native land as well as its story-teller.

More important for this study is the analogy between Edgeworth's novels and "legislative enactments." Here Scott invests the novel with authority beyond the literary field explored by Ferris. He seems a precursor of Robert M. Cover, arguing that the novel can be constitutive of *nomos*. This suggestion is explored by Avrom Fleishman in terms central to my argument:

By showing the shortcomings of the historical figures in his novels, and by leading his heroes through a pattern of education of moral and political values, Scott was adumbrating a *paideia* for modern life, filling the same social function that the heroic tales and epics of antiquity had played for their times.[19]

Fleishman's discussion centres on aristocratic values; Jeanie Deans's heroism depends on aristocratic patronage for its effect, but the novel's rhetoric of value transcends particular classes. In her case the exemplary "pattern" is not one of education, but of integrity in a world of compromise and of orderliness resisting disorder. In comparing novels to legislation Scott suggests an expansive conception of narrative function. First, he assumes that fictional narrative has a cognitive aspect, as a source of understanding not limited to the specific actions and characters it describes. In this condition it approaches that generality of statement characteristic of legal discourse. Second, it assumes the propriety and propounds the advantage of using literature in the service of political aims. The cognitive capacity of narrative does not just enable the imaginative creation of normative worlds, but places these literary creations within and recognizes their potential to change current world-views.

So conceived literature becomes an instrument of political action as well as paideic articulation. Scott recognized that the social context afforded no special privilege to writers: in his *Lives of the Novelists* he records how Defoe was commissioned to travel to Scotland to "promote the Union" in 1706.[20] So adverse was the climate of opinion in Edinburgh that he received a death threat. Scott deplores his project, yet praises Edgeworth's. The explanation for this inconsistency probably rests on the imaginative licence of novels and Scott's own support for the English in Ireland. A further example shows that while accepting the political implications of Edgeworth's novels, Scott had, much earlier in his career, resisted those of Godwin's *Caleb Williams*. In the *Edinburgh Review*, he summarizes the "moral" of the story, that a man might be "regularly conducted to the gallows for theft or murder which he has never committed," as "mischievous," but proceeds:

our sense of the fallacy of his arguments, of the improbability of his facts, and of the frequent inconsistency of his characters, is lost in the solemnity and suspense with which we expect the evolution of the tale of mystery.[21]

This response highlights the imaginative force of literary forms, the possibility that the pleasures of fiction are sufficiently powerful to cause the suspension of disapproval as well as disbelief. Effie Deans, like Caleb Williams, is convicted of a murder she did not commit. Scott's tale, like Godwin's, is a "call upon the justice of the country." And the historical novel, like "legislative enactments," is a means of normative reconstruction, a rhetorical "Act" to promote the constitution of a new world.

By reorganizing two stories from the national past into a novel offered to the English and Scottish, *The Heart of Midlothian* extends the individual reading experience into a social process. Implicit in Scott's analogy between the two discourses is the notion that literature is not simply the product of a solipsistic writer or the possession of a solipsistic reader, but is communal, transactional, political. In the next section I discuss how Scott represents law in his novel and to what extent the values and methods of legal discourse are taken over by the narrative.

II

*The Heart of Midlothian* is presented to its readers as a narrative drawn from the annals of Scottish law. The story of Effie and Jeanie Deans is one of the "notable trials" which have taken place in "the Heart of Midlothian" and which form the evening's entertainment in chapter one of the novel. This chapter, "Being Introductory," frames the story by telling how Peter Pattieson, Scott's fictional narrator, came into possession of the tale and by placing it in a comic version of the complex of legal and literary discourses mentioned above.

The story emerges from a series of witty and imaginative conceits instigated by the virtually briefless barrister, Hardie: on Dunover as the conventional (and unrecognized) "worn-out litigant"; on the qualities of the Tolbooth's "heart"; on the "Last Speech, Confession and Dying Words" of the soon-to-be-demolished gaol; and finally on his projected narrative anthology, the *Causes Célèbres of Caledonia*. The last initially seems a conventional allusion to the French compilation discussed in chapter two, but when fully developed, it culminates in a contest of modes, an ironic vindication of "narratives of notable trials" over mere fiction. Hardie argues that the State Trials and Books of Adjournal contain "'new pages of the human heart, and turns of fortune beyond what the boldest novelist ever attempted to produce from the coinage of his brain.'"[22] By contrast, the novelist is doomed to repeat the stock devices and formulaic structures of romance. He concludes, "The end of uncertainty . . . is the death of interest; and hence it is that no one now reads novels." There is an element of inversion here as well as of hyperbole: if fiction is predictable and law uncertain, then indeed may the law reports be more interesting than novels. This opposition is modified in answer to Halkit's objection that Hardie is a novel-reader himself, in the admission that the seniors in the law, bar and bench, read novels and, perhaps obliquely referring to the anonymous "Author of *Waverley*," write them too. According to this mock debate between the lawyers, law and fiction become compatible

enterprises, their texts assisting each other. Halkit suggests that Hume's
*Commentaries* might "form a sort of appendix to the . . . circulating library,"
and Hardie's response, that his erudition would not be wasted in such
a usage, defends legal narrative in the very discourse of romance:

> When I come to treat of matters so mysterious, deep and dangerous, as these
> circumstances shall have given rise to, the blood of each reader shall be
> curdled and his epidermis crisped into goose skin. (1.23)

Though comic in its effect, this introductory blurring of narrative
genres is significant in several ways. First, it foreshadows Scott's own
intermingling of history and fiction in the historical novel; second, it
highlights the process of narration, the construction of stories out of
facts which have been organized in accordance with legal principles to
form a legal narrative; and third, it overturns the expected relationship
between genre and reality by asserting that legal narratives reveal not
society in its ordinary and orderly aspect, but the strange, individual
and the passionate, "curious anomalous facts in the history of mind."

   What I have called the blurring of narrative genres in Scott represents a particular adaptation of the novel's traditional practice of
advertising itself as history, or biography. Hardie's conceit recalls such
antecedent games as the opening of the Preface to *Moll Flanders*: "The
World is so taken up of late with Novels and Romances, that it will
be hard for private history to be taken for genuine . . ."; but it also
invokes the contemporary conventions, the thrilling terrors, of Gothic
romance. To these influences must be added a new sense of history:
the representation not of the immediate past of an individual life, but
of the more or less remote past of a society. The historical novel brings
together the contradictory impulses of history and fiction, which spring
from research and invention respectively. James Kerr has discerned:

> a tension between Scott the historical romancer, the trickster who writes a
> history in accordance with his own wishes, attempting to fool the credulous
> reader with his clever illusions of the past, and Scott the realist, writing a
> straight narrative of the past, faithfully depicting things as they were.[23]

Kerr proceeds to argue that Scott effectively "reemplots" certain historical crises (particularly the Jacobite rebellions in Scotland) by grafting them onto a romance pattern, thereby transforming a violent into
a sentimentalized past.

   It is precisely this element of composition, of creating with literary
forms, which is ignored in Hardie's assertions that the law reports
contain stories which outstrip those of novelists. Writing of Scott's own

novels, James Fitzjames Stephen provides a more accurate assessment of the relative interest of the two texts and a reminder of the constructedness of narrative:

Who would infer from one of the trial scenes which occur in almost every one of the *Waverley Novels*, what a real criminal trial was like? The mere *coup d'oeil* presented by the judges, the barristers, the prisoner, the witnesses, and the crowd of spectators, might be pretty accurately represented to any sufficiently imaginative reader by the account of the trial of Fergus MacIvor and Evan Macobich. The *State Trials* would give a juster notion of the interminable length of the indictments, the apparently irrelevant and unmeaning examinations and cross examinations of witnesses . . . ; but to anyone who seeks mere amusement, such reading is intolerably tedious, and even when accomplished it gives a very faint representation of the actual scene as it appeared to those who sat or stood, day after day, in all the heat, and dust, and foul air of the court-house at Carlisle or Southwark. . . .[24]

Stephen's real interest is in the difference between reading about a trial and being there (in "The Relation of Novels to Life"), but his remarks are incidentally pertinent to the different representations of law in fiction and in factual reports. He argues that because novels lack the involvement in "real and serious business," in the issues at stake of an actual lawsuit, they must generate alternative sources of interest: "more points of interest, more dramatic situations, the circumstances are more clearly defined, more sharply brought out"; and alternative modes of treatment, which he summarizes as *suppressio veri* and *suggestio falsi*. While Stephen's criticism suffers from the limitation of regarding novels as "mere amusement," his recognition of the artful creation of "interest" and the bloodless abstractions of the law reports is a salutary corrective to the amusing fancy of Hardie.

Alexander Welsh's discussion of Stephen's *Introduction to the Indian Evidence Act* demonstrates that the juristic and critical did not necessarily go hand in hand, that Stephen illustrated evidentiary principles through cases presented in narrative form, betraying no awareness that they were constructs, but merely assimilating case and narrative.[25] Stephen's blindness here is attributable to the strong part played by the construction of narrative in the trial process, as Welsh notes: in coming to a decision, a tribunal must build up, mentally, but often articulated in speech, a complete, chronological, coherent, account of a situation. Law reports customarily include a narrative summary of the facts of each case. Narrative is implicit in forensic practice; and provides a ready medium for representing legal action.[26] Scott himself entertained hopes of writing a narrative compilation of notable Scottish trials.[27] To put this wish into the mouth of a character in the framing chapter of a narrative which unites two such *causes célèbres* is to make this historical novel a vehicle for exploring the development of particular rules and of the *nomos* which generates them.

For Stephen, as for Hardie, legal narrative is dramatic, in contrast to the ponderous court-room reality of the former and the tame novel-reading judges of the latter. Stephen ascribes the drama to the novelist's armoury. Hardie regards it as the product of history. Ultimately, the function of mixing history and romance is to comprehend, to find an appropriate form for the violence of the past. When Peter Pattieson suggests that Scottish jurisprudence will offer little in the way of drama, on account of the "sober and prudent habits" of the people, Hardie speaks of Scotland's recent civilization and long history of civil dissension, out of which background emerge "crimes of an extraordinary description" (1.22). Both Enlightenment and Romantic discourse may be traced in this argument: the traditional, value-laden distinction between barbarism and civilization is modified by an awareness, developed in the Edinburgh Enlightenment, of historical change, of stages in the development of whole societies, yet the endorsement of Scotland's progress is combined with an imaginative interest in the passionate past, characteristic of Romanticism. This dualism in Scott has been recognized by many critics.[28] Its relationship to the novelist's fusion of history and romance has been discussed by George Levine, for whom the fiction enables Scott simultaneously to realize and to distance the individual danger and social turmoil of Scotland's history.[29] In terms of legal narrative, the historical novel enables the representation of ancient lawlessness and the ultimate triumph of law; the cultivation and containment of an excitement of the illicit; and the displacement of social conflict.

The introductory chapter of *The Heart of Midlothian* might be expected to offer a contrast with the violent legal plot which follows it, to reinforce the proposed contrast between past and present. The setting of rural Gandercleuch seems opposed to the crowds which gather at Edinburgh's Tolbooth and Grassmarket; and the evening's conversation between Peter Pattieson, the two lawyers and the erstwhile prisoner, Mr. Dunover, after the overturning of the coach provides a model of amicable hospitality which anticipates the communal harmony of Knocktarlitie. However, just as the ending is interrupted by the shooting of Staunton, so is the beginning marked by disputes which require legal resolution. The inability of Halkit and Hardie to secure a coach results in two lawsuits: first, an action for damages against the coach-line; and second, a brief in the electoral dispute of Bubbleburgh and Bitem. As these names and that of Mr. Dunover suggest, Scott is here satirizing the law, especially in its prolongation of the dispute beyond the parliamentary term which was the object of the initial election. The severity of his critique is mitigated, though, by the narrative pleasure in the success of Hardie and Halkit and their consequent assistance to Dunover, whose fortunes are thereby renewed. Satire is accordingly tempered with the happy ending of romance. The total effect is of a prelude, in a minor key, to the conflicts and heroism to follow.

If this structure undermines the possibility of a disjunction between barbaric past and civilized present, it by no means denies the reality of change. The child murder law under which Effie was condemned to death has been replaced; the exclusive jurisdictions of aristocratic landlords have been repealed; and the "Heart of Midlothian" itself, Parliament, court and prison, is demolished. The novel functions as an alternative to the "Last Speech" of the Tolbooth, capturing for the national memory – like Muschat's Cairn in chapter xv – the desire for justice and the infamous misuses of legal power.

### III

The fictional historiography of the Porteous and Deans cases builds from its outset on Hardie's promised connection between violent crime and the social history of Scotland. The origin of the Porteous affair is located in a widespread Scottish resistance to the imposition of customs and excise duties, which manifests itself in sympathy for the smuggler Wilson. These imposts are seen as unjust economic domination by Plumdamas and his fellow Edinburgh business-people. The narrator's comment, that while contraband trade "strikes at the root of legitimate government" and injures the fair trader, the regulation of customs was regarded by the Scots as an encroachment upon their "ancient liberties" (II.28), attests to the existence of two attitudes and suggests the source of the conflict between them. The novel records, but explicitly dissociates its own discourse from this historical instance of civil disobedience. The Wilson story provides a good example of Cover's thesis that laws render actions and situations meaningful: the imposition of customs duty at Scottish ports is an assertion of jurisdiction,

of the right to rule, over Scotland. The contraband trade is seen by
its Scottish practitioners and supporters as a means of resisting the
Union, of denying the legitimacy of the government. The plot of *The
Heart of Midlothian* employs this law to begin the Porteous case and to
end the case of Effie Deans. In a significant repetition-and-reversal
pattern, both Wilson and, later, Donacha plan to rob an official carrying government money; Staunton is an accomplice in the former case,
the victim in the latter. Through this fable structure, Scott underlines
the truth of Butler's arguments against smuggling, rehearsed, ironically, to Staunton just before his death: "'if they have mingled in
the scenes of violence and blood to which their occupation naturally
leads, I have observed that, sooner or later, they come to an evil end'"
(II.497). A much larger breach of the territorial sovereignty of Britain
than smuggling occurs within the narrative's time frame, but is dis-
tanced from its action: the Jacobite uprising of 1745. The novel's treatment of customs is consistent with Scott's interest in promoting the
Union in the manner of Maria Edgeworth. His legal narrative begins
where law begins, with the foundational issue of jurisdiction, with the
constitution (literally the setting up) of the nation. Having placed these
in issue, he moves to a fuller explanation of the connection between
politics and law, between history and crime, in the Porteous affair.

The case of Porteous is "memorable in the traditions of Edinburgh
as well as in the records of criminal jurisprudence" (III.33). Scott collects and repeats various beliefs and practices from Scottish folklore, but the use of fiction to keep these traditions alive entails their
"reemplotment," their appropriation in a new story, their evaluation
and adaptation. This process is traceable in Scott's treatment of the
Porteous mob, which begins with the tradition of licensed misrule, of
"holyday" skirmishes between the "rabble of Edinburgh" and the City
Guard (III.34). Here the discourses of lore and law meet. The narrator's unreflecting use of the term "rabble" implies a higher valuation of
social order than of violence and an assumption that the lower classes
need to be controlled. The ritual and spectacle of public executions is
another example of the combination of custom, morality and the control of force in the creation of a normative world, as Douglas Hay has
demonstrated.

A crucial reversal in the attribution of order and disorder is central
to Scott's presentation of the Porteous mob. At Wilson's execution,
Porteous is described as *fey* or deranged in appearance and his firing
into the crowd is a wild, disorderly, and therefore criminal act. By

contrast, the mob which captures the city and hangs Porteous is, for most of its duration, disciplined and temperate. This presentation assists in the justification of the mob's action, but it is combined with other paideic factors. First, Scott presents the pardoning of Porteous as a political act emanating from London which interrupts the machinery of Scottish justice, the due processes of which have already established a true verdict and imposed the expected sentence. Second, the law in this instance is thought by characters within the novel to embody the higher law of moral right, the divine law: the reprieve is "'against law and gospel'" (IV.44); the mob sees itself as executing "the judgment of Heaven" (VI.63); and in response to Butler's arguments for mercy, one member replies, "'The laws both of God and man call for his death'" (VII.71). Against this moralistic rhetoric, the imputed policy considerations of the government seem unacceptably pragmatic and out of touch with the normative principles of the Scottish people.[30] This last is, indeed, Scott's third stratagem, to convert the mob from a lower-class rabble into a body which transcends the class divide, which includes or at least expresses the will of the burghers of Edinburgh and thus stands for a united Scottish people: "'I'll ne'er believe Scotland is Scotland ony mair, if our kindly Scots sit doun with the affront they hae gien us this day'" (IV.47). The failure of the official enquiry into the riot to find the leaders also attests to the communal milieu, not the governmental imposition, of law.

Yet this sympathetic portrait of the Porteous mob is not unequivocal. Butler argues for mercy and lawful action and Scott focalizes through him the horrifying image of the body being hacked on the gibbet. Unlike the law, which seeks order, the mob seeks vengeance, blood for blood. Ultimately, the unauthorized execution seems a parody of the official justice processes, with its makeshift gallows, its reluctant confessor and criminal-hangman. For all its respect for private property and courtesy to travellers, it is presented as riot and insurgency. The problem for the narrative is to represent and comprehend the mob's sense of the justice of its mission whilst retaining a retrospective detachment and valorization of law. The mob is accorded limited approbation for its orderly method while the transgressions against moral and social order inherent in its aims are also noted. The latter depends not only on the rhetoric of vengeance, but also on images of revolution. For the mob breaches the walled city of Edinburgh and storms the prison: the Tolbooth, as prison and former court and Parliament, is a symbol of authority, a citadel of law and government.[31]

When the city magistrates resume power next morning, they feel "the fragility of its tenure" (vii.72). Yet the mob's orderly progress and dispersal undermines these implications of revolution. Where the government's reaction is to deploy increased force against the city, the narrative shows the people to be in need of justice, not of force. The mob, through its orderliness, imitates civil society. In its misguided, because riotous, quest for justice, it mirrors the government's mistaken action in reprieving Porteous (cf. the epigraph to chap. vii: "The evil you teach us, we will execute."). The novel therefore questions what the government would consider assumed, the legitimacy of the constituted authorities. It reveals the importance of ideals of justice as well as the application of force in the creation and maintenance of a *nomos*.

IV

The Porteous and Deans stories are connected through Effie's imprisonment in the Tolbooth at the time of the riot. This link is extended through Butler and the Saddletrees. The effect of this reemplotment of the originally unrelated source story of Helen Walker is to convert a private history into a "national story."[32] The channels for conversion of private into public are religion and law. Butler attempts as a family friend to visit Effie, but as a minister is co-opted by the Porteous mob. Saddletree neglects his personal business for his hobby-horse, the impersonal formulae of the law; meanwhile, Effie, his employee and wife's relative, languishes in prison. Her secret love for Staunton and her concealed pregnancy are claimed for communal scrutiny by the law, acting, once again, under the higher law expressed in the Bible.

*The Heart of Midlothian* presents the narrative context in which the Child Murder Statute of 1690 has its meaning. In his own annotation,[33] Scott describes the Act as a response to "the great increase of the crime . . . ," but, in her interview with the Queen, Jeanie avers that the crime is itself a response to social conditions. The Biblical injunction against adultery, Jeanie's "seventh command" (xxxvii.367), is rigorously enforced by the puritan Kirk-sessions through "the stool of repentance." Such is the shame and fear of this public punishment that offenders are thrown even further into secrecy, driven by the righteousness of their elders to compound their "light" actions with the heavy guilt of killing their offspring. This punitive, legalistic enforcement of morality – of which David Deans's outburst against dancing is a small example – breeds (the metaphor is apt) the crime of presumptive murder. This Act addresses the possibility of concealment by requiring the defendant-mother to prove that she has done the "natural" thing of communicating her situation to another or be adjudged guilty of murder. What it overlooks is its own complicity in a system which represses the "natural" confidences that it claims to value.[34] This self-contradiction gives point to the exchange between the Saddletrees:

". . . The crime is rather a favourite of the law, this species of murther being one of its ain creation."
"Then if the law makes murders," said Mrs. Saddletree, "the law should be hanged for them." (v.55)

For as the complete history of Effie's case proves, the forms of the law do not allow the truth of her situation to emerge. Scott's annotation proceeds to describe two developments in the history of this law, the possibility of consenting to banishment and the alteration of the Act making banishment the official sentence. Though this law is traced to the sacred narrative of the Book of Exodus, its content and method of application is shown to vary according to the history of the Scottish people. The legislative history thus indicates the history of society, that progress toward civilization proposed by Hardie in the opening. This annotation serves what Fiona Robertson calls a "socially normative function," in that it "help[s] to construct a culture and its history."[35] However, in this instance the relation between passion and law is not merely oppositional. The Kirk sought to curb passions by initiating and then invoking the approach of law; but the single-minded purity and grim severity of the project suggest a displacement rather than a defeat of those same passions. When the Tolbooth is breached, the narrator notes how its criminal population flees in search of "hidden receptacles of vice," but Effie, devoid of passion and of hope, is so imbued with the tenets of the normative world of Kirk and state as to feel an outcast even before her trial. In this inverted condition she remains a prisoner.

This historical and critical perspective on the statute is achieved because the novel, in its action as well as its annotations, undermines the presumptions on which the law rests. Those presumptions are challenged at Effie's trial by her counsel, Fairbrother, but his approach is rejected by the judge:

The present law, as it now stood, had been instituted by the wisdom of their fathers, to check the alarming progress of a dreadful crime; when it was found too severe for its purpose, it would doubtless be altered by the wisdom of the legislature; at present, it was the law of the land, the rule of the court . . . (XXIII.234)

In this statement is expressed both respect for legal forms and faith in social and legal progress. By the time Scott writes, the wisdom of the legislature has acted. This historical dimension enables Scott to maintain, in his representation of the trial, a sense of the injustice of the particular case and, at the same time, admiration for the Scottish criminal justice system. While in the earlier chapters of the novel a critical awareness of the politics of law prevails, the trial of Effie Deans is approbatory and idealized in much of its narration.

The narrator begins with a detailed description of the scene, including explanations of legal terminology and practice:

> The crown-counsel, employed in looking over their briefs and notes of evidence, looked grave . . . ; on the other [side of the table] sat the advocates, whom the humanity of the Scottish laws (in this particular more liberal than that of the sister country) not only permits, but enjoins, to appear and assist with their advice and skill all persons under trial. (XXI.213–14)

Professional and national pride animate this account. Having devoted one chapter (XXII) to the first stage of the trial, the "interlocutor of relevance," the narrator begins chapter XXIII with this *caveat lector*:

> It is by no means my intention to describe minutely the forms of a Scottish criminal trial, nor am I sure that I could draw up an account so intelligible and accurate as to abide the criticism of the gentlemen of the long robe. (XXIII.223)

This playfully defensive rhetoric effectively anticipates the criticism of Fitzjames Stephen. More immediately, the final cryptically familiar reference to lawyers not only designates but defers to part of the narrative's likely readership. It simultaneously establishes the goals of intelligibility and accuracy, and attempts to excuse their absence by a statement of contrary intention. The generic consequence of this verbal shuffling is to invoke and yet qualify one of the criteria of realism, that close observation and accuracy of detail which the narrator has already demonstrated. The passage has three major functions: it playfully conceals the lawyer Scott behind his schoolmaster-narrator, Peter Pattieson; it attempts to accommodate the needs of two disparate sections of his readership, to please the lawyers and to "apprise the southern reader" who is less well-versed in northern law; and finally it serves, albeit indirectly, to signal that a variety of narrative modes, not just realism, may be employed. Within the trial scene, sentimentalism and melodrama are also relied on, while romance and fable assume great significance as the novel proceeds. Both Graham McMaster and James Kerr argue that the latter two modes take over from realism as the aesthetic mainspring of the novel and that this transformation is expressive of a desire to imagine a new society and indicative of Scott's dissatisfaction with social reality.[36] Kerr criticizes the novel's ending as a flight from history, while McMaster does not so privilege realism. An examination of the presentation of law in the novel's transactions between history and paideic vision suggests that realism itself may be an appropriate form for presenting the law's embodiment of communal ideals as well as its expressions of state power.

The normative centre of the trial, and, I would argue, of the novel as a whole, is Jeanie's evidence. It provides a model of true testimony which the narrator seeks to emulate. Her conspicuous truthfulness, her scrupulous attention to the relationship between language and reality is both recorded in and made a principle of form for the novel. In this respect, the novel's practice foreshadows the analogy formulated later in the nineteenth century by George Eliot:

my strongest effort is . . . to give a faithful account of men and things as they have mirrored themselves in my mind . . . I feel as much bound to tell you what that reflection is, as if I were in the witness box narrating my experience on oath.[37]

I shall argue below that *The Heart of Midlothian* develops its own evidentiary model, but that a more comprehensive notion of "testimony" is invoked, which witnesses not only to facts as *Adam Bede* does, but to other kinds of truths.

This sense is most clearly summarized in David Deans's remark, "I have been constant and unchanged in my testimony" (xviii.196). In the evidentiary discourse of *The Heart of Midlothian*, Jeanie is a witness not merely through her language, but through her actions and principles. The moral element in this conception of "testimony" gives rise to the need for romance and fable as well as realism in Scott's legal narrative.

This complex of legal and moral discourse is made part of modern readers' preparation for the novel. In the "Introduction" Scott briefly recounts the story of Helen Walker, the original of Jeanie Deans, and the activities of his informant, Mrs. Goldie. He concludes: "The reader is now able to judge how far the author has improved upon, or fallen short of, the pleasing and interesting sketch of high principle and steady affection displayed by Helen Walker" (p. 5). This willingness to improve upon the factors in order to highlight the moral lesson of the story shows that Scott's realism is tempered by other goals. In one of the characteristic strategies of legal narrative fiction the reader is here constructed as and invited to function as judge. Judgment is, in this instance, a process involving both aesthetic and moral considerations. The effect of the invitation is to declare and to place in issue the authority of the text, both the text of the various legal utterances and that of the novel too. This paradox conceals an expectation that the reader will assent to the novel's paideic formulations, because it presents reading as a normative activity. In the appropriate distinction of Paul Ricoeur, what is invited is not a hermeneutic of suspicion, but a hermeneutic of restoration. A similar attitude prevails within the narrative, in its evaluations of law.

An evidentiary motif is strongly present in the narrator's discourse. It appears significantly in the device of annotation: not only in the numbered endnotes which Scott appended to the Magnum Opus edition, but also in the parodic pedantry of Cleishbotham's occasional subscriptions to the narrative, which are their obverse. They have the effect of authenticating as well as explaining, through their fullness, attention to detail and citation of sources. In many cases, the notes tell other stories, thereby helping to place the main story more securely in its social context and affirming the cognitive power of narrative itself. The two most important examples, which we have already discussed, are note 10, an "authentic account" of the Porteous enquiry compiled by the Solicitor-General and quoted in full, and note 23, which details the history of Scotland's child murder law, a more authoritative account than that provided by Bartoline Saddletree. The mixture of satire and historical realism in the narrative is indicative of its specific criticisms and general endorsement of the law. While the annotations are directed to the establishment of facts, another aspect of the narrator's discourse highlights the process of inference and judgment which is enabled by the provision of factual evidence. For example, a hypothetical stranger is imagined among the crowd expecting the official execution of Porteous as the vehicle for inferences, interpreting the "evidence of his ears," which suggest sorrow, and his eyes, which see indications of vengeance on the faces in the crowd (IV.40); again, when the mob breaks into the Tolbooth, the scene is depicted in terms of evidentiary process:

oaths and maledictions, which would but shock the reader if we recorded them, *but which serve to prove*, could it have admitted of doubt, the settled purpose of soul with which they sought his destruction (VII.66; my italics)

and later, the narrator suggests that Muschat's Cairn was built "in testimony of abhorrence" to his crime (XV.151).

In adopting this discourse, the narrative clearly shows the influence of Scott's legal background and shares some of the epistemological interests and assumptions of the law. First, in its careful collation and processing of information, it emphasizes the goal of truth. The description of the Porteous mob has often been called comprehensive and fair, but this effect is achieved by notation of the sources and limits of Butler's knowledge and by the explicit drawing of inferences from designated phenomena. A contrast is discernible between this instance and the presumptions which the law invokes to condemn Effie. In this respect, the child murder law is singular: the trial of Porteous for murder is described as "a long and patient hearing" (III.38) after which the jury must evaluate contradictory evidence before arriving at a verdict consistent with the narrator's previous description of the event. Yet there are further differences in the treatment of these two trials: the fate of Effie's child is not finally revealed until well after the trial and subsequent transformation of Effie and Staunton. This deferred revelation creates both mystery and doubt as to Effie's guilt or innocence, for both reader and characters. While the statute itself makes the baby's fate irrelevant, the novel keeps the issue alive through Jeanie's contact with the Murdocksons. The evasions, distortions, madness and death of these characters are such obstacles to knowledge that they function as the opposite of the testimonial devices described above. They parallel the veil of silence which covers the Porteous mob. *The Heart of Midlothian* therefore exhibits one of the major concerns of legal narrative fiction, the question of whether truth is found and justice is attained through legal processes.

The novel's appropriation of the testimonial model suggests that it shares the law's assumption that reality is ultimately knowable: throughout, faces, actions, words and even rocks are shown to be intelligible or capable of supporting valid inferences by the protagonist and narrator and by the application of the categories of the law. The latter, though valid in the trial of Porteous, are so constructed as to be incapable of yielding the truth in Effie's case. Other instances in which signs, including speech, are misconstrued are Butler's assumption that Robertson is about to commit suicide in chapter XI, the discussion between Jeanie

and David Deans over her testifying in court, the various inferences
drawn from Jeanie's references to adultery during her audience with
the Queen, and the long-held belief that Effie's child is dead. These
examples suggest that knowledge and communication are not auto-
matically attained, but are dependent on a context of shared values,
pre-eminent among which is fidelity to truth, and on the practice of
rational enquiry rather than assumption. In all these examples the
truth is finally revealed: epistemological uncertainty is therefore provi-
sional and temporary. If the existence and identity of the Whistler
seems to become known only through a series of lucky coincidences,
that is not an exception to the principle, I would argue, but an example of the consequences of abandoning truth and reason.

v

Knowledge and moral conduct are linked in *The Heart of Midlothian* by
virtue of the religious world-view of the characters (aspects of which
the narrative itself shares). Jeanie expresses the link most succinctly in
her reasons for refusing to testify that Effie told her of her pregnancy.
When Robertson suggests that "the retainers of the law" would overlook such a falsehood, Jeanie cites her duty to God:

> He has given us a law . . . for the lamp of our path; if we stray from it we err
> against knowledge. (xv.157)

Knowledge here is less a human acquisition or faculty than a part of
divine revelation. It is a guide for conduct which imposes meaning on
experience rather than a hypothesis to be tested by experience. The
conjunction of law, light, the true path and knowledge in Jeanie's
statement suggests that she inhabits and is the vehicle for the definition
of a *nomos*. The basis of her world of meaning is fidelity to God's law
and a belief in the providential order of human life. Jeanie's action is
twofold: first, her truthful evidence at Effie's trial and second, her
heroic walk to London in quest of a pardon. Both entail that living
witness or testimony through conduct articulated by David Deans, in
which the individual life is dedicated to the fulfilment of a vision of
righteousness. Where her father's vision is of an exclusive Covenant,
which finds expression in a purist isolationism that is slowly broken
down by the problematic situations of the plot, Jeanie's vision is a
product of the action and is interventionist, an attempt to influence, or

in Cover's terminology, to "transform" an injustice in society. In order to fulfil her vision, Jeanie must convince not just Queen Caroline, but all those she encounters from the moment she forms her plan: Butler, Dumbiedikes, Madge and her would-be captors, the Reverend Mr. Staunton and the Duke of Argyle. Jeanie must persuade them by word and deed of the practicability and propriety of her attempt to seek a pardon as well as its abstract justice. As Judith Wilt points out, this process requires the transformation of Jeanie in the eyes of other characters and of the narrator: the walk to London makes Jeanie a hero rather than the conventional heroine she has been and will become again.[38] Just as her mission achieves its end, so its end transforms the pilgrim: from cowfeeder's daughter to symbol of Scottish virtue and courage.

The allegorical possibilities of Jeanie's walk are underlined by the novel's allusions to *The Pilgrim's Progress*. She leaves the imperfect world of her family home and passes through unknown country, finding sources of guidance, defeating the snares of Meg Murdockson, to arrive finally at her goal, which is both spatial, London, and normative, justice tempered with mercy for her sister. Meg Murdockson's attempt to stop Jeanie is expressive of the novel's anti-*nomos*: captured by thieves, Jeanie is led away from her true path to a forest hideout. Her struggles to escape occasion the most explicit references to Bunyan's narrative. Walking with Jeanie, Madge devises a game in which their meanderings are reconceived as the journey of Mercy and Christiana in the second part of *The Pilgrim's Progress*. Jeanie exploits the game to extend the walk and thereby regains the road and village of civil society. Here Jeanie succeeds in distinguishing herself through tidy clothes and quiet demeanour from the wildness of Madge. At their separation, Madge's utterance, "'God help me, I forget my very name in this confused waste'" (XXXII.312), encapsulates the desire for normative order. Waste and confusion are the opposite of the peace and prosperity which characterizes Jeanie's life at Knocktarlitie. This normative order is the reward for the quest she has undertaken.

The novel does not portray comprehensive national progress towards a new paideum. The violent depredations of the gang of Donacha invade and disrupt the orderly life of the Butlers. The narrative presents this gang as barbaric inhabitants of a physical and normative wilderness in a development of its order-disorder imagery. In this context it is noteworthy that one of the original meanings of *nomos* in ancient Greek was "pasturage."[39] As this image pattern is used in the story, there is no simple dichotomy between the two states of society: if the identity of the Whistler is unknown, so are those of Sir George and Lady Staunton. This system of contrasts functions to produce an ideal communal order and its extreme opposite and to show law and other social practices mediating between these poles.

Madge's recognition of the "confused waste" is both a personal cry for help and a statement of sibylline wisdom applicable to others. The narrator presents her as mad, yet she is the vehicle of this insight into a condition that describes the mob which kills her as much as it describes herself and her mother's underworld society. The incorporation of such arcane formulations suggests that the novel is normatively inclusive, giving space to and thereby engendering sympathy for a wide range of speakers and their experiences. It contrasts in this respect with law and religion, the normative projects of which result in the exclusion of characters like Effie and Madge. In consequence, the novel admits some hope of redemption to the outcasts from civil society: thus Jeanie attempts to communicate and win the confidence of the Whistler, unsuccessfully; and Madge shows more than the vestiges of a puritan moral education in her familiarity with *The Pilgrim's Progress*. The latter example is not fanciful: Madge's application of the story to her own situation is, as Jeanie recognizes, a "serious" attempt to "obtain the pardon and countenance of someone whom she had offended" (XXXI.304). As such, it is a sustained attempt to understand reality through narrative, similar to the narrator's own comparison between Jeanie at Muschat's Cairn and Christiana in the Valley of the Shadow of Death. The novel does not forget Madge's name, but derives much interest from her lively eccentricity. She becomes a means of introducing the "carnal wisdom" of folklore and of sympathetically presenting the experiences of loss, abandonment, heightened desire and madness. While Hardie claims that these can be read in the annals of the law, they are there confined, dismissed or repressed by legal disclosure. Within the novel, the experience of individuals finds greater scope: the explanation of Madge's involvement in the removal of Effie's child, the madness which grew from the taking of her own child and the loss of her lover, being a late, but crucial, revelation. Yet, even in this novel, the possibility of redemption within society is not realized for Effie or Madge. The normative inclusiveness of the novel comprehends them, but also marginalizes them.[40]

In this respect the novel assumes a quasi-legal function, that of attempting to repel or dispel normative disorder. Daniel Cottom argues, as foreshadowed above, that this project is undermined in the Waverley novels by a recurrent presentation of law as problematic and violence as a means of recovering truly personal relations. The latter does not really apply to *The Heart of Midlothian*, probably because the central characters are women, whose position in an economy of violence is traditionally that of victim. Nevertheless, he argues that Jeanie's attainment of justice supports his general thesis on two grounds. First, the interview with the Queen is seen as extraordinary. A similar argument is made by Kerr to the effect that Jeanie's quest is individual, not representative or an appeal on behalf of her class, not radical but conservative of the political order.[41] Kerr's use of constitutional discourse serves as a reminder that the royal prerogative of mercy is traditional, not only to British law but to all systems which have the Bible as a normative source. Jeanie herself cites the example of King Ahasueris to Butler, who wrongly regards it as no precedent for the present instance. Her obtaining a pardon is unusual as an action in her life, but as a legal remedy, it is not.

Cottom's second argument is that the pardon is dependent on personal contact and that its orality is expressly set against the predominantly written basis of the legal system. This offers a false dichotomy: it ignores the central function of Jeanie's oral testimony at the trial; moreover, before arranging the interview with the Queen, the Duke of Argyle consults the papers relating to the case and, in doing so, honours the written pledge of assistance given by his ancestor to Bible Butler. Writing and speech are interdependent in these episodes: even personal interviews take place in legal, political or familial contexts. The Queen and Jeanie speak as monarch and subject, in almost completely different discourses, the former sophisticated and political, the latter naive and moralistic. As at the trial, Jeanie's final resort to emotion and sympathy finds a common human chord, but it harmonizes with the political advantage of restoring the Duke's support for the Queen. Cottom's postulation of pre-social, purely personal relations is therefore overstated: even the Duke's subsequent patronage of Jeanie's family takes place within and serves to validate a social order. Writing, then, is not a modern imposition, but part of the heritage and the resources of that evolving order. It includes the royal pardon as well as the child murder statute, and the sacred text of the Bible as well as the specific, fictional narrative of *The Heart of Midlothian*. Law and narrative fiction are therefore two related aspects of society's quest to dispel normative and physical disorder. The interplay of violence and law in the novel does not mean that the quest has failed: only that its challenge is accepted by the novelist and his readers.

For Jeanie's achievement does not purify the state or establish the *nomos*. Kerr speaks of the "pastoral" setting at Knocktarlitie and both he and McMaster note the displacement of the 1745 uprising from the novel's final locale. Karl Kroeber argues that the pardon and subsequent action indicate a union of personal morality and social lawfulness.[42] But the microcosm of Knocktarlitie is no more immune from disorder than the other worlds of the novel. Duncan of Knockdunder may be a comic despot, but he remains a despot, sharing his name with Donacha Dhu (Duncan the Red) whose activities he tolerates, ignoring both the Commandments and Acts of Parliament; and claiming to act instead under the personal authority of the Duke of Argyle in his ancient, exclusive jurisdiction. This assertion recalls Hardie's distinction at the beginning of the novel between modern lawfulness and the violent and passionate past, in which he cites the hereditary jurisdictions as enabling many daring and violent crimes and resting their investigation in "ignorant, partial or interested" judges (1.23). The abolition of this system in 1748 was an attempt to curb the power of the Scottish chieftains and prevent further rebellion. Ross reports that after initial reservations the Duke of Argyle "came out in favour" of the proposal. In the light of Hardie's remarks and, later, Butler's opposition, Duncan's intention to hang the Whistler seems a barbaric survival, comparable to Donacha's plan to rob Staunton.[43] The latter's death at the hands of his own son is the product of this lawlessness. While undoubtedly melodramatic, this action replicates the normative chaos of the opening chapters of the novel. Jeanie's attempt to deal kindly with the Whistler is a misplaced paideic gesture. In describing his later history (or oblivion), the rhetoric of the novel is virtually absolute in its opposition of civilization and barbarism, summarily consigning him to "a tribe of wild Indians" where he cannot be traced, but with whom he is fit to associate (LII.506). His Butler cousins are, however, accounted for, one becoming a lawyer and the other a soldier. That these two supports of the secular state emerge from the religiously-minded Butler and Deans families foreshadows greater access to power for the sons of Jeanie, and more generally adumbrates the emergence of a modern or "imperial" *nomos*.

The moral which is appended to the novel by Peter Pattieson is a final, if comic, reminder of the cognitive capacity of narrative. An adequate interpretation of the story requires that to the moralizing be added an understanding of law, as the normative expression of social understandings, and as a subject for the application of power. Scott's novel brings together history and dream in an attempt to narrate the development of the modern Scottish *nomos*. As an intervention in British culture, it fulfils the author's analogy between novels and laws. It offers a critical account of the errors of the past and demonstrates the possibility of change by the heroic example of Jeanie. Through its adoption of moral and legal discourses, the novel aligns itself with the normative institutions of law and religion. It shares some of the pre-suppositions of these discourses: the belief that a true and authoritative account of events may be constructed, that conduct may be judged according to shared moral principles.

This alignment raises a particular question for legal narrative fiction: does the novel share the law's belief in the social practice of seeking both to understand and to regulate human behaviour by reference to pre-existent categories? Legal discourse is characteristically general-ized, a single formulation which attempts to cover a potentially limitless number of cases, and imperative; whereas the novel, as the discussion of Effie and Madge has shown, focuses on, begins from, individuals and is expository. Yet this opposition cannot be sustained: laws are operative when applied to particular cases; and novelistic representa-tion entails mediating between specific details and general forms and conventions. While later novels distinguish their own practice from the methodologies of law, *The Heart of Midlothian* employs the discourse of evidence and of Enlightenment theories of social development, and searches among the genres of history, romance and fable for an adequate narrative structure. However, it also satirizes the excesses of formalism in law and religion in the characters of Saddletree and Deans, suggesting that form alone is incapable of achieving justice.

The novel comprehends another response to situations, another aspect of reality, the unpredictable emotions of human beings. Such emotional expressions are social as well as individual: for example, the "deep groan" which passes through the court after Jeanie's evidence and the comparable, collective, non-verbal utterances of the mob after Porteous's reprieve.[44] These signify the release of a response more basic than those expressible in the word of God or government, and prepare the reader for the melodramatic moment of David Deans's fainting at the feet of his accused daughter. This outbreak of emotion in the otherwise repressive Cameronian and in the midst of formal legal proceedings undermines the authority of pure legalism. Yet such is the omnipresence of the novel's rhetoric of order that even here Jeanie's "deep and firm mind" ensures that sympathy does not degenerate into the disorderly emotionalism of Staunton. Law and sympathy, form and feeling, must, it seems, interact with each other.

In this light, the novel may affirm the normative project of law and criticize the law relating to child murder. The latter is an overly-formalistic and therefore repressive law, which provides an inadequate, formulaic account of Effie's behaviour and of the fate of her son. Overall, *The Heart of Midlothian* does not provide a radical critique of the citadel of Scottish law, but an account written from within the discourse, one which might be addressed to the Bench. It not only records the passing of its eponymous Tolbooth, but it helps to design the new court of justice. The architectural metaphor was used by Scott in praise of his law teacher, Baron Hume: Scottish law "resembles some ancient castle, partly entire, partly ruinous, patched and altered during the succession of ages," to which Hume gave "a methodical plan."[45] Scott, through his novel, has recommended some alterations to the law and society he loved, has honoured its traditions and sought to improve the light and heating.[46] In this respect, *The Heart of Midlothian* foreshadows another novel that tropes *nomos* through buildings, *Bleak House*, in which the illegitimate child – relegated to the margins of Scott's narrative – holds the key.

## CHAPTER FOUR

# *Reformist critique in the mid-Victorian "legal novel"* – Bleak House

A reviewer of the first number of *Bleak House* anticipated that Jarndyce and Jarndyce would "doubtless be a famous cause – and take its future place beside the Common Pleas case of Bardell v Pickwick in the Law Reports of Fiction."[1] This prediction has proved true in the long term.[2] When the serialization of the novel was completed, the same reviewer criticized Dickens for failing "to keep the mighty mystery of Iniquity and Equity perpetually before the reader," and for giving, instead, "the first concern and sympathy . . . to Lady Dedlock's secret."[3] These remarks provide a compact starting-point for a critical and historical discussion of the representation of law in *Bleak House*. In the first section of this chapter I explore the mid-Victorian evolution of a subgenre based on "the Law Reports of Fiction," and argue that although *Bleak House* emerged from this generic field, its critique of the English legal system and *nomos* is more profound than that of *The Heart of Midlothian*. The specific focus of this critique, the Court of Chancery, had become a national scandal, obstructing inherited notions of justice and resisting attempts at reform. The sense of contradiction expressed in the phrase, "the mighty mystery of Iniquity and Equity," is emplotted in *Bleak House*, which presents the stories of the institution's victims as evidence of the need for reform, but which also recuperates part of the tradition of Equity as an alternative to Chancery. That alternative is best embodied in Esther Summerson. Esther's recovery of family represents, it is argued in the last part of the chapter, a type of world-building which is set against the destructive and entropic tendencies of Chancery.

I

The existence of two major Victorian connections between literature and law is indicated by these phrases, "the Law Reports of Fiction" and "the mighty mystery of Iniquity and Equity." The former phrase expresses the reviewer's expectation of the realistic presentation of legal proceedings, while the latter evidences the contemporary dismay at the injustices wrought by the Chancery Court. The two phrases may be thought to point in opposite directions, one towards the law as it is, the other towards the law as it should be. However, such a dichotomy would be over-simplified, for the allusion to *The Pickwick Papers* suggests a realism alloyed with comedy and satire, while the wordplay of "Iniquity and Equity" bespeaks an awareness that error and evil may likewise be illustrated through comedy and satire. In this context, the "mystery" of Chancery is not insoluble: rather the institution may be understood and remedied.

As a formulation, "The Law Reports of Fiction" seems to derive from the title of *The Pickwick Papers*, chapter xxxiv, "Is Wholly Devoted to a Full and Faithful Report of the Memorable Trial of Bardell against Pickwick." The hyperbole of this title, however, invokes an eighteenth-century tradition of fulsome titles not only of novels, but more importantly of sensational pamphlets and broadsides. Narratives of trials and criminal biography formed a notable species of publication in this medium.[4] The restrained expression of "the Law Reports of Fiction," by contrast, invokes the authority of professional and official case reports, which were largely a nineteenth-century development.[5] As a genre, the law report combines discourse, legal reasoning from principle and precedent, with the narrative recitation of facts. To juxtapose such historical narrative with "fiction" is to play the same games with genre as Scott's advocates with their "Causes Célèbres of Caledonia." The results of this juxtaposition are twofold: the law becomes an object of entertainment through the mimicry of stereotypes; and fiction becomes a medium for authoritative representations of law.

*The Pickwick Papers* employs mimicry not only of the forms of the common law trial, but also in its portrait of the judge. Dickens's Mr. Justice Stareleigh is a comic imitation of both the name and the manner of the real Mr. Justice Gazelee.[6] This impulse famously reappears in the Skimpole-Leigh Hunt portrait in *Bleak House*, and also in the attributed link between Caroline Chisholm and Mrs. Jellyby. Lord Denman, who is reported to have read his copy of *Pickwick* on the bench, condemned the Jellyby portrait and Dickens's criticisms of Chancery in a pamphlet on *Bleak House*. Despite satirizing the law, for example, the sharp practices of Dodson and Fogg, or the absurdities of the rule that parties to a case were ineligible as witnesses, the Pickwick trial shares the geniality of the other sketches in the novel and presented no threat to the legal system or profession. Indeed Dickens made comic play of the "case" and its "report" in a speech to the United Law Clerks' Society dinner in 1849.[7] *Pickwick* was easily conscripted into a tradition of legal humour which stretches from *Jorrocks's Jaunts and Jollities* to A. P. Herbert's *Misleading Cases*, which depends upon detailed representation of institutional usages, of the peculiar, that is to say both the characteristic and the strange, features of the English legal system. Such stories, in consequence, offer increased delight to those familiar with the details alluded to, the legal community whose functions and knowledge are thereby invoked as well as imitated.

The mimetic impulse in the "full and faithful report" blossomed with the mid-Victorian novel's dominant aesthetic creed of realism, and fictional narratives involving legal proceedings or questions or actions occurring in a legal milieu flourished. Of this literary interest, Northrop Frye has commented that there is hardly a British novelist in the nineteenth century who does not make a major character out of the law.[8] The cultural context for this literary interest will be examined shortly, but here it is proper to note that the law was strongly present in various conceptions of the real.

A significant example of this trend, and an important precursor of *Bleak House*, is Samuel Warren's best-selling novel, *Ten Thousand A Year* (1840–1). It concerns an upstart shop assistant's claim to a landed estate, engineered by fraudulent solicitors, Quirk, Gammon and Snap. The legal and social ramifications of their roguery are fully detailed. The law is presented as an effective underpinning to all actions and arrangements within society. The narrative is supplemented by numerous footnotes detailing the cases and statutes applicable to the actions described; thus verifying both the accuracy of the account and the meaning of the various events. The effect is to endow the legal (and other social) details with normative force. The law becomes a subject for approbation, not merely description: "Both were men of rigid integrity: 'tis indeed a glorious thing to be able to challenge the inquiry – when, for centuries, have other than men of rigid integrity sat upon the English Bench?"[9] Such laudatory comments by the narrator and the use of authenticating notes to the text were devices of Scott's narrative. They reveal the part played by legal discourse in constructing conceptions of reality in the nineteenth century. Scott and Warren worked within this discourse, being lawyers as well as *littérateurs*. (Warren was the author of a standard text on *The Duties of Attornies and Solicitors* and *A Popular and Practical Introduction to Law Studies*.) *Ten Thousand A Year* was one of many novels that centred upon claims to estates, from *Wuthering Heights* to *Orley Farm* and others by Anthony Trollope. *Bleak House* is, therefore, illustrative of a general interest in both the law and the ideology of family succession in the Victorian novel.[10]

This interest is exposed in an anonymous review of *Tales by a Barrister*, of which two editions were published in 1844 and 1847. The reviewer suggests that the *Tales* herald a welcome new sub-genre of narrative fiction, "the *legal* novel."[11] This is defined not merely by subject or milieu, but by its avowed inculcation of "some *legal* moral," a narrow definition which, the reviewer recognizes, excludes the works of Fielding, Scott, Edgeworth and Warren! The article is interesting in its very proposal of a sub-genre and in its conservative didacticism. The reviewer argues that such fiction will acquaint readers with legal rules and thereby help to protect their property and reduce ignorance in a "nation . . . where the strict impartiality of the law is every one's boast." This statement is comparable to Scott's posited connection between *Waverley* and the Union of Scotland and England in the way its paideic expression is so openly tied to the interests of the propertied classes, to an ideological position. The tales themselves concern the loss of property by generally imprudent owners who fail adequately to protect themselves against exploitation by unscrupulous agents. The accuracy in legal detail, the verisimilitude of character and manners, is emphasized by the reviewer as the foundation of a prescriptive commentary on social organization. He comments disparagingly on the Reform Bill (which "deluged the House with brisk Vestrymen"), but also on the "prolix and tautologous jargon" of the law.[12] In one of the tales, a solicitor advises against his client bringing a suit in Chancery, whereupon the reviewer considers the validity of complaints against the Chancery Court and offers his own plan for reform. Thus, the "*legal* novel" is conceived as a vehicle not merely for the representation of the law, but for its criticism.

In the matter of Chancery reform, *Tales by a Barrister* and *Bleak House* are as different as they are similar. Where the former *speaks* of such reform in an overwhelmingly realist and normative representation of the English legal and social system, *Bleak House* abjures both discussion and the intricate details of legal process in favour of a dramatic and symbolic expression of Chancery's effects in society, of society imagined as a "Chancery world," to use a phrase by Q. D. Leavis.

Though Dickens is associated with some of the most famous cases in "the Law Reports of Fiction," he is not a writer of "legal novels" as conceived by the anonymous reviewer of *Tales by a Barrister*. He is considered disdainfully as a writer of "laboured" sketches.[13] This criticism has affinities with the charges of exaggeration and simplification made against Dickens by Fitzjames Stephen and Anthony Trollope. Patrick Brantlinger argues that such criticism entails a dual commitment – aesthetic and political – to realism, or "things as they are."[14] In this argument, which will be more fully considered in the chapter on Trollope, the dominance of realism in English fiction from the 1850s onwards is related to the decline of what Brantlinger calls "the spirit of reform." This spirit, which had prevailed since the 1820s, is defined as:

the belief that social improvement, and especially the improvement of the working class, can be brought about by some form of political action, whether through legislative and administrative channels, or through social work and private charity.[15]

Brantlinger notes how the novel came to be used in various campaigns for improved penal laws, factory conditions and treatment of the insane, along with journalism and official reports. Some such novels presented emotive rather than systematic cases for reform. Brantlinger notes, for example, how Lytton's *Paul Clifford*, a "Newgate novel," advocates penal reform while ascribing criminality to individual moral, rather than social causes. Despite these defects, the "novel with a purpose" was an important literary mode, numbering among its practitioners Frances Trollope, Elizabeth Gaskell, Charles Reade, Harriet Martineau and Dickens.[16]

This tradition provides a more secure basis than the conservative "legal novel" for an examination of Dickens and the law. English law is not, for Dickens, the guardian of liberty, but a defective system kept in place by vested interests. In his journalism and his fiction, he campaigned against "abuses." Looking back from *Bleak House* and Lord Denman's criticisms of it, he generalized this pattern:

The most serious and pathetic point I tried with all indignation and intensity to make, *in my first book*, (Pickwick) was the slow torture and death of a chancery prisoner. From that hour to this, if I have been set on anything, it has been on exhibiting the abuses of the Law.[17]

As the above discussion of *Pickwick* may show, the possibility of retrospective special pleading exists here.

Dickens was no blind follower of reformist programmes. The genealogy of law reform is, in nineteenth-century England, Benthamite in inspiration. The Royal Commissions into such aspects of the legal system as the criminal law and the Court of Chancery were attempts to rationalize their operation. Dickens's critical response to this approach is illustrated by his attack in *Oliver Twist* on the New Poor Law of 1834, one of the first achievements of the reformers in Parliament. If the critique of Utilitarianism in *Hard Times* is taken as the yardstick, Dickens appears ardently anti-Benthamite. Yet, as Marjorie Stone has demonstrated, the novelist and the philosopher could, on occasion, attack the same targets with the same weapons. Her example is the campaign against "legal fictions," the presumptions and false averments by which the law adapted itself to new demands over the centuries.[18] Bentham's insistence that such fictions were lies and absurdities is taken up by Dickens in many passages in the novels and journals and extended to include fictions operating in social life. However, Bentham's attitude to imaginative literature – his celebrated comparison of poetry to push-pin – is emphatically resisted by Dickens, as the famous satire on "Facts" in *Hard Times* shows: such facts are not self-sufficiently true and provide no adequate explanation of the world, much less any conception of how to reform it. Imagination and values are the discourses of Dickens's reformism, "the romantic side of familiar things."[19] The "abuses of the law" that Dickens exhibits may be targets of Benthamite critique; his radical attitude to social problems may be the product of his association with radical journals like the *Daily News*, as the legal historians Maine and Dicey suggest;[20] but the humanitarian and imaginative treatment of such problems highlight aspects of them that the Benthamite reformers never noticed, and locate problems in the operation of industrial society that the Benthamites had no means of seeing. Brantlinger summarizes this difference by arguing that the Benthamite radicals were strong in their systematic analysis of social institutions, but lacked a means of recognizing inequality and basic injustices, while the "sentimental radicals" like Dickens, possessed an awareness and a vocabulary for injustice, but were not systematic or intellectually coherent in their critiques of social institutions.[21] This difference emerges most clearly in respect of Chancery, where, I shall argue below, Dickens adheres to a notion of Equity which Bentham rejected as irrational.

The "topicality" of Chancery Reform in 1851 has been demonstrated by Butt and Tillotson:

Dickens's indictment of Chancery . . . followed in almost every respect the charges already levelled in the columns of *The Times*. In both we read of houses in Chancery, and wards in Chancery, of dilatory and costly procedure, of wasted lives, and of legal obstructionism.[22]

*Bleak House* was recognized, but by no means universally applauded, as a contribution to the reform of Chancery. While the *Illustrated London News* believed that Dickens's influence was, as always, "pure, beneficial and elevating," many reviews criticized the lack of novelty, the lateness, of his exposé. For example, the *Spectator* regarded Jarndyce and Jarndyce as "stale and commonplace satire upon the length and expense of Chancery proceedings." The *Eclectic Review* wrote that Dickens "only exhibits in a stronger and more romantic light what has been pretty well made known before through the earnest prose of plainer men." For *Bentley's Monthly Review*, his lack of professional understanding was fatal: "so much energy spent in a vain attempt to crush the giant of Chancery"; and concluded that Lord St. Leonards would be a "more effectual" Chancery Reformer. *Blackwood's Edinburgh Magazine* was more balanced: "even admitting that Mr. Dickens comes late into the field, it is not to be denied that, for the purposes of his story, he makes very effective use of his suit in Chancery."[23] The charge of lateness is difficult to credit when it is remembered how long and hard the process of Chancery reform was: from Lord Eldon's inconclusive Chancery Commission of 1824 to the final establishment of a single system of courts exercising common law and equity powers in 1875; even Parliamentary Acts were resisted, such as that of 1833 abolishing the Six Clerks' Office, which required another Act in 1842 to achieve its aim.[24] Such obstructionism is revealed for readers of the novel not simply through the satire on Mr. Vholes, but in Dickens's Preface, which travesties a public defence of Chancery by the Vice-Chancellor, Sir William Page-Wood.[25] Dickens suggests that the Judge is so steeped in the usages of his court as to be blind to its faults. Chancery reform was still a matter of debate, despite the overwhelming (and eventually successful) movement for change. The criticisms quoted above may seem to repose little faith in the novel of reform ("a vain attempt") but, from another viewpoint, the insistent demand for novelty suggests an expectation that the novel should be at the very front of social progress. Addressing this issue of the effectiveness of *Bleak House* in his *Lincoln's Inn Essays*, Sir Gerald Hurst K. C. concludes that while the legislative reform of Chancery had already begun, Dickens's work:

contributed in some measure at least to mould the minds of the men who
mattered . . . its version, however extravagant, of the abuses of Chancery was
sufficiently biting to stir even the complacency of vested interests and for this
reason deserves a place among those classical works of fiction . . . which have
helped practically to make a better England.[26]

The ideal of "a better England" animates both the law reform movement in general and Dickens's *Bleak House*. This idealism is recognized
in Butt and Tillotson's use of criminal discourse: "Dickens's indictment
of Chancery" and "the charges already levelled in . . . *The Times*" cap-
ture the sense of positive wrong which it was the aim of reform to
redress. *Bleak House* may be viewed then as a critical intervention in
debates about social organization, rather than as a linguistic, revolu-
tionist or pessimistic attack on all social structures.[27] That Chancery
reform proceeds from an ideal is one of the implications of the wordplay of the *Athenaeum* reviewer quoted in my introduction. The "mighty
mystery of Iniquity and Equity" conjoins similarities in sound with
opposites in meaning to express the paradox of Chancery: that the
Equity court, in defiance of its name and its jurisdiction, delivers
"Iniquity" or injustice. The result of the conjunction is to create two
senses of equity, the ideal and the institutional. The former signifies
justice and mercy, the opposite of the fixed rigour of the law. The
latter signifies the Court of Chancery, established to give effect to the
ideal, but by Dickens's day a by-word for injustice and as bound by
precedent as the Common Law it was designed to supplement. The
existence of equity as an ideal is important both for the novel and for
Chancery reform.

In *Bleak House* the impersonal narrator's opening account of the
court in session expresses outrage at the impenetrable technicality of
the proceeding, with barristers "running their goat-hair and horse-hair
warded heads against walls of words, and making a pretence of equity"
(p. 6). "So much has this public institution perverted its purpose," John
R. Reed observes, "that it *begets* injury and injustice instead of curing
them."[28] Listing the consequences of the Chancery suit, the people
whom the "unwholesome hand" of Jarndyce and Jarndyce has been
able to "spoil and corrupt," the narrator concludes that it has affected
the mentality of those even "in its outermost circle of evil," who "have
been tempted into a loose way of letting bad things alone to take their
own course, and a loose belief that if the world go wrong, it was, in
some off-hand manner, never meant to go right" (pp. 8–9). The "shirking
and sharking" sponsored by Jarndyce and Jarndyce are unambiguously

"bad things" which must be corrected. This reformist imperative is underwritten by the narrator's rejection of any elevation of Murphy's law ("if something can go wrong, it will") into a metaphysical principle. *Bleak House* is, therefore, imbued with "the spirit of reform."

The paideic vision of the law reformer is illustrated by Brougham's six-hour speech to the House of Commons on 7 February, 1828 on the need for reform. In his peroration, Brougham cites Napoleon's boast that his greatest achievement was his *Civil Code* and urges England's sovereign to dream of a similar boast:

> that he found the law dear and left it cheap; found it a sealed book – left it a living letter; found it the patrimony of the rich – left it the inheritance of the poor; found it the two edged sword of craft and oppression – left it the staff of honesty and the shield of innocence.[29]

He specifically excluded equity from his speech because the 1824 Chancery Commission had already reported on some reform needs. Twenty years on, Chancery was still unreformed, and Dickens could work Brougham's antitheses into a more urgent critique. For Bentham the notion of a supplementary equity jurisdiction was irrational, a sign of the absence of a scientific system of legal rules.[30]

The achieved reforms of the law imply a belief in the fundamental soundness of the legal system; but they also imply an acceptance that the ends and means of the law are under human control, and that a duty exists or social policy demands that the law be turned into an effective instrument of justice. An analogy may be drawn here between law reform and the repairs and renovations undertaken by John Jarndyce at his eponymous home. With all its successive additions, its design seems "delightfully irregular" (p. 62); yet it has been made habitable and becomes the setting for a new family life by Jarndyce's efforts after the neglect of the previous occupant, the distressed litigant, Tom Jarndyce. Chancery reform, then, is not only a procedural matter, but an attempt to reactivate the jurisdiction of equity, to overturn the warning of honourable Chancery practitioners, "Suffer any wrong that can be done you, rather than come here!" (p. 7). One consequence of stressing the paideic element of Chancery reform is to reclaim as a critical issue "the general belief that Dickens's object in writing *Bleak House* was to get the Chancery Court reformed,"[31] because the social as well as the symbolic significance of Chancery is necessary to an understanding of the novel's representation of law.[32] As Cover argues, real and ideal are connected by the bridge of law.

Chancery became a bitter jest, even the name of a wrestling hold, because it travestied its own promise of justice. Something of the manifold physical and spiritual, ethical and financial, experience of injustice is revealed in Dickens's response to his own abortive suit for injunctions and then common law damages against the piracy of *A Christmas Carol*:

I shall not easily forget the expense, and anxiety, and horrible injustice of the Carol case, wherein, asserting the plainest right on earth, I was really treated as if I were the robber instead of the robbed.[33]

It is sometimes suggested that this righteous disappointment is the source of an irrational hatred of Chancery which devalues *Bleak House*.[34] This judgment denies the historical record of Chancery abuses, and rests on expectations of normative realism and perhaps on a deterministic psychology of literary creation. The opening of *Bleak House* displays a mimetic interest in the Chancery scene, but this mimesis competes for the reader's attention with the symbolism of the fog and the tone of portentous sonority of the narrative voice. The conventions of the "legal novel" appear to be invoked, but the respectful commentary of Scott and Warren is replaced by majestic irony: "And hard by Temple bar, in Lincoln's Inn Hall, at the very heart of the fog, sits the Lord High Chancellor in his High Court of Chancery" (p. 6). Likewise the details of legal office are presented with disdainful vagueness: "there are two or three maces, or petty-bags, or privy purses or whatever they may be" (p. 7). However, this dialogical representation of Chancery also leaves *Bleak House* open to the larger discourse of equity. Specifically, I shall argue that Dickens's adoption of a reformist perspective entails a commitment to the ideal of equity. Accordingly, the next section suggests some ways in which the structure and rhetoric of the novel are informed by notions of equity that had developed in England. Importantly, in this view *Bleak House* is a product of *legal* history, as well as of literary history. It is impossible to say how much of the discourse of equity in the novel was intentionally used, but it is equally impossible, in view of Dickens's personal and journalistic experience of Chancery, to deny its significance in the design.

II

The classical notion of equity, defined by Aristotle as "a correction of law where it is defective owing to its universality,"[35] might be exemplified by the pardon of Effie Deans in *The Heart of Midlothian*. The residuary power of the monarch "to administer justice outside the regular system" is usually cited as the foundation of the Chancery jurisdiction in England.[36] Originally a court of conscience, the equity it administered was gradually refined into a body of principles, partly as a result of clashes with the Common Law courts and partly from the recognition that without principles, parties would not be treated equally. Equality, as Baker puts it, "was a requisite of equity." The eventual result of this development was a system rigid in its rules and procedures:

It is the height of irony that the Court which originated to provide an escape from the defects of common law procedure should in its later history have developed procedural defects worse by far than those of the law. For two centuries before Dickens wrote *Bleak House*, the word "Chancery" had been synonymous with expense, delay and despair.[37]

This irony is underscored by the discrepancy between Chancery practices and the principles of the equity jurisdiction, set forth in the "maxims of equity."[38] Among the maxims, the following are particularly telling for present purposes: equity will not, by reason of a merely technical defect, suffer a wrong to be without a remedy; he who seeks equity must do equity; he who comes into equity must come with clean hands; delay defeats equities; equality is equity; equity looks to the intent rather than to the form; and, equity acts *in personam*. These illustrate the conscientious, substantive and idealistic expectations which equity imposed on those seeking its assistance and the standard of justice which it set itself. With the defects of Chancery, some of the maxims began to function ironically. The Jennens case, the inspiration for Jarndyce and Jarndyce, was begun in 1798 and was still extant in 1915, when costs amounted to £250,000.[39] In such an example, the maxim, "delay defeats equities" ironically applies to the court's own dilatoriness, which denies its suitors' justice.

The amplitude of the maxims' application was also limited by the kinds of case able to be brought before the court. From the sixteenth century most Chancery cases concerned land or "real property" and as the court rigidified its practice, this limitation became entrenched. In consequence, the equity jurisdiction protected the land-owning class, but not others. According to Blackstone's *Commentaries*, the Chancellor was "keeper of the King's conscience; ... general guardian of all infants, idiots and lunatics; and [had] the general superintendence of all charitable uses in the kingdom." This jurisdiction derives from the

monarch's duty as "*parens patriae*," parent of the nation.[40] Douglas Hamer
comments that the "basic principle of the Court of Chancery, that the
socially weak must have a protector-at-law in the monarch, operated
only where real estate was concerned." Lord Eldon ruled, as part of a
policy of "crystallizing" the equity jurisdiction, that he should not exercise these powers unless a case of disputed property was before him.[41]
The Chancellor is guardian-at-law to Ada and Richard because they
are heirs to the Jarndyce estate. He discharges no such responsibility
with respect to Jo, or Charley, or Guster, or Esther. The apostrophe
following Jo's death, "Dead, your Majesty. Dead, my Lords and gentle-
men," invokes the consciences not only of all "men and women," but
especially the Queen as *parens patriae* and those in power under her.
That the exercise of the *parens patriae* jurisdiction is seen in the Lord
Chancellor's careful and kindly enquiry into the appointment of John
Jarndyce as guardian of the wards serves only to emphasize the need
for and existent limitations on such power. Jarndyce becomes guardian not only to Rick and Ada, but to Esther and, through her, to
Charley and others. This extension of compassion and charity makes
him a supplementary Chancellor-figure, one who is perhaps more
effectual, though sometimes, when the "east wind" blows, as problematic as his prototype. The function of guardian is therefore drawn from
the equity tradition, but is given a far wider range of operation than it
had in Chancery.

Yet even this is recognized as second best. The notion of surrogate
parenthood is criticized from the beginning by Esther: "The Lord
High Chancellor, at his best, appeared so poor a substitute for the love
and pride of parents" (p. 31). Jarndyce himself hopes that his guardianship will "heal some of the wounds made by the miserable Chancery
suit" (p. 43). The Chancellor's surrogacy is vitiated by its origin in
Jarndyce and Jarndyce. As Ada writes to Richard, the suit "had its
share in making us both orphans" (p. 466). Jarndyce and Jarndyce is
largely responsible for Richard's unsteadiness: when the Chancellor
reproves him as a "Vexatious and Capricious Infant" who does not
know his own mind, Richard's riposte, "a pretty good joke . . . from
that quarter," is pertinent criticism (p. 300).

Ultimately, *Bleak House* idealizes responsible parenthood and family
life while multiplying instances of abandonment, neglect, infertility,
poverty, disease and death. Like the ideal of equity, family "love and
pride" is the desired Other in a world of broken relations. The novel
seeks to inscribe the care and protection of children into the *nomos*.

The power of the Chancellor over guardianship is the one room in the "bleak house" of the law adapted to the purpose. Dickens's awareness of this power may be traced to *The Autobiography of Leigh Hunt*, wherein the model for Harold Skimpole laments the removal of Shelley's children from their father's custody by the Chancellor:

the reader, perhaps, is not aware that in this country so justly called free on many accounts, and so proud of its "Englishman's castle" – of the house which nothing can violate – a man's offspring can be taken from him tomorrow who holds a different opinion from the Lord Chancellor in faith and morals.[42]

The interest here is not the merits of Hunt's defence of Shelley (or of Dickens's disloyalty to Hunt), but the dialectical contrast with Dickens's view of the "condition of England" in general and of the value of the Chancellor's guardianship function. The passage gives to the novel's portrayal of Skimpole as parent a special sharpness, but most importantly it links the idea of parenthood with the image of the home as sanctuary. Esther betrays a consciousness of the rights of the householder and parent when, at the Jellybys', she is "in two minds about taking [the] liberty" of bathing Peepy (p. 46), but knows that nobody will notice.

Further, this legal cliché is shown to function negatively in *Bleak House*, through the forcible entry into houses by bailiffs and such self-appointed moral guardians as Mrs. Pardiggle. The fractured families are also those whose dwellings are most exposed or liable to invasion, which is not only a sign of the novel's socio-economic realism, but an image pattern of emotional, psychological and also political significance. Most precarious in this respect are the brickmakers' wives and children. This domestic setting is invested with political awareness: of the arrogant paternalism of Mrs. Pardiggle; of the brickmakers' radical resistance; of the "triple jeopardy" of the brickmakers' wives, poor, grieving, and battered; of the effects of economic depression and the lack of self-determination evident when brickmakers cannot house their families properly. The disturbing scenes in which Bucket arrests Gridley and later Trooper George by disguised entry into George's and the Bagnets' homes are further examples of this correspondence. By contrast, Charley's efforts to protect her siblings by locking them in is a telling image of determination and a successful adaptation, perhaps inversion, of the skills of a bailiff. Needless to say, her father has easily gained access to Skimpole's. If, according to the mythology of English law, an Englishman's home is his castle, then the novel's imagery of homes vulnerable to invasion and of "decaying houses" in Chancery forces a reconsideration of the security afforded by the law. In consequence, the decrepit slum of Tom-All-Alone's comes to stand not only for the deranged obsession of Tom Jarndyce, but for the rotting structure of Chancery. By extension, English law is not the protective walled city of Heraclitus, but a "bleak house" in which victims like Jo are "moved on" by officers of the state.

The distinction between Chancery practice and the ideals of Equity has far-reaching consequences for an understanding of *Bleak House*. A further illustration of this "pretense of equity" is afforded by the maxim, "Equity acts *in personam.*" Simply put, this refers to the nature of equitable remedies, which order named persons either to perform an action that, in conscience or justice, they ought to perform, or to desist from any unconscionable or unjust action. In *Bleak House* Chancery barely acts at all; instead it is presented as feeding off the estate, as concerned only with the self-maintenance of the suit and the profits to the legal officers. Dickens begins the action of the novel at a time when the only question in dispute in the legal action is that of costs. The reader is never informed what substantive orders were made in answer to the questions originally brought before the court. The equitable action ordered by the court is irrelevant when there is no estate left to be distributed after lawyers' and court costs have been deducted. The late discovery of a final will, which seems to supply the details upon which the court has ruled and the money has been spent, simply confirms the futility of the Chancery action. As D. A. Miller suggests, Jarndyce and Jarndyce is not resolved, merely ended by the exhaustion of the estate in costs.[43] This is the only appropriate outcome for a court obsessed by procedural issues and clogged by procedural inefficiency. The objective correlative of this wasteful system is, of course, Krook's rag and bottle shop, a business without turnover, much less profit, "'of so many kinds, and all, as the neighbours think (but *they* know nothing), wasting away and going to rack and ruin, that that's why they have given me and my place a christening'" (p. 50).

The only exception to the substantive inaction of Chancery is the order appointing John Jarndyce guardian of the wards. The Jarndyce household, under the superintendence of Esther, is a model of sympathy and efficiency, in contrast to Krook and his eponym. In consequence, Jarndyce's role as supplement to the Lord Chancellor is extended, and Bleak House becomes an alternative Chancery. It becomes the centre of a network of fellowship and charity, in which Jarndyce's quiet generosity

and Esther's unpretentious practicality provide conscientious and effective assistance to those of their acquaintance in need. The hallmark of
this assistance is personal action and immediate relief. In its conversion
of ideals into reality, it contrasts with the distant dream and present
mess, the torrent of words and paper, of both Chancery and Tele-
scopic Philanthropy.

This contrast recalls Cover's image of law as a bridge in normative
space, stretching across a gap between a present reality and an envisaged ideal. The reactivation of equity by Jarndyce and Esther constitutes such a bridge. It is possible to trace an "alternity" in the structure
and image-patterning of *Bleak House* in the contrast between the "fog"
and the light and warmth connoted by the sounds of Esther's surname,
"summer-sun." Her activity and performance of her "duty" may be
seen as opening up the possibility of a new world, especially as the
emblem of that duty is her keys. Janus-like, keys have a double significance, of locking and unlocking. Esther and Jarndyce, by their actions,
use the keys as instruments of opening, not closure. In this respect, their
munificence is contrasted with the penny-pinching Smallweeds, with
Tulkinghorn's locked boxes of aristocratic secrets and with the accumulated junk of Krook's shop. A variant of this pattern is provided by the
closure of the right-of-way, which is the subject of a ridiculous dispute
between Boythorn and Sir Leicester. The non-communication between
these hyperbolical opponents, like that between the brickmaker and
Mrs. Pardiggle, contrasts with the connections achieved by Esther with
Jo and the brickmakers' wives.

The significance of seeing the Esther-Jarndyce principle as a bridge
is confirmed by the gulf posited by the narrator between Jo and the
cross on the dome of St. Paul's Cathedral, "so golden, so high up, so
far out of his reach" (p. 243); an emblem not of religion, but of confusion. Jo is not the only character who experiences this: all the Jarndyces,
and especially Richard, find that the "great suit" is a veritable maze,[44]
the exploration of which only increases perplexity; Esther is mystified
by her likeness to Lady Dedlock, as is Guppy; Krook does not understand the documents he collects or the letters he laboriously copies. On
this basis, J. Hillis Miller has argued that *Bleak House* is "a document
about the interpretation of documents," in which reader, author and
character are all interpreters of "signs and tokens."[45] He argues, like
Cover, that systems of law "give actions and documents a meaning,"[46]
but, distrusting systems, concludes that *Bleak House* is poised between a
traditional belief in them and a tendency to put all interpretation in

question. This opposition pays insufficient attention to the presentation of Chancery's institutional failure to perform the required acts of
interpretation.[47] The acquisition of meaning is expressed in the novel
by the plot, which emphasizes *anagnorisis*,[48] and by the narrative scheme,
in which a character whose existence was sought to be erased is elevated to the ontologically supreme status of co-author.[49] Esther's narrative, like the plot of the novel, opposes the hermeneutic failure of
Chancery. Moreover the cognitive function of her narration is combined with affective developments: speaking of her own experience,
she proposes a link between the quickening of the affections and of the
understanding. By this process, in equity and in private life knowledge
is connected with the novel's moral imperative of charity. Esther narrates the parallel growth of her emotional security and knowledge of
her own identity. Part of her "duty" is to lessen the confusion of others
by teaching them to read.

What the novel repeatedly calls "Esther's Narrative" not only
describes her own "progress," but also provides a new perspective
from which the confusion wrought by Chancery may be judged. As
autobiography, Esther's narrative represents a completely different story-
telling practice from that adopted in the Court of Chancery. Evidence
in Chancery was always written, not oral. Holdsworth describes the
process by which Chancery obtained its formal "depositions": witnesses were required to answer, without legal assistance, "lengthy and
minute" interrogatories written by the plaintiff's lawyers; their answers
were written down by commissioners, not verbatim, but in the third
person and often rephrased. Holdsworth concludes "that there was
every chance that in the course of this transcription its effect would be
materially altered."[50] The unusual "double narrative" of *Bleak House*
may be seen in part as a reaction to this artificial and indirect form of
testimony, an ironic commentary on, if not an intentional disavowal of
it. Esther's narrative is a first-person statement, integral to, but part
of a larger document, in her own words, preserving all her significant
evasions, hesitancies, qualifications and avowals. Its inclusion has pro-
voked much comment about the relative status of the two narrators,
their contrasting voices and the consequential articulation by Esther of
alternative values.[51] What an evidentiary analysis of her narrative adds
to the critical understanding of the novel is a sense of the importance of the individual witness. Esther's narrative asserts the value of
personal expression over the formal reconstructions of Chancery.
Moreover the elevation of the individual in the narrative system is an

embodiment in the form of the value of personal action in the social system. Above all it endows the illegitimate orphan with the right to speak in the cause of her own life. Esther's narrative is a vindication of her identity, a proof that she is not *filia nullius*, the daughter of *Nemo*, nobody. It is a rewriting of the repressive history of Miss Barbary. Ironically, it effectively takes the place of the deposition she could not give in explanation of her interest in Jarndyce and Jarndyce.[52] With the impersonal narration it supersedes the mountainous writing and rewriting of that case. As evidence, Esther's narrative also stands in condemnation of the rejection of Jo as a witness at Nemo's inquest.

## III

*Bleak House* includes the evidence of Jo's grateful remembrance of Nemo, just as it includes Sir Leicester's grief at the death of Lady Dedlock. It is often praised for the comprehensiveness of its social analysis, for anatomizing the "condition of England."[53] A similar, totalizing ambition is listed by Holdsworth as one of the "abuses" of Chancery: "the rigid rule that, if it acted at all, it must assume entire control. It would not, for instance, decide a single doubtful point . . . without administering the whole estate."[54] The rule arose from a desire to do "complete justice," but the result, for Holdsworth, was Jarndyce and Jarndyce. Does *Bleak House* replicate the plenipotentiary defects of its referent? Hillis Miller argues along this line in his discussion of the theme of interpretation. He suggests that the novel is "a model in little of English society," but proceeds to examine not the society, but the structure of its literary model: "*Bleak House* has exactly the same structure as the society it exposes."[55] Interpretation is a characteristic common to literature and law, and therefore a central concern of the "legal novel." However, Hillis Miller's conclusion is predicated on a thematization of the world as a text, an approach that his namesake, D. A. Miller, points out is resisted by the novel itself. D. A. Miller avers that "the current critical fondness for assimilating form and content" must account for novelistic assertions of the difference between them. In this respect, as foreshadowed above, he emphasizes how Chancery profitably defers the work of interpretation rather than carrying it out. He himself considers the relationship between the length of Jarndyce and Jarndyce and the length of *Bleak House* and sites their qualitative difference in their endings, the case lacking and the novel supplying meaning through resolution. In addition, the pleasure of reading Dickens's account of Jarndyce and Jarndyce contrasts with the weariness of Chancery litigants wading through another round of paper-work in their protracted cause. In a similar way, the totality of *Bleak House* depends upon a selection of incidents and characters being carefully built up into a pleasurable and meaningful whole, of disparate scenes, the connections between which are gradually revealed; while the "monument to Chancery practice" begins with an entire property which it gradually wastes, with a cast of beneficiaries which it expands at will, and occupies an infinitely extensible duration.

While pointing to the novel's difference from the social institution which it represents, D. A. Miller nonetheless connects the literary form with the world. Specifically, he regards the novel as the product and agent of Foucault's age of "discipline." In this argument the novel is one among many systems for the bureaucratization of power. The reading of novels, especially in the serial form of their first Victorian readers, "trains us to abide in Chancery-like structures."[56] The novel cannot be read at one sitting, but must be laid aside for work, thereby helping to perpetuate the public-private, work-leisure dichotomies of industrial societies. The ending, finitely deferred but always promised, delivers gratification to subservient readers. (The existence of resistant, unsatisfied readers like Lord Denman or the anonymous reviewers quoted above cannot be explained by this model.) Miller relies on simile, rather than on historical exemplification: "Chancery-like structures" are illustrated by the queue, "getting us to wait, as it were in its very long lines," and by the trust that the reader learns to place in the "machinery of distribution," which will deliver the promised next instalment.[57] The invocation of queues seems so trivial as to be a parody of micropolitics. The use of the present tense elides current and Victorian readers.

The implication that nothing has changed, endemic in New Historicist criticism, contrasts with the claims of Hurst that the legal abuses have gone and that there have been revolutionary changes in the social and physical environments of the English courts: "To modern England, poor Jo speaks from a dead world."[58] Each of these views is extreme and simplistic, one overly deterministic, one too sanguine in its belief in social progress. In their "defence," it should be said that Miller recognizes that *Bleak House* demands a reformed Chancery, and Hurst acknowledges the effects of historical change. Hurst's complacency may be traced to his inability to see that Chancery is a symbol as well as a legal institution, the significance of which transcends historical time and place. His own historical situation, writing in the late 1940s, may have fostered the illusion that the only bleak houses then in England were those bombed by the external enemy. By contrast, Miller's limitation is that he sees Chancery too much in its symbolic, too little in its historical aspect. For him, Chancery functions less as a Court of Equity than as a thematization of the disciplinary system. In *Bleak House* Gridley's anger is directed at this deterministic and exculpatory invocation of "the system" by individuals working within it (p. 193). His violence exposes the coercive power of the court, which has imprisoned him. While Foucault makes the prison the prototype of the normalizing institutions diffused throughout society, its usage in the forced restraint of force should not be overlooked. Further, its disciplinary regime is unsuccessful, as is Chancery's. The power of the system, then, is great but not absolute. A fully political reading of *Bleak House* must attend not only to its inscription of disciplinary modes, but also to what David Suchoff calls "the oppositional force of narrative," its critical representation of the *nomos*.[59]

*Bleak House* incorporates this conflict by making the Chancery officials and practitioners respond to Gridley's demands with bemusement and intransigence. Between its injustice to litigants and its imperviousness to criticism, Chancery seems to hold no prospect of change. There is no reformist lawyer in the novel; the reform process forms no part of its plot. Yet the discourse of reform is implicit in the lawyers' very avoidance or denial of it, in their expressed consideration for Mr. Vholes's daughters, and in Conversation Kenge's embarrassed explanation of the end of Jarndyce and Jarndyce. The case for reform is established in the novel through the narrators' discourses and through the dramatized misery of the litigants and self-interest of the practitioners. Dickens derives from the lawyers' travesty of professionalism the rule that "the one great principle of English law is, to make business for itself" (p. 482). Of this predatory attitude, the characterization of Vholes as a vampire seeking respectability is an expressive Victorian adaptation of an old satiric type. The altruism of Jarndyce is the ethical accompaniment of his distancing himself from the court. His refusal to take Chancery on its own terms provides the foundation for a counter-discourse and an alternative ethos. In its general orientation Jarndyce's Bleak House is one of Cover's "isolationist" nomic communities – but his intervention to protect Ada and Rick is a "redemptive" action. Rick's entanglement and death plots the partial failure of the redemptive enterprise. The conflict between him and Jarndyce and their eventual reunion confirms the value of isolationism: entanglement means death while isolation enables them to "begin the world" afresh (p. 763).

However, this desire must contend with the novel's valuation of practical charity and its insistence on the inescapability of the past. The latter is indicated in numerous related ways: in the psychological revelation of Esther's narrative as well as in her discovery of her parents; in the belated recovery of Nemo's identity as well as the exposure of Lady Dedlock's secret. The novel thus asserts the futility of attempts to erase personal history. This principle is also attested in the "genealogy" of Bleak House itself, the fact that architecturally and in its contents it allows the prosperity and decline of the Jarndyces to be traced. If John Jarndyce's presentation of a replica of Bleak House to Esther and Woodcourt seems to trap them in the past and to problematize his whimsical generosity, it must be remembered that the house and the family have changed before and will probably change again. Though there is an element of the conventional romantic ending of the attainment of love and stability, the new Bleak House enables Esther's history to be incorporated in their new life rather than superseded or made irrelevant.[60] As such, it provides an appropriate setting for the active amelioration of Esther's charity and Woodcourt's medicine. Their approach is less to "begin the world" afresh than to repair the old one. For this remedial work, a doctor is a more significant choice of agent than a law reformer.

Woodcourt's ministrations, like those of Jarndyce and Esther, work "little by little" and promise no appreciable effect on the powerful monolith of Chancery. "Deadlock," or lack of progress, seems to dominate the social system. Coodle and Doodle have presided over ruinous governments, but according to Sir Leicester Dedlock no-one else is qualified to govern the country. Chancery is a monstrous source of inefficiency and injustice, but according to Kenge a great country cannot have a little system. Parliament and Chancery are stiff-jointed survivals, like Deportment: in Hillis Miller's analysis, metonyms for a society deadlocked by an archaic and self-serving ruling elite.[61] Through this rhetoric of contiguity Dickens builds up a picture of the British Constitution and body politic. For example, Sir Leicester regards an interminable Chancery suit approvingly, as "a slow, expensive, British, constitutional kind of thing" (p. 15). To countenance criticism of the status quo is to encourage revolution, personified as "Wat Tyler." As

Susan Shatto has noted, this and other expressions of Sir Leicester, such as "the floodgates are burst open" (p. 504), were part of the conservative reaction to the 1832 Reform Bill, expressing fear of the rising tide of democracy.[62] In this light, it is significant that Chesney Wold is in flood when the novel opens.

The most explicit development of the body politic imagery occurs in the description of Sir Leicester's gout. In a satiric extension of the hereditary basis of aristocratic society, Dickens includes the disease in the Dedlock patrimony, something handed down throughout time "beyond which the memory of man goeth not to the contrary" (p. 196). This phrase, a misquotation from Blackstone's *Commentaries*, applies the language of custom sanctioned as law to the ills of the body. As an internal inflammation, the Dedlock gout is a variation on the "Spontaneous Combustion" of Krook, the pseudo-Lord Chancellor. The latter is overtly symbolic, "the death of all Lord Chancellors in all Courts, and of all authorities in all places . . . where false pretences are made and where injustice is done." Like Jo's death, it is reported rhetorically not to the common reader but to the monarch, or to the reader as democratic ruler. It is not described but diagnosed: "inborn, inbred, engendered in the corrupted humours of the vicious body itself" (p. 403). This death has been interpreted as having revolutionary implications: for Edgar Johnson, it is a prophecy that society's injustices are so oppressive that they can only be cured by "the complete annihilation that they will ultimately provide by blowing up of their own corruption."[63] Dickens's resort to Spontaneous Combustion, a fictitious natural process makes the death of the corrupt order an organic necessity, not the result of a political action. Krook's death therefore functions less as revolutionary prophecy than as apocalyptic warning. The death of the old and the birth of the new are alike imaginable only as nightmarish fantasy.

A more realistic nightmare, one that eventuates, is the smallpox infection passed from Jo to Charley to Esther. The prophetic future tense which imagines the pestilence moving from Tom-All-Alone's "up to the proudest of the proud, and to the highest of the high" (p. 553) dispels Sir Leicester's presumption that disease and death are levellers that yet respect class distinctions. Once again, disease is political:

There is not an atom of Tom's slime, not a cubic inch of any pestilential gas in which he lives, not one obscenity or degradation about him, not an ignorance, not a wickedness, not a brutality of his committing, but shall work its retribution, through every order of society. (p. 553)

The first figure whom the narrative finds moving through this portentous setting is, significantly, the physician. At first anonymously, he
attends to the brickmaker's wife; then, seeing and chasing Jo, he is
named. This meeting between the doctor and the diseased is important for the contrast it affords between Bucket's and Woodcourt's treatment of Jo. The former is feared for his unsympathetic "moving on" of
the boy, while the latter helps him to find shelter and companionship.
Though medically unavailing, Woodcourt's political and ethical action
of attending the poor and treating them with dignity is of great significance. It represents an inversion of the analogy drawn by Socrates in
Book V of the *Republic* between a just city and a healthy body: in such
a city the legislator is like a doctor, healing society; but in an unjust
city, the legislators are inactive, the people are sick and the doctor
must dispense medicine, comfort, wisdom and law.[64] In *Bleak House*
England requires not a reformist lawyer, but a physician and surgeon.
The sickness motif is so thoroughly connected with the ethical concerns of the novel that Esther, in the most horrific nightmare of her
illness, dreams of herself as one of a set of gleaming beads, from which
she prays to be taken off (p. 432) – a reversal of her normal cultivation
of helpful connection with others.

IV

The ideal society in this novel is defined by Esther as the family,
a co-operative and loving union. As D. A. Miller has argued, family
domesticity serves as a refuge from and alternative to the public world
that is "in Chancery."[65] Jarndyce and Jarndyce introduces conflict into
the family: Richard, when he is absorbed in the case, loses the ability
to see his guardian as anything but a competitor, an "interested party."
Esther forces him to see this: "'Are division and animosity your natural terms, Richard?'" (p. 464). Rick's admission that the suit "puts us
on unnatural terms" becomes only "another reason for urging it on!"
For Esther it is a reason for abandoning it. It is possible to argue that
Esther has it completely wrong, that the "Chancery suits have all
originated in family quarrels – Jarndyces', Miss Flite's, Gridley's."[66]
This argument makes it easy to absolve Chancery and to blame the
litigants for their own misery.[67] It also ignores the evident need for
courts to determine real disputes: Jarndyce and Jarndyce really had its
origin in an unclear will. The ambiguity of documents and the competition over financial and other resources are the sources of legal cases.

The latter problem is evaded, indeed effaced, in *Bleak House* by the apparently illimitable funds of John Jarndyce. While there is a fount of generosity in the family, while the distribution of wealth extends to whoever comes under notice, the problem of scarcity and competition does not exist, and the reality of conflict can be displaced into the category of the unnatural. It is essential to note, though, that the Bleak House community has had to be created, by renovating the home, by intervention in Chancery, by paying for Esther's education. The novel therefore presents the ideal family as something retrieved from the social and moral chaos. The plot of Esther's life is one of finding and making her own family. Nevertheless, the task of building a family unit is made easier – and the experience of family life looks rosier – in the benevolent environment created by John Jarndyce's wealth. As *Bleak House* elides the need for Chancery reform with the "natural" death of corrupt systems, so it replaces the fraught rejection of Esther's childhood with a "family romance."

The process of transformation is, in each case, entrusted to a guardian. A reformed Chancery would provide true, equal, effective guardianship. Esther's accession to a family of her own is presided over by Jarndyce. In each of these cases there is a problematic paternalism at work: the only alternative to the gouty and self-serving elite is the ironmaster, whose superintendence of the marriage of Watt and Rosa is the same species of patronage as the Dedlocks' and John Jarndyce's. The ruse whereby Jarndyce "transfers" (almost in the legal sense) Esther's plighted troth from himself to Woodcourt is arrant paternalism. Indeed it clarifies their relationship from that of lovers to that of father and daughter. Further, the presentation of the new Bleak House constitutes a dowry, given by a father through his daughter to her husband. If, as the rationale of the Chancery jurisdiction suggests, the need for guardianship is to ensure the protection of the young or insane, then this extension of the activities of guardian into the arrangement of marriage, whatever its generosity, replicates the legal subordination of women in Victorian society, and affirms paternalistic power.[68]

To infer from this conclusion that nothing changes in Esther's life or in a reformed Chancery is too sweeping. For Esther to marry Woodcourt, not only does Jarndyce have to recognize the falsity of his "suit," but Mrs. Woodcourt must undergo a change of values in a particular which ramifies throughout *Bleak House*, the importance of noble blood or aristocratic lineage. Esther's illegitimate birth would bar her from Lady Dedlock's admittedly worthless share in the Jarndyce estate, and closer to home, from a middle-class marriage with Wood-court. Sir Leicester's ideology of class purity is a means of maintaining political hegemony, and one of its effects is to imbue the middle classes with a false consciousness of the value of gentility. Jarndyce's pertinent question to Mrs. Woodcourt, "What is the true legitimacy?" mounts a challenge to this ideology and hegemony, forcing her to choose between her prejudicial reverence for "blood" and her observation of Esther's evident loving and dutiful character. The question demands that Esther be valued not by her social status, but by her personal qualities. The structure of the novel underwrites this changed valu-ation by making Esther one of its narrators, ensuring that we see things from her "point of view" and more than this, that we experience her struggle to achieve a belief in the validity of her own perceptions. While her narration is still self-deprecating ("As if this narrative were the narrative of *my* life!" [p.27]) Esther progresses from burying her doll to marriage and motherhood, from the periphery to the centre of an emotional circle which changes its quality from disgrace to rich happiness.

The question, "What is the true legitimacy?" also applies to the body politic. The novel challenges social and political institutions to legitimate themselves rather than to rely on inherited authority. Law, fashion, parliament, all "things of precedent and usage" (p. 10), have their injustices, pretensions and irrelevances exposed. Even the funda-mental law, the regulator of political power, is an unwritten and inher-ited body of practices, and is described with ironic invective as "that inestimable jewel to him (if he only knew it) the Constitution" (p. 198). Jo, to whom this passage applies, is as ignorant of the Constitution as the Constitution is of him. The rhetorical power of both the imper-sonal narrator and Esther is directed against the rhetoric of the ruling class: it questions the equitable professions of Chancery, the repres-entativeness of the "representative government" and the sincerity of religious Missions and proselytes; it deflates Blackstone's eloquence by applying it to gout; it rewrites the Authorized Version of the Bible and the Book of Common Prayer to accord with realities ("here they lower our dear brother down a foot or two: here, sow him in corruption, to be raised in corruption" (p. 137);[69] and it shows the anachronism of conservative clichés by investing Chesney Wold with the damp of the already-breached floodgates. Thus, in the year of the Great Exhibition, *Bleak House* seeks to inject into the self-congratulation of the British people a questioning of the comprehensiveness of their vision; amid the economic well-being it seeks to promote a "legitimation crisis."[70]

As an answer to "the Condition-of-England" question, *Bleak House* portrays English society "in Chancery," dominated by and characterized by the dead hand of the court. Against this, Dickens sets the "progress" of Esther Summerson and, through her, the reclamation of the ideals of equity. The upshot of this two-fold presentation is to override any static assumptions underlying the "Condition of England," to insist on the necessity of change by using the temporal properties of narrative. Thus *Bleak House* acknowledges the obstructive ambitions of institutions like Chancery and people like Sir Leicester, but in its representation of a succession of incidents it brings the Jarndyce case to an end, transforms Esther from orphan to mother, brings down the house of Dedlock and otherwise exposes illusions of permanence, restores lost children to their families and destroys attempts to bury the past.

Although the original Jarndyce will is said to have been made "in an evil hour" (p. 88), wills in general provide an opportunity to confer benefits on others and to link past, present and future. The nature of these benefits is expanded by the novel beyond the material: Jo and George make wills, while in her last chapter Esther writes of having little money but being rich in the love and praise of other people. George's will is an acknowledgment of the family ties he foresook for so long, and he guards against any possibility of cutting out others from his mother's estate. In this, one of the concluding episodes of the novel, the link between the law of succession and the ideal of the family is reaffirmed: not the division and animosity of the Jarndyce heirs, nor the exclusive and self-valorizing heritage of the Dedlocks, but the co-operative arrangements of the Dedlock servants and their progressive offspring are presented as a sign of what families can achieve under the law if, to use a slightly different sense of the word, they have the will.[71]

Dickens's choice of the story of a disputed will is, therefore, a significant vehicle for the promotion of an ideology of the family in the context of a general critique of society. It suggests, in particular, an older and more generalized sense of the word "estate," meaning not property, but a state of life, one that incorporates both classes of society and personal well-being. Jarndyce and Jarndyce, as noted on page 81, is based on the Jennens case. A sidelight of this case was the formation of the Jennens Society: payment of the membership fee

entitled subscribers to investigation of any possible claim that might be
made of their kinship with Jennens and hence a share in his estate.[72]
The opportunism, greed and fraud of this venture have their echo in
*Bleak House* in Guppy's quest for "information" and the Smallweeds'
visit to Sir Leicester. More importantly, however, the real beneficiary
of the Jarndyce case is the orphan who finds her family in a most
unexpected "connection" and who tells us that the money does not
matter.

## CHAPTER FIVE

# Representation, inheritance and anti-reformism in the "legal novel" – Orley Farm

*Orley Farm* (1861–2) occupies an important place in what the reviewer of *Bleak House* called "the Law Reports of Fiction." Trollope's novel opens by stating that its ideal title would be "The Great Orley Farm Case" and warning readers that the less cumbersome actual title behoves no pastoral plot, but refers, like *Bleak House*, to a piece of real estate which has become the subject of an inheritance dispute. Just as the title *of* the novel may mislead, so the title *to* the property may not be what it seems. The self-conscious deliberations of the narrator playfully indicate the fictionality of the story, but in a move typical of Trollope, they lead smoothly into a narrative discourse which asserts its own historicity: "certain legal questions which made a considerable stir in our courts of law."[1] In this formulation the prescriptive "legal novel" inspired by *Tales by a Barrister* meets the sensationalism of the *Causes Célèbres*: rebellion and passion are domesticated, reduced to the genteel crime of forgery by a wife of her husband's will, with redress sought through law and conscience. Reviewing *Orley Farm* in *The Times*, E. S. Dallas whimsically reflected on the paideic possibilities of such fiction:

> The legal student need no longer study his cases in thick volumes bound in yellow leather . . . ; he may study them in the loves of some Edwin and Angelina. If he looks for legal commentaries, he will find in the same pleasant pages abundance of useful reflections, illustrating perhaps not what the law is, but something much better – what it ought to be.[2]

This juxtaposition of two normative forms, law reports and romantic love, suggests that the love plot may be a metonymic figure for a society ruled by law, that marriage functions as the exemplary relationship of a well regulated society. The norm of a peaceful community is certainly mediated in *Orley Farm* with more directness and confidence than in either *The Heart of Midlothian* or *Bleak House*. However, just as the love of "Edwin and Angelina" is here juxtaposed with several dysfunctional relationships, so the social ideal must survive the experiences of crime, resentment, mockery, and failure.

Dallas's distinction between "what the law is" and "what it ought to be" encapsulates all the major issues to be addressed in this reading of *Orley Farm*. Taking "law" as norm, the plot rests on a conflict between the infraction and reassertion of conceptions of right. Second, the novel registers the "spirit of reform," the narrator attacking a number of legal institutions, but satirizing the official reform movement itself. Finally, there is the question of whether the law as represented in the novel is "true." The reception of *Orley Farm* was notable for criticisms of Trollope's law and lawyers. In this chapter I shall examine the most important of these attacks, not only because they show where the interests of law and fiction coincide and where they differ, but because they provide evidence of the development of the configuration of law and literature in the nineteenth century.

I

It is a critical commonplace that the novels of Anthony Trollope focus consistently and complexly on men and women whose lives are spent in and around such institutions as the Church of England and the Houses of Parliament. Asa Briggs, for example, has written appreciatively of how the novels reflect Bagehot's description of the English Constitution.[3] This reflectionist approach must be supplemented by a sense of the selective and constructive work of the novels. Nevertheless, Trollope's exploration of the interactions of public and private life in the sites of power of nineteenth-century England make his novels an appropriate choice for this study. They contributed, in ways I hope to show, to the "world-maintaining" function of the *nomos* through their presentation of the *imperium* of the legislators and divines (and less often of the *paideia*). Moreover, this engagement with the normative and the Machiavellian is extended by a recurrent interest in the institution of the law. According to Gerroulds' *A Guide to Trollope* there are eleven court-room scenes and in excess of one hundred lawyers or judges depicted in the novels:

Trollope loved his lawyers, and, although he frequently allowed them to play fast and loose with English law, they were individuals he delighted to portray. He followed them to their dingy offices and even to Court, not contenting himself, as he did with his Members of Parliament, with confining himself to their social life.[4]

While this contrast perhaps rests on too narrow a concept of "political" behaviour, it remains true that Trollope's novels evince a close interest in the professional life of lawyers and in the operation of the law. The Gerroulds assert that the novelist's primary concern is with character rather than the accurate presentation of legal action, an argument also made by recent critics.[5] *Orley Farm* offers an unrivalled opportunity to examine this issue: claims of legal inaccuracy have loomed large in the critical reception of the novel, some of which may be ascribed to authorial ignorance and some attributed to characters themselves "playing fast and loose."

Moreover, the legal content of *Orley Farm* is fundamental and extensive. The story depends on a forged codicil which leads to both an inheritance dispute and a criminal trial for perjury. The relationship between the accused Lady Mason and her leading counsel, Mr. Furnival, involves professional and sexual interests and so raises a real problem in barristers' ethics.[6] The portrait of Furnival is only one among a gallery of barristers and solicitors, the former ranging from the idealistic radical, Felix Graham, to the rough criminal defender, Mr. Chaffanbrass, and the latter from the genteel Round to the grasping Dockwrath. Together they form a fair representation of the "legal world" of England. The ideology and usages of this professional group are contrasted with those of continental Europe at an international congress on law reform held in Birmingham prior to (and juxtaposed against) Lady Mason's trial. The central issue is whether lawyers should be primarily concerned with finding the truth or with promoting the interests of their clients. The narrative therefore incorporates a discourse on the law as it should and should not be, as it is and might become. Through multiple plotting the action is broadened beyond the formal legal system to encompass social norms: the maintenance of principles and breach of duties derived from morality, religion, contractual relations and the ties of blood or friendship. In this dimension "law" becomes metaphor and metonym for society's normative project.

Stephen Wall has written that "matters of legal principle are raised sufficiently often in *Orley Farm* for the critic to be tempted to posit an integrating concept, to sense the consoling presence of a structuring theme."[7] Wall depreciates this line of enquiry as being inconsistent with Trollope's fidelity to the claims of individual character at the expense of abstract patterning of action. Thus, while Wall acknowledges the novel's concern with "the relationship between moral principles and professional ethics," he explores this through various characters' attitudes. When the issue becomes important to the resolution of the plot, when the barristers work to secure an acquittal for the guilty Lady Mason without believing her to be innocent, Wall stresses Trollope's recognition in chapter xiv that "All our motives are mixed." He argues that Trollope accepts the necessity of compromise, indeed that the novelist is himself compromised in that he has willed Lady Mason's acquittal, an outcome occasioned by Trollope's preference for the felt claims of her character over those of poetic and natural justice. I would argue that these entities cannot be so separated, that Trollope's ending (which includes not only the acquittal, but the surrender of Orley Farm and emigration of Lady Mason and her son) represents the author's notion of a just outcome for Lady Mason. This fusion of character and action, of sympathy and judgment, derives from legal notions of property and personal responsibility and from moral notions of mercy and atonement as much as from an aesthetic based on character. *Orley Farm* may not console us with a single unifying theme, but it challenges us by its championship of the individual and its attack on conventional advocacy in the name of truth. By combining these goals, Trollope makes legal ideas matter both to society and to novelistic practice. For the practice of advocacy and the ideal of truthful representation become issues for the writer as well as the lawyers. While the plot of *Orley Farm* and its narrative commentary pose questions about "the morality of advocacy,"[8] the reception of the novel by its first critics had as one of its foci the counter-suggestion that Trollope's presentation of the trial process and the work of the advocates was inaccurate and misconceived. In returning the novel's challenge the critics remind us that "representation" is both a legal and an artistic function. *Orley Farm* is therefore the site of a "contest of faculties," namely a clash between literary and legal practices.

II

A belief in fidelity to truth lies at the core of Trollope's rhetoric of value in *Orley Farm*. Both the court actions place in issue the truth or authenticity of the codicil and Lady Mason's evidence in support of it. The burden of the narrator's attack upon the English system of trial and advocacy is that it prevents the truth from emerging. Thus the idealism of Sir Peregrine Orme is ironized: "'My love, what is the purport of these courts of law if it be not to discover the truth and make it plain to the light of day?' Poor Sir Peregrine! His innocence in this respect was perhaps beautiful, but it was very simple" (II.161). And John Kenneby's simple desire to tell the truth is ridiculed by Moulder with his usual cynical epithet: "'Gammon! What do they care for truth?'" (II.209–10) This idealism is preserved in legal narrative fiction which centres on barrister-heroes such as Perry Mason or Rumpole, whose forensic skill enables the truth to emerge through the trial process. Trollope, however, eschews such a possibility by having Lady Mason confess her guilt privately, to Sir Peregrine, before the trial. This act of truth-telling, the dramatic centre of the story, reveals her legal guilt, but through a morally-admirable gesture. It elicits from the Ormes, and eventually the reader, a complex response of refined judgment and enlarged sympathy. More importantly for present purposes, the reader is placed in possession of facts which the court must, without the benefit of the confession, somehow discover. Only through this plot structure, as the *Saturday Review* noted in 1862, can Trollope maintain both his high valuation of the truth and his low opinion of the court system.[9] What this structure minimizes, despite the twenty years of Lady Mason's possession of Orley Farm, is any recognition that the truth may be difficult to access. In her close study of language and speech in *Orley Farm* Glynn-Ellen Fisichelli notes the "layers of ambiguity" in the evidence, but minimizes their effect, uncritically adopting Trollope's valuation of the trial as "a system gone corrupt."[10] As McMaster observes, the difficulty arises from an unreflective use of the omniscient point of view: "The problem of achieving total insight into a character is no problem for Trollope since, like God, he is the creator. He does not, at least at this early stage, consider that in life no such insight is available." Later, in *Phineas Redux*, the accused is indeed innocent, despite appearances of guilt, and Chaffanbrass becomes a kind of barrister-hero in proving this. In general, though, Wall's suggestion that Trollope hankers after a world of "transparent straightforwardness" is appealing.[11]

The ideal of truthfulness is not only the concern of the novel's content, but an implicit claim of its narrative mode as well. For the narrator of a realist novel is assumed to be telling a true story and, indeed, often proclaims the truthful superiority of realist narration over the falsifications of romance. One of the major analogies through which this assertion was made in the nineteenth century, apart from Stendhal's image of the "mirror in the roadway," was that of forensic evidence. George Eliot's formulation in chapter 17 of *Adam Bede*, which conjoins the images of mirror and witness, has been previously quoted (see chapter three above) but the comparison was invoked in respect of Trollope's narration in *Orley Farm* by the *Spectator* reviewer:

> Mr. Trollope never for a moment loses the nice discriminate style of "articulately-speaking men," – separating event from event, thought from thought, with the manner of a distinct witness who wishes to give the most perspicuous evidence, not of an artist the glow of whose conception has for the moment struck fire from his own mind.[12]

This appeal to evidentiary discourse is grounded in a dream of language as transparent medium.[13] Yet for all its commitment to telling the truth, *Orley Farm* has been criticized for offering an *untrue* representation of English law in action. Many, though not all, the critics have been lawyers. Barrister-writers were not uncommon contributors to the great nineteenth-century reviews, and a number of leading literary editors and critics had trained as lawyers. Their arguments deserve investigation because the novel's rhetorical emphasis on the ideal of veracity and its high mimetic form may make true representation of law a literary concern and not a mere matter of legal quibbling. To explore this issue I proceed first to a discussion of some of the points so criticized and then to the general considerations.

Criticism of the law in *Orley Farm* has focused on three areas above all: first, that Trollope does not present sufficient evidence to prove the charge of perjury against Lady Mason; second, that Chaffanbrass's cross-examination and Furnival's address to the jury go beyond the acceptable bounds of conduct for barristers; and, third, that Trollope generally misconceives the function of counsel in a criminal trial.

The "charge" of insufficient evidence is made by E. S. Dallas in *The Times*.[14] He argues that apart from Lady Mason's confession, which does not form part of the case against her (because it was made to Sir Peregrine who is not called as a witness, and because the accused was not permitted to testify in a criminal trial until 1898), there is little evidence of her guilt. Dallas distinguishes between a fact and evidence thereof. The evidence of perjury is not strong: the date of the deeds is circumstantial; John Kenneby's memory is shown to be unreliable; and Bridget Bolster limits herself to saying that she signed only one document, the nature of which seems doubtful. Dallas was not a lawyer, but he castigated Trollope's disregard of evidence as an abandonment of the principle of "innocent until proven guilty." Compared to this sane and otherwise laudatory review, an intemperate and legalistic discussion of the novel's treatment of law by Sir Francis Newbolt K. C. also examines the adequacy of the evidence. Newbolt is critical of virtually everything, from the inconsistent usage of "will," "codicil" and "deed" for "codicil" to the seating arrangements in the court. However, he believes the evidence is specifically deficient in that the prosecution fails to produce the record of the previous proceedings, thereby depriving the perjury trial of the supposedly perjured statements. If this is true, then Lady Mason has no case to answer. Unfortunately it is not true. Admittedly there is some confusion about this as Furnival quotes from Kenneby's previous evidence, saying that *he* will formally prove the record later. This would indeed be giving away a defence. Finally, however, the prosecution does "prove the circumstances of the former trial" (II.323–4), thus negating Newbolt's mock claim to the jury, "The case for the prosecution is that Lady Mason swore falsely, but neither before you, nor before the grand jury, nor before the magistrates, did they offer any evidence that she swore at all."[15] This misreading might be considered a trivial point, but I shall argue below that it and others like it are symptomatic of a larger failure to recognize novelistic conventions where they conflict with legal expectations.

As the novel is closely concerned with the perennial controversy of "the morality of advocacy," it is not surprising that Trollope's account of the actions of the defence lawyers should have drawn criticism. A brief comment by the former Chief Justice of the High Court of Australia, Sir Owen Dixon, is instructive. Introducing an examination of the inheritance problem set by the plot of *Doctor Thorne*, Dixon depreciates the trial scene in *Orley Farm*: "The cross-examination of the great Mr. Chaffanbrass is revolting. His questions are more than inadmissible; they are impossible."[16] Chaffanbrass's questions concerning what Bridget Bolster had for breakfast, and especially the offensive brandy, are not germane to the issues, but simply an attempt to discredit her. The reviewer of the novel in the *Saturday Review* recognized the abhorrent practice exposed by Trollope: "the irrelevant inquiries in which counsel indulge, in order to discredit and damage and annoy a witness whose evidence they cannot shake are often very cruel and very injurious to society at large."[17] Beyond these inadmissible questions lie the opinions and threats that Bolster would herself be tried for perjury if she lied, which are statements rather than questions, and objectionable as an attempt to bully the witness. Is it, however, objectionable in the novel rather than in a court? As *Orley Farm* provides so many examples of breaches of norms, from Lady Mason's crime to Dockwrath's invasion of the "commercial room" of the tavern, Chaffanbrass's disregard of the rules of advocacy is functional to the plot as well as illustrative of Trollope's case against cross-examination. The narrator reprobates this bullying in his discourse, emphasizing Chaffanbrass's attempt to becloud rather than reveal the truth. Nevertheless, in demonstrating the outrage, he invests the contest between Chaffanbrass and Bolster with dramatic intensity. The conflict inherent in the trial situation is exploited by the fullness of the scene; indeed that conflict is temporarily incarnated in the battle between the barrister and the witness. Chaffanbrass's conduct, "impossible" in law though not in fact, obeys a number of literary imperatives. The irregularity charged against Furnival is more straightforward. Having elected to call no witness on behalf of Lady Mason, he himself gives evidence during his speech to the jury. He tells them of his own recollection of the trial over the validity of the will, and then of his own knowledge of Lady Mason's character: "I have known her intimately during all those years – not as a lawyer, but as a friend – and I confess that the audacity of this man Dockwrath, in assailing such a character with such an accusation, strikes me almost with admiration" (II.329). All critics are agreed that, however attractive as oratory, this is evidence.[18] Such a basic confusion of categories is improbable as well as illegitimate.

Nevertheless, this mistake arises out of Trollope's conception of the role of the barrister as the unprincipled partisan, the hired assassin, of his client. A system which elevates the duty to one's client over the duty to pursue the truth must, under this theory, allow all means to the client's end. On the contrary, the barrister is an officer of the court, and is under an obligation not to mislead the court or to adopt any unfair or illegal practice. Moreover, the premises and assumptions of Trollope's attack on barristers are misconceived. As Fitzjames Stephen explains it in "The Morality of Advocacy," the English system of law is private: the machinery of justice is set in motion by private parties.[19] The system is therefore adversarial. The parties may instruct lawyers to prepare and present their cases before duly constituted and independent tribunals. In short, the functions of advocate and judge are separate. Mr. Furnival's suspicions or opinions concerning Lady Mason's guilt are therefore irrelevant. Neither is he allowed to make enquiries independently of the instructions he is given. Stephen admits that different obligations would arise under a public system of law, such as the public, inquisitorial procedures of Europe. Lucius Mason's statement that "'lawyers are all liars'" (I.22) is the most extreme utterance of the narrative's anxiety. He is completely if understandably wrong in his judgment of the situation. He, like the narrator, assumes that a lawyer somehow knows that a client is guilty. As Fitzjames Stephen says, few clients have such candour. Most are entirely convinced of the rectitude of their positions, or the innocence of their actions.[20] An exceptional case was that of *Courvoisier* in the 1840s. During his trial for murder, he told his barrister, Phillips, that he had killed the deceased, but that he wished to defend the case. Phillips was told by the judge to continue the defence so as to ensure that the case was proven and that no defence was available, but to make no statement or implication suggesting the innocence of the accused.[21] This case was famous within and without the legal profession, and remained a conversation topic for many years. Interestingly, *Orley Farm* contains its own example of the absurd speculation to which the abandonment of this principle leads, when Mrs. Furnival asks Sophia, "why are they allowed to try her" if she is innocent? This question is the obverse of that propounded throughout: if she is guilty, why are they allowed to defend her? It reveals once again that Trollope has forgotten the distinction between fact and evidence, between charge and conviction. Dallas concludes that Trollope's case against advocacy is facile: "it was not worth his while to run the risk of spoiling a good story, which he has very nearly done, by indulging in such easily-written claptrap."[22] Coral Lansbury's modern comment that "Trollope belligerently chose to misunderstand the system of advocacy" is no exaggeration.[23]

The result of this survey of inaccuracy and misconception in the representation of law in *Orley Farm* is that while some of the alleged errors affect the novel's sense of verisimilitude or the cogency of its argument against the conventions of English law, many others are consciously placed as the misdeeds of particular characters and form a coherent part of the plot. The result or overall effect is a novel which engages its readers (both lay and legal members of the expanding English polity) in a controversial area of legal policy, drawing on a traditional moral conundrum, on satiric characterization and above all, despite occasional lapses, on a convincing representation of legal and social reality.

The tendency of the barrister-critics to magnify the legal faults of the novel and to attribute them to a failure of realism by the author has important implications for the configuration of law and letters. For it appears that as the novel approaches its fullest treatment of legal subjects and usage of legal discourse – and as the realistic novel achieves critical acclaim for its comprehensive sense of the real – so the lawyers

begin to depreciate its imitation of legal reality and fail to understand
the bases of its artistry. To illustrate this conclusion I turn first to
David Skilton's discussion of the *Saturday Review* notice of *Orley Farm*.
The reviewer's complaint that the novel's "excitement is got over early
in order that the trial may bear an instructive character" is censured
by Skilton as "a particularly blatant example of a critic's attention
being deflected by non-literary concerns," because Trollope's prime
interest is the character of Lady Mason, not suspense.[24] Sir Francis
Newbolt provides an extreme example of "non-literary concerns"
because of his exclusively legal interests. Discussing the perfunctory
treatment of the grand jury in *Orley Farm*, Newbolt writes that Trollope
"seems never to have heard of depositions, of names of witnesses on
the indictment, and the freedom of the grand jury room," and to have
rushed past this obstacle in quest of his trial scene. No detail is given in
the novel of the grand jury, except that it had "returned a true bill."
This might be an oversight on Trollope's part, but most likely not. For
there are compelling literary reasons why the novelist should avoid
minute details of legal form and the repetition of information necessitated by the series of tribunals before which an accused person
appears. Like Scott, Trollope explicitly declines to provide an exhaustive
account of the legal process. As he writes on the page preceding the
reference to the grand jury, "a considerable amount of time was spent
in preliminaries. But we, who are not bound by the necessities under
which the court laboured, will pass over these somewhat rapidly"(II.278).
A similar decision to summarize governs the presentation of the original proceedings twenty years earlier (1.3,5). Newbolt's critique is therefore literalistic and formalistic. While the judicial process may require
the repetition of each detail at each stage, for purposes of formal proof,
the novel reader does not need to be told repeatedly of each event in
the chain making up the story. Indeed, repetition is acknowledged as a
problem by the self-conscious narrator: "Many of the points of this
case have already been named so often, and will, I fear, be necessarily
named so often again that I will spare the repetition when it is possible" (1.257). The narrator may pass over whatever is unimportant in
the chronological unfolding of the story, but the trial process requires
retrospection, minute exactitude and multiple retelling. In this instance,
the different narrative practices of the law and the novel derive from
the different values of the two discourses.

     There may be a perverse appropriateness in Newbolt's legal mis-
reading of Trollope's novel: the lawyer's sardonic strictures harmonize

in their wrongheadedness with Trollope's caricature of advocacy. Nevertheless, Newbolt's difficulties with the conventions of fiction should not be trivialized or personalized. Writing some fifty years after the novel's publication, Newbolt demonstrates the advancing separation of legal and literary discourses. Though he published his essay in a literary and a legal journal, it is clearly affected by the rise of professional specialism in the later nineteenth century in its exclusion of novelistic concerns.[25] The early signs of this process may be seen in Trollope's contemporary critics.

We have seen, in chapter three of this study, how Fitzjames Stephen demonstrated the differential "relation of novels to life" through an examination of the unreality of the trial scenes in the Waverley novels. Six years later he criticized *Mary Barton* and other "novels with a purpose" in his defence of "the morality of advocacy."[26] Technical criticism was not confined, then, to *Orley Farm*. Indeed, relations between the barrister-critics and Trollope's novels have a dialogical explicitness and a narrative completeness which reveals much about the theory and the production of fiction in the mid-century. The review of *The Three Clerks* in the *Saturday Review* criticizes as misconceived Mr. Chaffanbrass's defence of Alaric Tudor, and asks, "Why do not novelists consult some legal friend before they write about the law? Is it impossible to find a barrister who... would bring his skill... to bear upon the correction of the layman's mistakes?" In his next novel, *Doctor Thorne*, Trollope playfully addressed this idea, without following the suggestion: "I know that I am wrong, my much and truly-honoured critic, about these title deeds and documents. But when we've got that barrister in hand, then if I go wrong after that, let the blame be on my own shoulders – or on his." This intervention in the narrative is predictably censured by the *Saturday Review*'s article on the novel: not only is the advice not taken, but the problem is aired in a way that breaks the illusion of the reality of the story.[27] It is noteworthy that *Doctor Thorne* presents a problem requiring legal solution. As mentioned above, Sir Owen Dixon set himself the task of construing the will in question and finding its legal consequences. He concluded that Trollope's solution was substantially correct, and he praised the novelist for posing such a problematic situation for the law.[28] Equally important, though, at this point, is the profound appeal of complex legal cases to a novelist. A case is essentially a story, the action of which has not only to be discovered through evidence, but understood through interpretation. Little wonder that Trollope was led to another legal controversy in "the great Orley Farm case," with results that we have noted. Trollope was stung somewhat by the criticisms of *Orley Farm*, for in *Phineas Finn* he wrote of:

those terrible meshes of the Law! How is a fictionist, in these excited days, to create the needed biting interest without legal difficulties; and how again is he to steer his little bark clear of so many rocks, – when the rocks and the shoals have been purposely arranged to make the taking of a pilot on board a necessity?[29]

Finally, in *The Eustace Diamonds*, Trollope employed such a pilot, the barrister Charles Merewether, to write the opinion on Lizzie Eustace's title to the diamonds.

This fascination with the law and these attendant difficulties were not peculiar to Trollope. I referred in the opening to the Preface to *The Woman in White* and Walter Hartright's announcement that the story will be told by a number of witness-narrators followed by an assurance that the accuracy of legal material has been approved by an experienced solicitor. Again, George Eliot sought the help of a barrister, Frederic Harrison, so that the legal ramifications of the plot of *Felix Holt* would be authentically represented in the novel. On the basis of these examples, Kenneth Graham suggests that in the 1860s a "doctrine of verification" obtained among critics and novelists, not only with respect to law, but to whatever historical or factual *milieu* was presented. "Detailed verisimilitude is demanded, and any offences against it are considered fatal to the work: reviews abound with triumphant discoveries of minute inaccuracies."[30] Not only is this obsessive and narrow "realism of correspondence" responsible for much of the criticism of *Orley Farm*, but in licensing the reduction of literary to legal values it is one of the sources of the breakdown of the configuration of law and letters. Thus, the reception of *Orley Farm* supports G. M. Young's nomination of 1860 as the "date of that rift in English intelligence when learning began to fragment into specialism."[31] It is ironic that as the novel aspires to its closest possible representation of legal action, and perhaps its greatest interest in *nomos*, barristers attempt to use the public sphere of the reviews to reclaim the discourse of the law as their private province.

Nevertheless, one of the major appeals of Trollope's novels has always been what David Skilton calls their "perfect illusion of reality."[32] He argues, however, that this effect is constructed not through a "realism of reference" but through a "realism of coherence," through the internal consistency and completeness of the fictional world rather than its verifiability. In particular, Skilton argues that the Trollopian world is an "autarky" – one whose norms of behaviour and standards of judgment are so fully set out that the reader need not refer to those of the external world in order to understand the action or the fate of the characters. The novel is in effect self-governing, though there is a certain correspondence between its social and normative structures and those of Victorian society.[33] In this argument the complaints of inaccuracy are immaterial to the novel's verisimilitude. Thomas Pavel has, however, urged otherwise in respect of Balzac's representation of law:

> The Balzac world version would be equally affected by the discovery that Napoleonic civil law was in fact quite different from its description in the novels, and by the realization that all texts and passages referring to Vautrin were interpolated later by some other writer.[34]

That no such radical vitiation occurs in *Orley Farm* may well be related to the fact that its so-called errors concern procedure and value judgments about the morality of advocacy rather than positive statements of substantive law. Nevertheless, Pavel's argument is important for recognizing the element of law in the wide sense of "the way things are" in realism as well as for retrieving accuracy as an issue in modern criticism. Pavel's analogy reminds us that texts are embedded in worldly contexts, that the story of *Orley Farm* springs from a question of documentary authenticity, that the novel's rhetoric of value centres on truthful utterance, and its own representation of the law in action has been impugned as untrue. The cross-currents of representation and misrepresentation, of fact and fiction, of law and art provide the swirling context for the critical understanding of *Orley Farm*.

I have been using "representation" as a term in the discourse of art, meaning the copying or reproduction of a thing through painting or some other medium. However, "representation" is also known to legal or political discourse: first, in the sense of someone standing in the place of some person or group, and speaking or voting on their behalf; and second, as the placing of facts before another by means of discourse. Each of these meanings depends on the substitution of the person, thing or fact by another person, by an image, or by words. W. J. T. Mitchell has described as "unavoidable" the links between "aesthetic/semiotic and political forms of representation." He postulates a common, triangular structure for them: "representation is always *of* something or someone, *by* something or someone, *to* someone."[35] *Orley Farm* exhibits the various forms of representation, either in its story or its discourse, and it brings them into relationship with each other. The narrator offers a verbal account of a *cause célèbre*, a reproduction of the case, to the reader. Personal representation by characters acting on behalf, or standing in the place of others is exemplified by Moulder and Kantwise, sales representatives of commercial firms; by Furnival as Parliamentary member for the Essex Marshes; and in a technical legal sense the heir of Orley Farm is his father's representative. Furthermore, the barristers may be described as representing Lady Mason, though as she is herself present in court, they are not strictly her representatives. In what they say, however, they make verbal representations about her actions, her character, her innocence, just as Kantwise represents his iron furniture as the newest and tastiest article on the market. On this last sense is the argument against lawyers mounted, that they misrepresent the truth in what they say (see the narrator's comment on Furnival's speech to the jury: II.331) and in their taking on cases in the truth of which they have no belief. As we have seen, this argument rests on a gross misconception of the function of the barrister in an adversary system, in that the latter is retained by the client to promote (or defend) his or her legal interest. The specific functions of legal representation therefore entail a partiality which is incompatible with the objective or consensual truth-claims of artistic representation. For the realist novelist is bound to tell the truth like a witness on oath, and any misrepresentation might amount to artistic failure. I have argued above that Trollope's inaccuracy (to use a neutral word) is not of this character or extent. Nevertheless the question is raised; there is a case to answer. Not that the author is to be sent to trial, at the hands of Newbolt K. C.; but legal and novelistic practice are juxtaposed against each other. The mimetic theory of art and the English system of advocacy are brought into conflict by the novel's determination to evaluate the ethos and truth-claims of the law.

While there are structural similarities between artistic and legal representation, then, important differences emerged in the practice of the two forms in nineteenth-century England. However, the literary representation of legal representation did not occur from a transcendent position. We have seen how, in attempting to expose the barristers, the novel itself occasionally falls short of its own creed. More than this, in attempting to express its own views about advocacy and about Lady Mason, the novel finds its practice being modified. For the narrator-as-witness occasionally adopts the language of persuasion and the position of a partisan; in short, becomes an advocate. In rendering Lady

Mason's thoughts and actions after her confession to Sir Peregrine, the narrator's language sometimes merges exposition and justification. For example, in chapter LXIII, "The Evening before the Trial," her mental condition – her preparation, resolutions, fears for Lucius – is presented through a combination of direct narration and *style indirect libre*. The narrator takes the unusual step of referring the reader to Millais's illustration of the sorrowful Lady Mason (II.230), a stratagem criticized by Wall as evincing Trollope's failure fully to reveal her inner life early in the novel.[36] While this may be true, it also incorporates two significant rhetorical gestures which characterize the narrator as an advocate. First, the reader's active participation, indeed co-operation, is invited in the construction of an image of the heroine. Second, the drawing itself becomes evidence in the narrator's quest to invoke sympathy for Lady Mason. Together their effect on the reader is comparable to that of a barrister asking a jury to behold the pitiable creature in the dock. The reader is constructed as someone needing to be persuaded. The narrator moves from overt judgment ("It would be wrong to say that she was in any degree a hypocrite") to direct appeal ("O reader, have you ever known what it is to rouse yourself and go out into the world on your daily business, when all the inner man has revolted against work . . . ?" [II.232]). This self-presentation of the narrator as advocate is perhaps the final impression left by the novel, for in the penultimate chapter the narrator apologizes somewhat disingenuously to the reader and asks explicitly, as he does with another heroine, can you forgive her? While not yielding any ground in his argument against the morality of advocacy, Trollope finds the function of advocate indispensable to the practice of legal narrative fiction. Indeed, in his marshalling of narrative and commentary, in his manipulation of evidence and action, he is, as Lansbury has suggested, closer to traditional advocacy than he realizes.[37]

Advocacy may be viewed as an extension of the narrator's usual functions. The need for narrative advocacy in *Orley Farm* emerges out of the telling of Lady Mason's guilt. This disclosure enables that "full intimacy" with a character prized by Trollope, but it also exposes Lady Mason to possible condemnation by conventionally moralistic readers. To obviate such antipathy, the narrator must mount an argument on her behalf. Importantly, his advocacy can be distinguished from Furnival's, because it does not involve prevarication. The advocate's frankness must however be set against the narrator's earlier reticence: as Trollope later admitted, the revelation of guilt forecloses some of the story's suspense.[38] The two functions work well together, however, at the trial itself when the reader is made to share the characters' forebodings and eventual surprise or relief at the verdict. The advocacy is, of course, left to the lawyers at this point, but in its necessarily temporal development the trial has a narrative structure. In this structure the preliminaries, including Sir Richard Leatheram's opening speech, form a prologue, foreshadowing the narrations and counter-narrations of the witnesses and their cross-examiners, and the verdict is the climax. Leatheram's address to the jury not only outlines the evidence to come, but recreates Lady Mason's crime. Here, repetition is functional, for the lawyer's narrative is so full of imaginative insights – including the Biblical model, Rebekah – that Lady Mason feels her guilt has been discovered. Nevertheless, as James Boyd White has shown, a trial is a forum for competing stories.[39] Lady Mason's answer is shown not only by her advocates, but through the implicit messages of her manner, her appearance, and her attendance by Mrs. Orme and Lucius. Trollope registers the communicative and persuasive power of Lady Mason's unyielding countenance when she raises her veil, when she outfaces Joseph Mason, and by her sustained composure throughout the trial. In exploiting the semiosis of spectacle, Lady Mason is both artist and advocate, representing herself as determinedly upright and fearlessly innocent.[40]

### III

The dramatic, indeed histrionic, possibilities of the English trial process contribute largely to Lady Mason's acquittal. As I have shown with respect to Furnival and Chaffanbrass, the novel both relishes and censures such performances. The inquisitorial model of Continental Europe is offered as a quiet, earnest, rational contrast. Trollope's argument for reform of criminal advocacy is expressed through the novel's action as well as its rhetoric by the participation of Lady Mason's legal advisers in the international congress at Birmingham. The novel's aspersions against English trial advocacy gain greatly from the juxtaposition of Lady Mason's case with the meeting of the reformers. The conflict is set in train when Furnival goes to Birmingham to talk to old Round, and in their negotiations about Joseph Mason they routinely disparage the conference. As the trial approaches, Felix Graham sets his own misgivings in the context of the congress: "'After all that we said and did at Birmingham, it is odd that I should so soon find myself joined with Mr. Furnival'"(II.257). Devotion to reform is unexpected in a Trollope novel. The conventional view of Trollope's politics and poetics is one stressing his conservatism: Patrick Brantlinger compares Trollope's political novels with Dickens's reformist novels, and writes of the conservative critiques directed at the latter: "In Stephen, Bagehot and Trollope, the advice 'to be realistic' means either to acknowledge the righteousness of the Constitution and the status quo, or else to stop meddling with politics in fiction."[41] Yet, as we have seen, *Orley Farm* opposes some fundamental principles of British law, such as the presumption of innocence. Moreover, in doing so, it remains a realist novel, for it invokes the discourse and institutions of reform current in England in the 1850s and 1860s. The Birmingham congress, as Skilton notes,[42] alludes to the annual proceedings of the National Association for the Promotion of Social Science, an organization which brought together bodies and individuals interested in social reform. Trollope's method of writing about reform contrasts strongly with the pathos and invective of *Bleak House*, a novel which excludes all reference to the long-standing Chancery reform movement.

However, if *Orley Farm* avoids the excesses of Mr. Popular Sentiment (Trollope's caricature for Dickens in *The Warden*) it by no means dispenses with satiric hyperbole. For Trollope invests the Social Science Association (as it was commonly called) with a fictitious radicalism. One of the Association's progenitors, Brougham's Law Amendment Society, gives by its title a clue to the aims and scope of the Association. It sought specific reforms in particular areas, such as Public Health, Penal Policy, Education, and Criminal Procedure. Recommendations for reform followed upon the enquiries and reports of qualified persons. The chosen vehicle of reform was legislation. The Association therefore operated "within the system" and sought to improve it. Trollope's depiction of the congress as verbose and impractical is a misleading evaluation of a body which achieved a number of defined goals, including the right of accused persons to give evidence at their own trial. Indeed, Trollope himself later proposed to the Association that it investigate the international protection of intellectual property.[43] More importantly, the rather cavalier disregard for fundamental principle evinced in *Orley Farm* is at odds with the cautious reformism of the Social Science Association.

A contradictory attitude to reform therefore pervades Trollope's novel: it propounds with forceful prejudice the reform of English criminal trial procedure, and it criticizes the work of a major reformist body working in the field. It is not, of course, the function of a novel to formulate social policy in detail. Indeed the theoretical approach to social problems is deplored throughout Trollope's fiction.[44] Instead, *Orley Farm* examines a variety of attitudes to reformism through the thoughts of a number of characters. Thus Furnival's pragmatism and Chaffanbrass's boredom are registered along with Graham's optimism and von Bauhr's dream of "an Elysium of justice and mercy." That Trollope is less interested in ideas than in emotions and behaviour is emphasized by his omission of the content of von Bauhr's speech. Any conflict of ideas or intellectual debate is limited to the rather primitive clash of attitudes among the English listeners. The marathon address in German becomes an emblem of Babel; and the antithesis of narrative and forensic advocacy. Moreover, German thought is characterized as abstractly systematic and absurdly grandiose, not only through von Bauhr but through Lucius Mason's choice of "philology and the races of man" (along with scientific farming) as a profession. The presentation of von Bauhr's Elysian vision endows his reformist aspiration with some dignity by using him as a focalizer. However, the conceit of his ambition, symbolized by the bust in the garden inscribed, "To von Bauhr who reformed the laws of nations," severely limits the narrative sympathy. The narrator concludes by granting limited success to idealists, and that on a personal, ethical basis: "A man who strives honestly to do good will generally do good, though seldom as much perhaps as he has himself anticipated" (1.173). If there is self-delusion in von Bauhr's fancy, there is also an honourable and civilized ambition for "a reign of justice."

The problematics of the gap between ideal and achievement are further explored through Felix Graham's relationship with the Staveley family. On the one hand the growing love between Felix and Madeline overcomes all obstacles to reach the conventional happy ending, a forthcoming marriage. This is one paideic element permitted, almost compelled, by Victorian ideology. Felix becomes a welcome son-in-law despite his radicalism and his ugliness. Yet on the other hand, a certain expectation that he will begin to conform, to take up his profession in the usual way, is placed on him. On the evening before Lady Mason's trial, and having been given permission to address his suit to Madeline, Felix is told by Judge Staveley that "'many young men dream of a Themis fit for Utopia. You have slept longer than others . . .'" (11.258). Earlier, when discussing Felix with Madeline, the judge had remarked on his impracticality and determination to change the world: "'we all ought to do something to mend [the world]; but while we are mending it, we must live in it'" (II.183). This attitude is much closer to the imperial than the paideic aspect of the *nomos*: it is adjusting the world from within to make it go better; doing what can be done rather than dreaming what might be done; a practical rather than a prophetic attitude. Quite unlike Scott or Dickens, whose novels end with the creation of a domestic idyll, Trollope introduces into his romantic ending the need to make a living. *Orley Farm* therefore illustrates what George Levine has called Trollope's insistence on compromise, on the necessity of adjusting one's hopes and beliefs to the pressures of actual circumstances.[45] I shall discuss below the implications of this attitude for Felix's personal career, but first the public and political counterparts to the domestic and private experience must be explored.

To mend the world while living in it is to acknowledge the need to balance the aspiration for improvement with the desire for continuity. This Janus-like attitude is nowhere more succinctly expressed than in Trollope's own definition of his political position: "I consider myself an advanced, but still a Conservative-Liberal."[46] A similar consciousness of past and future, of advancing towards the millennium and applying the brakes to decelerate social change is manifest in the language in which reformism is rendered in *Orley Farm*. Von Bauhr dreams of "Elysium" and Judge Staveley invokes "Themis," the goddess of law. These classical allusions are typical of the novel's discourse: the French reformists are called "Ulpians, Tribonians and Papinians" (I.115) after three Roman jurists, while the collectivity at Birmingham are "Rustums of the law." One of the novel's final references to Graham as a reformer prompts him to allude to the need for a Hercules to clean out the "Augean Stables" of English law. This description of the unreformed law was coined by John Stuart Mill. Graham's adoption of the comparison is another example of Trollope's deployment of mainstream discourse as well as his own "classicism."[47] While Greek and Latin were the staples of European education in the nineteenth century – and *Orley Farm* contains quotations and tags which are interspersed throughout the narrative at appropriate places – their usage in connection with law reform is especially interesting. For its effect is to describe the reform movement in the language of the cultural tradition. While there is humour and irony in these heroic comparisons, there is also an implied affiliation between the reformers' dreams and inherited ideals. Robert Tracy has argued that Trollope believed that his civilization was a continuation of the classical one and that history was a progressive and providential order.[48] *Orley Farm* provides an acute example of the tension between the conservative's fear of change and the liberal recognition that all is not well in the present system, and between the anxiety to repeat the greatness of the past and the mistrust of abstract models of the future state.

IV

The novel therefore reveals a broadly evolutionary consciousness in its sense of the temporal development of law and social institutions. A more explicit and systematic examination of such legal evolution was undertaken by Sir Henry Maine, whose study, *Ancient Law*, was published contemporaneously with *Orley Farm* to great public and professional acclaim.[49] It is not known whether Trollope read Maine's work, but the latter's exploration of certain concepts and institutions of Roman law, notably property, wills and succession, seemed to relieve some of the mid-Victorian sense of normative instability, on precisely those subjects which are the staple of Trollope's fiction. *Ancient Law* is the *locus classicus* of the nineteenth-century concept of "succession" – that is, the transmission of rights – and of its important subset, inheritance, the transmission of rights of property.[50] According to Jack Goody, a system of inheritance "is not only the means by which the reproduction of the social system is carried out, . . . it is also the way in which interpersonal relationships are structured."[51] So conceived, the functions of inheritance suggest underlying affinities between the Lady Mason plot and the Birmingham conference and Felix Graham subplots, which I shall explore in the remainder of this chapter. Inheritance forms an element of Victorian fiction so often as to rank with the *Bildungsroman* as a culturally significant plot formation.[52]

The law of inheritance, then, seeks to reconcile continuity and change, for the inevitable changes in the constitution of family and society caused by death are addressed with a view to preventing the breakdown of order and custom. A person dies, but his property – and in the Indo-European tradition of Maine and the English novelists the property owner is male – continues. Etymologically, "property" means that which is proper to one; and it includes attributes such as rights, obligations and political freedoms as well as physical assets. All these survive. Michael Seidel has suggested that the "power of inheritance and primacy among children is discussed by jurists as part of a mystical code," and he quotes from a work by two successors of Maine, Pollock and Maitland's *History of English Law Before the Time of Edward I*:

To us it must seem natural that when a man dies he should leave behind him some representative who will bear, or some few representatives who will jointly bear, his *persona*. Or again we may be inclined to personify the group of rights and duties which are, as it were, left alive, though the man in whom they once inhered is dead: to personify the *hereditas*.[53]

Under this theory, Joseph Mason of Groby is his father's "representative" and Lady Mason's forgery is an interference with the *persona* of her late husband. This legal fiction or mythology would help to account for the sense of grievance felt by the elder son, were he educated in the law or in the traditions of succession. Critics who have examined Trollope's treatment of estates have concluded that he did regard inherited property as something transcendent, a trust involving obligations to the past and future of the family. Moreover, they emphasize that he believed in primogeniture as virtually a law of nature.[54] This conception of inheritance is embodied in *Orley Farm* through the three generations of Ormes living at The Cleeve, with the ageing Sir Peregrine wishing to hand over to his grandson and namesake. The Masons, by contrast, are *parvenus*. Joseph Mason has no tie to Orley Farm, and his reactions are based on greed and a hatred of his stepmother. Nevertheless, the seriousness of Lady Mason's crime is highlighted by this jurisprudential background. Not only is it an affront to Mason's pretended gentility; but to the county society it strikes at the root of continuity in the social order, at inherited titles and ideals. The crime therefore has social and political implications. Not only has Lady Mason violated the legal and moral foundations of landed society, but she has sought to subvert the patriarchal system of property. Her ostracism is the inescapable punishment following upon the strongly-urged surrender of the property.

Notwithstanding the narrator's advocacy in the service of a sympathetic evaluation of Lady Mason's character and actions, the denouement enforces the law of inheritance. While some commentators regard the ending as the supersession of legal failure by moral justice,[55] it is undeniable that the transfer of Orley Farm to Joseph Mason is in accordance with the true will of his father and with the underlying principle of primogeniture. The narrative desire for a just resolution of the plot depends finally on a legally-conceived and culturally-inherited sense of right.[56] In many nineteenth-century novels the inheritance convention functions as the reward of virtue or as a metonym for the maintenance of a certain social order.[57] *Orley Farm* demonstrates a complex and equivocal attitude to such conventional plot formations. Joseph Mason is morally repugnant, while Lady Mason is a "sympathetic criminal."[58] The family estate is returned to the heir, but the family itself is irrevocably sundered by twenty years of legal conflict and bitter recrimination. Unlike *Bleak House*, which deflected all questions of competition for resources in its quest for a loving family home, Trollope's novel is structured on the power of greed and need to overthrow moral rules and emotional ties. The Biblical story of Rebekah and her successful evasion of the rule of primogeniture serves Lady Mason as a precedent. Her justification is not endorsed by the narrative, in contrast, say, to Jeanie Deans's appeal to the example of Ahasueris, discussed in chapter three. For Robert Cover, the story of Jacob and Esau was one of a series of breaches of primogeniture which had to be understood in the light of the larger sacred narrative of Israel's destiny as the younger son among the nations. This narrative has no significance in the rhetoric of Trollope's novel, which, in its references to the racial identity of Lady Mason's solicitor, Solomon Aram, is tainted with nineteenth-century European anti-semitism. Moreover, in the world of the landed gentry and those aspiring to enter that class younger sons must accept the rigour of primogeniture. The story of Jacob and Esau therefore provides the novel with a traditional plot of two brothers in competition for a single estate, and of the crucial intervention of the mother. To paraphrase Dallas in his review, the patriarchal blessing occurs now not by imposition of hands, but by the disposition of property through a legal instrument.[59] In the modern retelling Esau retains the homelands and Jacob is compelled to wander bitterly to the end of the earth, specifically to that favoured penitential destination of the Victorian novel, Australia.

If the inheritance laws aim to provide social continuity in a changing world, then they may be taken overall as a force for conservatism. Trollope's employment of the inheritance plot is conservative in its ultimate commitment to primogeniture and in the normative value it places on family harmony and community morality. Drawing on the Blackstonian figure of the inherited mansion of the common law, Edmund Burke claimed that the model of inheritance provided the British with the basis of their evolving, unwritten constitution and law: "In this choice of inheritance we have given to our frame of polity the image of a relation in blood."[60] The criminal behaviour and accumulated resentment of the Masons shows that this paideic image does not always inform actual relationships. Burke proceeds to argue that English political liberties are also justified because they are inherited. This identification between the principles of land law and constitutional law is seen by J. G. A. Pocock as,

a genuine historical insight into the character of English political thinking. [Burke] says, quite explicitly, that it is the greatest accomplishment of our thought to have based our claim to liberty on an idea drawn from the law of real property.[61]

Pocock's use of the first person plural adjective suggests that Burke's view of the tradition remains valid and alive. It is surprising, then, that Trollope should manage, in presenting "the great Orley Farm case," both to endorse the law of inheritance and to disparage such evolved protections of liberty as the presumption of innocence and the right to cross-examine witnesses. That the author is aware of the constitutional ramifications of these aspects of criminal procedure is indicated by his willingness to burlesque them. He ironically impersonates a newspaper editor railing against "the antediluvian prejudices of the British grandmother – meaning the Constitution" (II.208) and he chooses the "low" or comic character Moulder to defend trial by jury as "the bulwark of the British constitution" (II.216). The narrator follows Moulder's invocation with a homely story of the child who complained about the quality of its bread and butter, only to be told by its mother to be grateful, and then comments: "Bread and butter is a great thing; but I would have it of the best that be possible." In Trollope's novel, then, respect for inheritance in family and state is tinged with a nineteenth-century belief in reform, or at least with a willingness to engage the novel in topics of legal controversy. The "bread and butter" analogy trivializes potential encroachments upon individual rights, a strange position for a writer who avowed himself a "liberal" – indeed a "conservative" one – and who himself takes up the defence of a mother who has stolen from a stepson in order to provide for her own.

To advocate "the best that be possible" is to temper idealism with pragmatism, to regard von Bauhr's paideic dream with suspicion while recognizing as complacent the English Bar's defence of its "bread and butter." The final expression of this attempt to embrace opposites and reject extremes is Felix Graham, who refuses to accept the conventions of English advocacy and whose love of Madeline is reciprocated. A number of critics are convinced that by marrying into the Staveley family he will begin to accept the norms of his profession.[62] While the plot undoubtedly moves towards the recognition of the need for compromise and of the need to earn a living, Felix does hold out in one important respect which has been overlooked and which is crucial for this study. When Madeline reports in the final chapter that her father would prefer him to give up writing, Graham refers to Aesop's fable, "The Fox Without A Tail," casting the judge in the title role. The moral of this story, "Distrust Interested Advice," suggests that the literary lawyer should not cut off his tail merely because his brethren have decided that literature is purely ornamental and gets in the way of specialist practice. This is presented lightly, but Madeline acknowledges that her fiancé has a right to choose for himself. Moreover, just as she strives to combine loyalty to father and lover, so the narrator places Felix in the vanguard of reform and, simultaneously, at the tail of the configuration of law and letters. As a writer and a lawyer, Felix Graham embodies the novel's quest to maintain the dialogue between law and literature, and to extend their common commitment to true representation as an instrument of justice.

The denouement of *Orley Farm* and the subsequent history of the configuration suggest, however, that Felix's task will be difficult, that one or other of the discourses will be relegated into second place. For while much of the rhetoric of the novel assumes the possibility of accommodating disparate impulses and finding an acceptable middle ground, the story insists that only one brother may inherit Orley Farm and one suitor marry Madeline. The ending of the novel registers both the pathos of disappointed hopes and the possibility of social fulfilment in the contrasted states of its principal families, in the dispersal of the Masons (and to a lesser extent the Ormes) and the unity of the Staveleys. *Orley Farm* comprehends the advocate's championship of the individual and the community's need for normative order, and it negotiates a precarious balance between the claims of tradition and reform.

## CHAPTER SIX

# Power, chance and the rule of law –
# Billy Budd, Sailor

Found a family, build a state,
The pledged event is still the same:
Matter in end will never abate
His ancient brutal claim.

This is the first of the two quatrains which comprise Herman Melville's
1891 poem, "Fragments of a Lost Gnostic Poem of the 12th Century."[1]
With its ellipticism and claim of incompletion, its scepticism and enigmatic wisdom, it affords a means of changing floors in "the house of
fiction," from the large public rooms of *Orley Farm* to the cramped,
secret quarters of *Billy Budd*. With Melville's novella we leave behind
the narrative amplitude and *sensus communis* of Victorian realism for the
compression and "indirection" of much Early Modernist fiction.[2] This
movement towards dramatic intensity is neatly captured in the poem's
opening, "Found a family, build a state," which condenses into a single
line a metonym developed by Scott, Dickens and Trollope for the
novelistic representation of growth, decay, continuity and change in
the *nomos*. The reconstitution of family in the conclusions of *The Heart
of Midlothian*, *Bleak House* and *Orley Farm* serves as a cell of normative
hope, of the possibility of reasonable reform, in a body politic variously
conceived as disabled by history, institutional sclerosis or unenlightened
self-interest. However, this residual optimism is denied in the second
half of the poem, as what is "pledged" by the establishment of *nomos* is
not the transformation of ideal into actuality, spirit becoming flesh in
a radically altered future, but "matter" reasserting "its ancient brutal
claim." Here, Tennyson's anguished vision of "Nature, red in tooth
and claw" is superseded by a frank recognition, axiomatic in expression, of the primacy of physical needs among human aspirations. The
source of this fundamental legal narrative, with its assimilation of the
human into the natural world, is neither Blackstone nor Bentham, but
Darwin.[3] The violence that Scott had sought to banish from the "united

kingdom," that Trollope sublimated into the sport of hunting, is, at the end of the century of reform, reinscribed into the literature of *nomos*. The poem's Gnosticism, its strange wisdom, arises from its juxtaposition of the normative and the physical, of creative and destructive intimations. To the post-Darwinian idea of the "law of nature" as a principle derived from invariable observation, Melville's poem attaches a deep-seated social pessimism.[4]

"Fragments of a Lost Gnostic Poem" was published in *Timoleon*, the volume Melville published in 1891, the year in which he annotated his manuscript of *Billy Budd* with "End of book." It is therefore likely that they are contemporary with each other. The meditative lyric and the novella share not only a fragmentary quality (*Billy Budd*, while "finished" in one sense, has been assembled by editors) and a sense of compression, but the tragic fate of Billy is, I will argue, another expression of Melville's pessimism and scepticism concerning the human potential to transcend through law the "brutal" claims of "necessity." The legal action of *Billy Budd*, set aboard a man-of-war in wartime, enables a confrontation between law, conceived as an instrument for the peaceful resolution of disputes and the containment of violence, and war, with its quest for supremacy by force and its individual and corporate invocation of the necessity of survival. These elements are brought together in martial law, the operation of which is used to justify Billy's hanging, and the representation of which enables a revaluation of the rule of law.

*Billy Budd* has attracted sustained attention from critics of "legal narrative" and historians of the changing relationship between law and literature. In various ways Richard Weisberg, Barbara Johnson and Brook Thomas approach it as an exemplary text in their studies of fiction and the law: I shall examine their arguments in detail during the course of this chapter, but here it suffices to note that for Weisberg, Captain Vere epitomizes a cultural tendency in modern law and literature to divorce rhetoric from ethics; for Johnson *Billy Budd* offers a paradigm of the process of judgment through Vere's attempt to foreclose the play of linguistic *différance*; and for Thomas it is the fictional text which best expresses the contradictions in late nineteenth-century American legal ideology.[5] Robert Cover, in a discussion cited appreciatively by Weisberg and Thomas, argues that Vere is a "fictional *type*" of the formalist judge, that is, one who applies the law despite the fact that its provisions or effects run counter to his or her own moral beliefs.[6] Cover and Thomas agree in nominating Melville's father-in-law, Chief Justice Lemuel Shaw, as the model for Vere, and his decision to enforce the Fugitive Slave Act despite his own opposition to slavery as analogous to the moral-legal dilemma faced by Vere. *Billy Budd* is *An Inside Narrative*, as its subtitle avers, not simply because it tells the hitherto suppressed truth about Billy's case, but because it makes an implicit critique of the legal ideology to which Vere and Shaw subscribe. Cover's *Justice Accused* is therefore a concrete example of his later, more general thesis that a law can only be understood in the light of a larger normative mythology. The fate of Billy Budd also casts its shadow over his later aphorism, "judges deal pain and death."[7] I argue that the trial and execution of Billy can only be properly understood in its martial context, which poses new questions for the sanctioned violence of the law. Is the "martial law" invoked by Vere to be understood in its original sense of law governing the military, or in its modern sense of the military rule of civilian populations? Melville's 1891 novella sets its action a century earlier, looking back not only to the Napoleonic war, but to the fictional representation of unequal justice and arbitrary force within England in Godwin's *Caleb Williams*. *Billy Budd* is a new "call upon the justice of the country," one which, I argue, substitutes the tragic figure of the speechless victim for the confident reformist rhetoric of *Bleak House*, *Orley Farm* or Melville's earlier treatment of "The World in a Man-of-War," *White-Jacket*.

I

For Robert A. Ferguson the significance of *Billy Budd* is that it provides the "most eloquent statement" of "the changing meaning of the law" in nineteenth-century America. Before discussing its historical significance, he offers a conveniently brief summary:

The essential action takes place in a paragraph and can be summarized in less. Billy Budd, innocence personified, kills the ship's master-at-arms, John Claggart, with a single impulsive blow when Claggart falsely accuses him of mutiny before their captain, Edward Fairfax Vere. Billy strikes because a stutter prevents him from speaking; he is then charged, tried, sentenced and hanged by Captain Vere and a drumhead court for the capital offence of hitting a superior.[8]

The succinctness of this account is useful for its precision of statement, which draws attention to the work's interest in the quality or the significance of its action ("a single impulsive blow," a false accusation) and the moral and psychological condition of its characters ("innocence personified"). I shall deal with these issues in a later section of this chapter. At this point, I wish to focus on the historical meaning which Ferguson, and other critics, draw from the story's dual insistence on Billy's personal "innocence" and his legal culpability.

Ferguson quotes Robert Cover in order to suggest that Captain Vere's "orchestration of Billy's conviction" represents "'a positivist's condensation of a legal system's formal character.'" Vere's speech to the court articulates eloquently and cogently a positivist and formalist justification for punishing Billy according to the letter of the law. His argument proceeds by refuting the claims of an alternative source of law, "Nature" or private conscience. The trial scene therefore puts in conflict two jurisprudential traditions, two ideologies of law, Natural Law and Legal Positivism:

> "If, mindless of palliating circumstances, we are bound to regard the death of the master-at-arms as the prisoner's deed, then does that deed constitute a capital crime whereof the penalty is a mortal one? But in natural justice is nothing but the prisoner's overt act to be considered? How can we adjudge to summary and shameful death a fellow creature innocent before God, and whom we feel to be so? . . . Well I too feel that, the full force of that. It is Nature. But do these buttons that we wear attest that our allegiance is to Nature? No, to the King. . . . [In] receiving our commissions we in the most important regards ceased to be natural free agents. . . . [S]uppose condemnation to follow the present proceedings. Would it be so much we ourselves that would condemn as it would the martial law operating through us? For that law, and the rigour of it, we are not responsible. Our vowed responsibility is in this: that however pitilessly that law may operate in any instances, we nevertheless adhere to it and administer it."[9]

Ferguson argues that in its marginalization of private conscience and exclusive attention to statutory requirements this passage recapitulates the transition from natural law to Legal Positivism as the dominant legal theory in America during the nineteenth century. One can readily see its appeal to Cover as a "condensation" of the legal reasoning which led Melville's father-in-law, Lemuel Shaw, to apply the provisions of the Fugitive Slave Acts, and return runaway slaves to their owners, despite his personal abhorrence of the institution of slavery.

The decline of natural law theory has another consequence for Ferguson, namely the end of the eighteenth-century configuration between American law and letters. The separation of law from moral philosophy was, he argues, part of a larger separatism between the specialist study of law and traditional cultural education. Law and literature become distinct, mutually uncomprehending fields. Ferguson claims, too generally in view of his treatment of *Billy Budd*, that with Melville, Thoreau and Hawthorne "a new aesthetic [which] excludes the legal mind" by interesting itself in the imaginary, the ambiguous and the private, which self-consciously breaks with tradition, begins to develop. Brook Thomas traces this emerging fiction and its links with the law and society, arguing in effect that separation but not divorce was the true relation between the law and literature, that the latter "did not so much exclude the legal mind as search for alternatives to it."[10] The law continued to shape, if indirectly or negatively, the fiction produced by writers in the age of legal formalism and positivism. This questioning of the legal heritage is visible not only in *Billy Budd*, with its highly articulated trial, but in "Bartleby" with its earnestly conventional lawyer-narrator reduced to helplessness before the mysterious quietism of the scrivener.

While Ferguson's primary focus is on early American lawyer-writers and on the civic culture they dominated, Thomas compares and contrasts legal and literary texts and emphasises the polyvocalism of nineteenth-century American culture. Thus, for example, in "The Legal Fictions of Herman Melville and Lemuel Shaw" he argues that "the ambiguity of literary texts might be better understood in terms of an era's social contradictions . . . and conversely that a text's ambiguity can help us expose the contradictions masked by an era's dominant ideology."[11] Noting Cover's treatment of the "moral-legal" dilemma faced by Shaw in the Fugitive Slave cases and by Vere, Thomas prefers to compare those judgments with Melville's "Benito Cereno" and to link Captain Vere with Shaw's judicial conduct in the *Webster* murder case. The latter was a controversial trial in which Shaw's direction to the jury was censured for its general partiality in favour of the prosecution. Of specific concern was a departure from precedent in which he ruled that only the fact of murder need be established beyond reasonable doubt, and that the involvement of the accused need only be proved to the jury's reasonable satisfaction. Thomas connects this willingness to change the law to meet present needs with Vere's manipulation of the drumhead court. He most impresses the court by "his closing appeal to their instinct as sea officers" which canvasses the practical consequences of apparent leniency in that mutinous year (p. 390); he in effect acts as witness, prosecutor and judge during the trial; and he thereby ensures that the court's order reproduces his own initial "prejudgment" of the case ("'Yet the angel must hang'" [p. 378]). Thomas's historical analysis of the trial scene therefore emphasizes not the triumph of formalism and positivism (which, with some qualifications as to dates, he accepts), but the way in which formalism serves as a mask, covering the mutation of forms for political purposes. *Billy Budd* therefore reveals the ideology of this approach to law, undermining its insistence on the imperative and neutral character of the forms, while showing its hold on the normative imaginations of officers and men alike. Billy's benediction, "'God bless Captain Vere,'" echoed by the crew, may be instructively viewed as an example of the false consciousness of a victim of an oppressive system. The ideology and Captain Vere's misuse of law are only aspects of a larger presentation, described by Thomas as "an account of how such behaviour is accepted by a culture even when it would seem to contradict the culture's definition of legitimacy."[12]

Before concluding the trial narrative with the formal conviction and sentence, the narrator digresses to compare the "harassed frame of mind" of Billy's judges with that of the Commander of the USS *Somers*, who in 1842 executed three men for conspiring to mutiny (p. 390). Melville's brother-in-law, Guert Gansevoort, was an officer on the *Somers* and a member of the drumhead court on that occasion. As many critics have noted, the Somers case was "reopened" by journalists during the late 1880s when Melville was working on *Billy Budd*, and it is a major source of the novel's legal action.[13] The narrator does not express an opinion on the case, "History, and here cited without comment," but in comparing the subjective perceptions of the two courts, does leave open the question of over-reaction: "But the urgency felt, whether well-warranted or otherwise, was much the same" (p. 391). Rather than trying to infer Melville's attitude from this indirect reference, Thomas turns to the "naval court of inquiry" referred to in the text, and to the literature supporting Captain Mackenzie's decision in order to show how, despite its irregularity, the hanging was vindicated. His chief source is an article by Charles Sumner in the *North American Review* in 1843, in which Sumner first discusses the Nore and Spithead mutinies in terms highly similar to *Billy Budd*. He then admits that Mackenzie acted beyond "'customary forms of law'" in not sailing to base before convening the trial, this being the requirement of the applicable statute. However, he argues that "the pressures of the situation demanded a trial at sea" and that this necessity should be judged not by an objective test, but by how it appeared to the commander at the time. He imports this criterion from the law relating to self-defence, arguing that the Captain's duty is to defend the ship. Thomas finds in this reasoning historical evidence of the contradictions in legal formalist ideology, for "although he violates the letter of the law, [Mackenzie] conforms to principles contained within the law itself." The breach of the law is justified as legitimate because it preserves social order, this being the law's overriding purpose.

The *Somers* case became a *cause célèbre*, not least because one of those executed, Philip Spencer, was the son of a cabinet minister. The issues were therefore openly debated in judicial, political and cultural forums, in contrast to the brief and misleading notice of Billy's hanging. Thomas argues that this silence, together with Billy's defective speech, functions as a political metaphor for the powerlessness of the seamen who are unable to protest against their own oppression. A crucial scene for Thomas is the disciplinary flogging which Billy witnesses the day after his impressment. He resolves that "never through remissness would he make himself liable to such a visitation" (p. 346). Thomas suggests that Billy is rendered easily controllable by "the accepted forms and usages of the navy," and that his silence in the face of this law is part of a general inability to say, "No," to any aspect of this unjust regime.[14] The stutter, therefore, is a "flaw" in moral and political terms, signifying a culpable willingness to let others, especially Vere, speak on his behalf. Thomas contrasts Billy's tacit acceptance of naval conditions with the outspoken defence of human rights made by Jack Chase (to whom *Billy Budd* is dedicated) in *White-Jacket*. The political and ideological implications of Vere's rhetorical skills and Billy's inarticulateness suggest strongly that they are conceived as representatives of the powerful and powerless classes. In retelling the story of Billy Budd as victim, Melville challenges Vere's law by means of what Thomas aptly calls "subversive indirection."[15]

This is a complex and subtle argument, which takes account of the narrative form as well as the legal content of *Billy Budd*. Thomas's phrase, "the accepted forms and usages of the navy," covers two source of law, however: the formal prescriptions of a statute ("forms") and the unwritten customs, the traditional practices, of naval punishment ("usages"). For the flogging scene differs from Billy's trial through its radical substitution of language with force. Although the "cat-o'-nine-tails" was prescribed for summary punishment under the Articles of War, it was not so much a modern formalist system of discipline as a customary spectacle of overwhelming monarchical power imposed on the bodies of recalcitrant sailors. Foucault, on whose distinction I am relying here, also draws attention to the *relationship* between military orders and the emergence of disciplinary modes of control: "While jurists or philosophers were seeking in the [social contract] a primal model for the construction or reconstruction of the social body, the soldiers and with them the technicians of discipline were elaborating procedures for the individual and collective coercion of bodies."[16] In *Billy Budd* the dual inscription of legalism and the lash, the mutual dependence of law and violence, takes place under the rule of martial law.

II

The distinction between law and war is confounded in Captain Vere's description of the Mutiny Act as "'War's child'" (p. 389). This reference to the Mutiny Act is one of the many errors of law listed by Richard H. Weisberg in his comprehensive technical legal analysis of the trial.[17] The Mutiny Act applied to the Army, while the Articles of War was the law governing the Navy. Both Vere and the narrator fall into this "error," perhaps because the action takes place "in the year of the Great Mutiny." To return to Vere's rhetoric, the personification, "War's child," is curiously coined in order to justify the exclusion of Billy's mental state as an admissible consideration for a court martial. In agreeing that the foretopman intended neither to mutiny nor to kill, Vere reflects on the normative quality of the court: "'before a court less arbitrary and more merciful, that plea would largely extenuate'" (p. 388). He links the court's harshness with the arbitrariness of war: just as the enemy will "'cut down in the same swath'" volunteers and conscripts alike, unconcerned by their varied commitment to the cause, so the mind of an offending crew member is of no interest to the martial court. "'War looks but to the frontage, the appearance. And the Mutiny Act, War's child, takes after the father.'" The analogy between the undiscriminating cannon shot and the judicial deliberation is disturbing as well as strained when considered against the careful reasoning of the earlier part of his speech. Is Vere's legalism a pretence, a mask for murderous resentment or military convenience?

Vere insists, with reason, that the circumstances of war affect the process of law: "'while thus strangely we prolong proceedings that should be summary – the enemy may be sighted and an engagement result.'" Weisberg notes that summary proceedings are not provided for in the Articles of War, so it is clear that this trial is an example of naval customary law, one of the "sanctioned irregularities" allowed the

Navy in the stress of its war effort. It is at odds with the pains taken by modern defenders and historians of court martials to show that military law is as concerned to protect substantive and procedural rights as its civil counterpart. James Stuart-Smith, for example, suggests that the military statute of Edward II was one of the first bills of rights; while Joseph W. Bishop contrasts the Mutiny Act with modern codes and finds it "somewhat primitive, even for that age."[18] He makes the important general point that in the Anglo-American tradition, military laws are promulgated by the civil authorities, so that, whatever conditions or restrictions may be necessary, in constitutional theory the law remains the "child" of Parliament and not of war. Captain Vere's reasoning, then, seems questionable.

The legal principle of looking "but to the frontage, the appearance" is examined by Warner Berthoff, who distinguishes military law from ordinary law, neglecting the constitutional tradition for a quasi-natural law of war:

> Melville is at some pains to present the martial law as morally *sui generis*, and in its own terms morally unimpeachable. . . . It is "War's child," . . . and must of its nature look "but to the frontage, the appearance" of things – and not wrongly. As against moral or divine law it can have no regard to questions of motive.[19]

By taking Vere's criterion at face value, Berthoff unites natural law and military necessity to preclude what the novella itself surely invites, and the Articles of War allow, the review of the judicial decision to hang Billy. Another writer, William Domnarski, places natural law and military necessity in conflict: "for Vere there was no choice because the wartime environment and threat of mutiny forced him to act as he did. . . . If the Bellipotent was in danger and Vere believed Billy innocent according to natural law, then the novel presents a classic case of principles versus circumstances."[20] In proposing this conflict as "the point of the novel," he condemns as irrelevant critics such as Weisberg who examine positive law in order to assess whether Billy "was properly charged, tried, convicted and punished" under the Articles of War.[21] When Captain Vere invokes such criteria of necessity as the proximity of the enemy and the threat of mutiny, he does so by limiting the operation of formal legal process. The legal basis for Billy's execution, the authorizing Act, therefore remains a crucial question for critics. Christopher W. Sten recognizes its importance when he argues that it was necessity which led Vere to manipulate the law so as to achieve Billy's death. Vere violated the Articles of War in holding a secret trial, with an irregularly composed court, upon which he urged a quick conviction. This action was necessary in the circumstances "to ensure the stability of his men and thence the safety of his nation."[22] By performing this difficult duty in full consciousness of Billy's "natural innocence," Vere enacts that sacrifice of the individual which is "the price of civilization." The narrative invites us to question this price and to "remake the world in a more benevolent image."

Sten's paideic conclusion sits uneasily with his justification of the execution. When law is conceived as *nomos*, the Articles of War must be taken to embody some of society's normative commitments. What the violation of the Articles implies is a lack of fidelity to those normative commitments on the part of either Vere personally, the naval establishment or the British government. C. B. Ives and Richard Weisberg both look to the moral psychology of Vere, respectively to suppressed affections and *ressentiment* of integrated humanity, for their explanations of his misuses of law.[23] While these readings properly particularize the character of Vere and the circumstances of this case, they do not provide a sufficient explanation for the historical data which Ives, at least, presents. Ives demonstrates that independently of what the Articles of War prescribed, naval commanders customarily exercised a wide disciplinary discretion, that, for example, the maximum summary penalty of twelve lashes was usually exceeded, and that the mandatory sentence of death for striking an officer was by no means always imposed. He explains this widespread latitude by reference to naval custom, which viewed sceptically the attempts by politicians and the Admiralty to regulate life at sea. Consequently, "a captain of a man-of-war was godlike and might exercise his disciplinary discretion, or even his disciplinary whims freely with little expectation of reproof."[24]

Vere's departure from the letter of the law may best be seen, then, as a sign of naval usage, of professional habits of thought and action, rather than of personal animus. Melville's record of his own "man-of-war experiences and observations" aboard a US frigate during 1843–4, *White-Jacket*, speaks of the "notorious lawlessness" of Commanders in terms of a sailors' proverb, "*the law was not made for the Captain*."[25] The experiences of witnessing a flogging and of hearing the monthly public reading of the Articles of War led to passionate, but well-informed, protests against the Articles as a legal regime. The burden of White-Jacket's argument is that this law is adapted from the British statute of the same name, and consequently that its provisions are inconsistent with the fundamental tenets of American democracy. For example, by preserving a general disciplinary discretion in the Captain it vests the powers of legislator, judge, and executive in one person; by exempting officers from some of its penal clauses it violates the principle of equality before the law; and by retaining flogging as the normal summary penalty it is comparable with "the penal laws that prevailed in England some sixty years ago," in that it makes no distinction between trivial and serious crimes. White-Jacket acknowledges that "the necessities of navies warrant a code for its government more stringent than the law that governs the land; but that code should conform to the spirit of the political institutions of the country that ordains it."[26] The explanation of this "monstrous grafting of tyranny upon freedom" is historical: "they are an importation from abroad, even from Britain, whose laws we Americans hurled off as tyrannical, yet retained the most tyrannical of all."[27]

This robust rhetoric is supported by detailed citation from the Articles of War and an informed discussion of constitutional and jurisprudential theories. Relevant historical examples and quotations from the best-known legal writers, such as Justinian, Coke, Hale and Blackstone, produce one of the most articulate evocations of *nomos* in nineteenth-century literature. Drawing on various sources such as natural law, traditional liberties, utilitarian policy-discussion, and chauvinism, *White-Jacket* combines the reformist passion of Dickens with the discursive realism of Trollope. With confidence, indeed normative fervour, he declares, "it is for America to make precedents, and not to obey them. . . . And we Americans are . . . the Israel of our time; we bear the ark of the liberties of the world" (p. 506). What this eclectic representation of law suggests is that there is no complete disjunction between what John P. McWilliams has styled the youthful radicalism of *White-Jacket* and the conservatism of *Billy Budd*.[28] The reformism of *White-Jacket* is animated by a paideic zeal to fulfil the promise of the Declaration of Independence. It is derived from the same Jeffersonian tradition that oversaw the incorporation of the Bill of Rights into the American Constitution, the protections of which it seeks to extend to sailors. Melville finished work on *Billy Budd* in 1891, the centenary of the Bill of Rights. By setting his novella in 1797, he invokes an historical context in which liberty is curtailed by war, as signified by Billy's conscription from the *Rights of Man* to the *Bellipotent*, and in which the Old World is the negation of the New World defined by White-Jacket. Indeed, one of the latter's favourite contrasts, between American constitutionalism and

the tyranny of the Russian czars, is indirectly repeated in *Billy Budd*
when the narrator compares the secrecy of the murder and trial
with "the policy adopted in those tragedies of the palace which have
occurred more than once in the capital founded by Peter the Barbarian"
(p. 381).

White-Jacket can only compare the "severity and unusualness" of
the Articles of War to the multiplication of mandatory death sentences
in the "Bloody Code" of England "some sixty years ago." During the
monthly reading of the statute the repetition of the phrase, "*shall suffer
death,*" at such short intervals reminds him of a "minute-gun" explod-
ing in the ears of the assembled crew. This transformation of legal
discourse into an effect of war has a "defamiliarizing" effect, enabling
White-Jacket to see through the Articles' normative pretensions to
the essential lawlessness of its excessive force: "Murderous! But then,
in time of peace they do not enforce these blood-thirsty laws?" He
answers this rhetorical question by alluding to the *Somers* case, and
concludes with a parodic oath: "By the main-mast! then, . . . I am
subject to the cut-throat martial law" (p. 659). Melville turns to the
Gothic mode, embodying the law first as monster and then as a
means of torture:

Afloat or wrecked the Martial Law relaxes not its gripe [sic]. And though . . . for
some offence . . . you were indeed to 'suffer death,' even then the Martial
Law might hunt you through the other world, and out again at its other
end . . . like an endless thread on the inevitable track of its own point, passing
unnumbered needles through. (p. 661)

After this temporary plunge into the solitary dark, he turns lawyer,
quoting the rationalist prose of legal authority against this irrational
system: "may we subscribe to the saying of Sir Matthew Hale in his
History of the Common Law, that '*the Martial Law, being based upon no
settled principles, is, in truth and reality, no law, but something indulged rather
than allowed as a law.*'" A longer version of this passage from Hale,
which dates from before 1676, is quoted in the *Oxford English Dictionary*
as part of its history of the phrase, "martial law." The quotation proceeds, "the Necessity of Order and Discipline in an Army is that only
which can give those Laws a Countenance." The two elements mentioned by Hale, the lack of settled principles and the governance of the
military, were to split apart in the next two hundred years. By the time
Wellington addressed Parliament in 1851 with the words, "Martial
Law was neither more nor less than the will of the general," the phrase
had acquired its modern sense of the suspension of civil law by military

power, and the rules governing the Army and Navy had come to be referred to as "military law." As E. P. Thompson has shown, with the development of the ideology of the rule of law during the eighteenth century, the use of arbitrary force masked as law came to be regarded as abhorrent, even in the military sphere. *White-Jacket* provides eloquent testimony to the emergence of a new kind of sea-lawyer. Martial law was pronounced by Blackstone and subsequent writers to be contrary to English law. Despite this, it was imposed on the civilian populations in the colonies of Ireland, India, Jamaica and South Africa at periods of crisis during the nineteenth century. When Melville came to write *Billy Budd* the modern sense of the phrase had become accepted usage, and even those lexicographers – like P. Austin Nuttall in *Routledge's Pronouncing Dictionary* (first edition, 1863) – who retain the old sense employ the pejorative language of modern legal discourse in doing so:

Martial law: in military service, an *arbitrary* law, regulated by *expediency* [my emphasis].

When Captain Vere describes Billy's case as one "'under martial law practically to be dealt with,'" and the pronouncement of sentence as "'martial law operating through us,'" he uses the older meaning, for which "Articles of War" is a synonym.[29] However, he invokes the phrase in the course of an argument that, as Thomas has shown, purports to adduce the binding, impersonal authority, the "measured forms," of statute law. The contradictions that White-Jacket exposes through argumentation are implicit in Vere's language when he applies modern notions of legitimacy to "War's child."

However, the effect of this superimposition of new ideas onto old practices is not a grafting of freedom upon tyranny, to invert White-Jacket's phrase, but an exercise of military power under the appearance of legal form. For in abjuring the commander's customary discretion as to punishment in favour of submission to the "mandatory" death penalty, Vere secures the best military disposition of Billy's case. His strict literalism in point of penalty is combined, as we have seen, with several procedural errors which constitute misuse of the law and which ensure prompt conviction and sentence. Legal process therefore becomes the vehicle of what Vere calls "military necessity," as the "practical" or expedient considerations of maintaining the crew in a state of efficient readiness to kill or be killed take precedence over normative demands for procedural correctness, an understanding of the nature of the crime, and an appropriate penalty. In this process of

nomic relegation, it is important to recognize, the law is by no means
an unwilling victim. Just as the Christian religion connives at its own
undermining by "serving in the host of the God of War – Mars"
(p. 398), so the common law, through Lord Mansfield, the Lord Chief
Justice, judicially upholds the custom of impressment (p. 337). This
interference with personal liberty is justified by the circumstantial
necessity of war, as is the secret practice of freeing prisoners before the
expiration of their sentences to man the fleet. The civil authorities,
who in constitutional theory control the military, subvert their own
legal system whilst purporting to defend it. What the narrator calls
"sanctioned irregularities" (p. 344) result. This is a "considerate" or
euphemistic term for breaches of the law committed by the authorities,
civil or military, in meeting the exigencies of war. When the war is
prosecuted on such a premise of normative compromise, the "necessity" of Billy's summary execution follows *a fortiori*. When the agents of
"sanctioned irregularities" board the *Rights of Man*, Melville dramatizes
the transformation of martial law from its old to its new sense, as its
influence begins to extend from the military to the civil sphere.

To sanction irregularities is to undermine the rule of law, for it
renders nugatory or at least unpredictable the discourse of "measured
forms" by which society is supposed to be governed. Such is the narrative's interest in the authorized breach of forms, however, that Vere's
phrase and his reading of the Orpheus story are quoted following a
"variance from usage" (p. 404). The drum beat to quarters is ordered
after the burial of Billy's corpse, one hour early, and is presented as
"evidence of the necessity for unusual action" (p. 404). The irony of
this juxtaposition is reinforced when the narrator displaces "the dis-
ruption of forms" from England to France. Law, then, is sacrificed to
order. The drum beat to quarters is one of two commands given to
quell the men's emotional responses to Billy's death and burial: in each
case an involuntary, collective utterance and movement signifies their
common revulsion, but the expression of such pre-military humanity is
checked by the word of command, which, in the narrator's telling
Latinism, "superinduces" an impulse of obedience. This channelling
of the crew's responsiveness is reductive, an Orphean "spellbinding"
applied not to "the wild denizens of the woods," but to men. Their
incipient resentment following the death of Billy may be compared to
the "practical grievances" (p. 333) and lurking discontent which produced not only the Great Mutiny, but the French Revolution, particularly as the volatility of their feeling leads the narrator to compare

them to "mobs ashore." The use of force to suppress the mutinies, and of "sanctioned irregularities" to prosecute the war, suggests that the narrator's contrast between the two nations, metonymically expressed through their flags, "the flag of founded law and freedom defined, [and] the enemy's red meteor of unbridled and unbounded revolt" (p. 333), cannot be sustained. Order rather than law is the highest value in this English *nomos*: freedoms are abrogated, and "strategic command[s]" are based on the semblance rather than on any real foundation of law.

### III

The appearance of legality in Captain Vere's execution of Billy confers retrospective irony on his claim that the Mutiny Act "'looks but to the frontage, the appearance.'" Vere's martial "vows" and membership of the aristocratic ruling class cause him to place trust in "appearances" in several ways. He consciously strives in his decisions not to undermine the impression the crew has of his complete authority: Billy's penalty may not be remitted lest it be taken to demonstrate that the officers are afraid of the crew's opposition; likewise no "visible" extra guard is appointed on the day of the execution. Vere's command therefore has a self-consciously rhetorical and hermeneutical aspect: it scrutinizes the expressive potential of all actions, gestures and words, and seeks by careful selection to control their interpretation by the crew. In a system which has forsaken its own paideic norms and the prospect of voluntary assent by the men, the desire to control thought as well as behaviour becomes paramount. The narrator registers this anxiety in his treatment of the crew's "confused murmur." It can only be "verbally rendered" through circumlocution and natural imagery drawn from the secret wilderness, "the freshet-wave of a torrent suddenly swelled by pouring showers in tropical mountains" (p. 402). Thus expelled from human language it is incapable of precise interpretation. From its ascribed primitiveness, however, a general sense of "capricious revulsion" is translated. In its formlessness and spontaneity this "thought or feeling," and its mode of expression, are disruptive of the "measured forms" of naval order, and are immediately silenced. Like the audible intake of breath that spreads when the Doomster rises to pronounce sentence on Effie Deans, this emotive utterance ought not to be viewed as revolt, but as an intelligently sympathetic response to an unjust hanging. However muffled and inarticulate, it is the expression

of a collective ethical consciousness that calls into question the pragmatism of their rulers.

What the military attention to "frontage" excludes is any consideration of Billy's intention. That he "'purposed neither mutiny nor homicide'" is known to the court, both from his own statement and from
Vere's evidence, but is taken to be irrelevant to the charge of striking
an officer. Charles A. Reich argues that Billy's lack of intention signifies his "innocence in being," which must be distinguished from his
legal responsibility for the act of striking and killing Claggart. For
Reich, all laws are condemned to rely on objective, external evidence,
on "the frontage, the appearance," rather than on the subjective intentions of the person charged. While acknowledging that Billy's act would
today be extenuated, his situation is yet representative: "although modern law is more flexible than the Mutiny Act, its basic approach is
similar; primarily it judges the action and not the man or his state of
mind."[30] Acts rather than minds are the law's focus because it must
apply universal standards of conduct and assumptions of rationality
and self-control throughout society. Reich proceeds to argue that *Billy
Budd* subverts the universalist and rationalist presuppositions of the law
through the insight it provides into Billy's character: by hanging him
for the unintended consequence of striking the malicious Claggart, the
law creates a "tragedy of justice." In this reading Melville's narrative
becomes a plea for the consideration of personal factors in legal judgment: the novella registers a sympathetic understanding of the various
influences on human conduct which the law should adopt. Captain
Vere's insight into Billy's innocence cannot be put into legal effect:
"Billy's execution is thus an image of society's failure to make its
actions fit its understanding."[31]

Reich takes Vere's pretence of legalism at face value, overlooking
the pragmatic military considerations that constitute the real "necessity" for the hanging. In doing so he compares Vere's reasoning with
the judgment of Lord Coleridge in the case of *Dudley and Stephens*,
where two shipwrecked sailors who had killed and eaten a third in
order to survive were convicted of murder. The judge ruled that the
law did not recognize the "natural" law of self-preservation or any
defence of necessity to commit a crime. It is an irony unrecognized by
Reich that the law admits a concept of necessity when it upholds the
legal system, but denies its benefit to individuals.[32] This predisposition
towards the claims of law facilitates his diminution of the place of
intention in the criminal law, for no crime can be committed without

the requisite mental state, the *mens rea*. If anything, the overemphasis on objective acts in the earlier part of Reich's article serves to highlight the contrasts he proceeds to draw between impersonal law and a desire for justice fuelled by the insights into Billy's character afforded by the narrative.

For the narrator, character precedes and explains action, "[t]he point of the present story turning on the hidden nature of the master-at-arms" (p. 354). Where for Vere the blow to Claggart's head is of prime importance, the narrator effects a normative reversal when he provides carefully executed portraits, with detailed focus on the heads, both physiognomically and psychologically, in an attempt to plumb the "hidden nature" of the three major characters. Though the histories of Billy and Claggart are obscure, the main features of their moral psychology, along with that of their Captain, are revealed. In the tradition of tragedy each is given a ruling passion, a flaw, or a characteristic that will have fatal consequences. However, the narrator's discourse of character is not ready-made or reductive, but a product of uncertainty, of speculation, of ponderous attention to complexity. By this means, the "blow" is particularized as the unique result of the interaction between the guileless "upright barbarian," Billy, and the unfathomable "Natural Depravity" of Claggart. When unforeseeable death supervenes, plot takes over from character as the dominant element in the fiction, as Barbara Johnson has noted, but character surely reasserts its importance when the Captain, whose response to the death raises doubts about his own sanity, must function as judge as well as witness. In focusing solely on the consequences of the blow, Vere eschews motive and other explanatory discourses as "'matter for psychologic theologians to discuss'" (p. 385). The "inside narrative" is full of such matter; indeed the phrase tossed aside by Vere, "'the mystery of iniquity,'" is apologetically invoked by the narrator in his search for an adequate moral lexicon to account for Claggart in chapter 11. He distinguishes knowledge of the world from knowledge of human nature, suggesting that the former may be acquired, while the latter is mysteriously innate. In an oblique commentary on the law's incomplete understanding of human nature, the "Hebrew Prophets" are considered better guides to the "obscure spiritual places" than are Coke and Blackstone. The crux of *Billy Budd* arises because Vere is invested with this insight: "something exceptional in the moral quality of Captain Vere made him, in earnest encounter with a fellow man, a veritable touchstone of that man's essential nature" (p. 373).[33] Yet, his

understanding of the characters of Billy and Claggart is kept separate
from his conduct of the trial. In this respect as in others the operation
of the law is impoverished by Vere's actions. Billy is constructed both
as an object of rigid discipline under the Articles of War and as the
sharer of an intersubjective encounter with Vere so sublime that the
narrative can only guess at its content.[34] A paradoxical conjunction of
sacrifice and sacrament is engineered, illustrating Reich's antithesis
between actions and understanding. Such understanding should preclude condemnation, should produce forgiveness; but martial necessity
precludes forgiveness, requires the death of Claggart's assailant.

The execution of Billy is therefore placed in a larger narrative context than that admitted by Vere. His restrictive focus on the blow and
its consequences is supplemented by an account of Claggart's motivation, of Billy's desperate inarticulateness and resort to violence, of the
historical circumstances as interpreted by Vere, and of the crew's intuitive but suppressed opposition to the hanging. Writing of Claggart's
"spontaneous antipathy" the narrator claims that in assigning this cause
to the lie about Billy he is combining psychological realism with "that
prime element of Radcliffian romance, the mysterious" (p. 351). The
realist project of rational explanation discovers its limit in the actions
of Claggart, Billy and Vere. Claggart's fundamental depravity produces a riot of irrationality under a rational surface; Billy, the most
opaque of the characters, is deprived of his innocence by the surprising
death of Claggart at his hands; and the humane intelligence of Vere is
constrained in its operation by the most conventional of political and
military assumptions. The narrative thereby defines the quality and
extent of consciousness as it is variously applied by the characters,
prospectively and retrospectively, to the central action. In revealing
the combination of voluntary and accidental factors in the constitution
of normative subjectivity *Billy Budd* illustrates William Domnarski's
claim that through character literature can offer "insights otherwise
unavailable" into the workings of the law.[35] Where the law, in the
person of Vere, excludes motive, intention and other subjective elements, this fictional narrative demonstrates their presence in and
value for the normative hermeneutic project of law. Reich's demand
that society's "understanding" – the insights of psychology, philosophy,
sociology and other contemporary discourses – be incorporated into
the "actions" taken in society's name by its legal agencies is therefore
an ethically and aesthetically sensitive interpretation of Melville's representation of law.

If this reading is placed in the larger terms of American cultural history, it can be seen as expressing the dominant nineteenth-century narrative of the conflict between Nature and Society, with Billy's natural innocence being sacrificed by the exemplar of social authority, Vere. One of the recurring themes of the legal culture of the period under review is the demand to historicize conceptions of what is natural. Indeed, the war in which the *Bellipotent* is engaged can be viewed as a conflict between competing claims of natural social organization or natural human rights. As I shall demonstrate shortly, Reich's interest in the subjectivity of the criminal can be traced in the criminology of Melville's last decades.

First, however, I wish to examine another anti-naturalist interpretation. In a deconstructive reading Barbara Johnson locates the cause of the failure of justice in *Billy Budd* not in persons or socio-political systems, but "within language itself."[36] She argues that "nature is authority whose textual origins have been forgotten."[37] She notes how linguistic spaces abound in *Billy Budd*, from Billy's stutter to the narrator's admission that though he "essay" Claggart's portrait, he will "never quite hit it"(p. 342). These produce "eclipses of meaning," "cognitive spaces," which are the cause of interpretation – by characters in and readers of the novel. Johnson believes that Melville is "asking us to understand" these gaps and spaces, is highlighting the "twisted relations" between cognition and action.[38] This pairing recalls Reich's distinction between society's action and understanding. While Reich assumes the possibility of reconciliation, Johnson problematizes the distinction and the very existence of such entities. Johnson may echo Reich's terminology, but as a post-structuralist her interest is epistemological, her attitude sceptical and her focus textual.

Among the categorical oppositions deconstructed by Johnson is that between guilt and innocence. Allegorical interpretations of the interplay between Claggart and Billy are undermined in Johnson's view by the narrative comment, "Innocence and guilt personified in Claggart and Billy in effect changed places" (p. 380). It is not, I believe, mere pedantry to note that Johnson capitalizes "innocence" and omits the qualifying introductory phrase, "In the jugglery of circumstances preceding and attending the event on board the *Bellipotent*, and in the light of that martial code whereby it was formally to be judged," from this quotation, for this recasting enables her to displace the legal code and the participants' acts from the interpretation of this peripeteia.[39] She concludes that this passage "invites and subverts" allegorical reading, invoking abstractions while denying them their stable embodiment in character. She prefers to view the opposition between Billy and Claggart in terms of "two conceptions of language, or . . . types of reading."[40] Billy is a literal reader, and believes in a "motivated" sign: he takes Claggart's "Handsome is . . ." remark at face value. Claggart is an ironic reader who, in believing Billy "a mantrap under the daisies," postulates an arbitrary relation between signifier and signified. Although an interesting contrast, this explanation anaesthetizes Claggart, neutralizing the antipathy which motivates his lie. Johnson proceeds to a study of "the linguistic implications of the murder," concluding that Billy's act illustrates the "radical *incompatibility*" of performative and constative language: "Billy performs the truth of Claggart's report only by means of his absolute and blind denial of its cognitive validity."[41]

At this point the linguistic model seems reductive. Johnson's trope of paradox captures nicely the complication, the inverted attribution, of guilt and innocence effected in the plot by Billy's fist. However, the act of striking Claggart is qualitatively different from the fomenting of mutiny alleged. Striking and killing a petty officer might constitute an act of mutiny, but circumstances here indicate that no intention to overthrow the lawful commander exists. Billy is guilty, but of what offence? By emphasizing plot at the expense of character and treating both these elements as functions of linguistic operations, Johnson evacuates all consideration of moral agency from the analysis of the "blow." While it is true that *Billy Budd* implicitly limits the sovereignty of volition in such agency, the understanding of the sailor's responsibility is not assisted by the abstraction of Johnson's argument. A crucial instance is her use of the term "murder" in "the linguistic implications of the murder." Claggart's death cannot unequivocally be called murder, because it is uncertain that Billy killed him with "malice aforethought," that is, with the intention of killing or of inflicting grievous bodily harm. Since the narrative supplies only a negative statement of his intent ("'Budd purposed neither homicide nor mutiny'") and the death is represented as the freakish result of a single impulsive blow, malice aforethought cannot confidently be inferred. Thus, unwittingly, Johnson joins Vere in simplifying the evidence and condemning Billy.

It is significant that the law relating to murder was the subject of many attempts at reform during the last two decades of the nineteenth century. Martin J. Wiener explains how "changing constructions of human nature, human agency, and the meaning of criminality" in these years prompted a major realignment in English criminal policy.[42]

He traces a movement away from Victorian notions of self-control and the conquest of "impulsiveness" to an Edwardian acceptance of various limits to personal autonomy. He shows how "more and more persons involved in the criminal justice system began to exhibit uneasiness over its 'rigid' conceptions of agency, and the 'unrealistic' demands it consequently placed upon many offenders' powers of calculation and will."[43] The possibility that an offender might suffer from or have been affected by mental disability or disturbance began to alter the way in which the law's "norm of personal responsibility" was viewed. The crime of murder attracted urgent concern because, like the crime in *Billy Budd*, its mandatory penalty was death. In 1881 the English Attorney General sought to amend the law by changing the definition of murder to require a wilful intent to kill. This attempt was rejected, but administrative measures were introduced to provide greater allowance for mental disturbance and inadequacy. This discourse was not exclusively one of mental defectiveness: the Attorney spoke of temporary and circumstantial, as well as congenital, conditions; and the concept of "adolescence," of youthful rebellion as a developmental stage, was introduced as part of this movement. Similarly, in the United States, according to Lawrence Friedman, "doctors and lawyers engaged in a grand and continuing debate about the meaning of criminal responsibility, and the scope of the insanity defence."[44] Of particular interest in this debate is the attempt to provide a medical foundation for temporary or partial occlusions of moral consciousness through such terms as "irresistible impulse." The legal recognition of "irresistible impulse" was pioneered by Lemuel Shaw. While subsequently introduced into some states other than Massachusetts, it remained a minority position in the nineteenth-century American criminal law.[45]

At the time of the composition of *Billy Budd*, then, the operation of the law was being changed to give effect to new social understandings. Melville dramatizes two contrasting "images of man" in the impulsive act of Billy and the "rigid" self-control of Captain Vere. The latter's attempt to impress the "measured forms" of an arbitrary legal system upon "primitive instincts strong as the wind and the sea" (p. 386) succeeds in the short term: Billy is executed and the crew's resentment quashed. The death-bed repetition of Billy's name, however, signifies the return of the repressed, a final, unconscious expression of sympathetic identification. Vere himself becomes the work's ultimate demonstration of the limits of the will when he joins Billy as a victim of the God of War. More generally, the novella is constructed upon a set of psycho-moral aberrations: Claggart's "lunacy is not continuous, but occasional, evoked by some secret object; . . . it is self-contained, . . . to the average mind not distinguishable from sanity" (p. 354); Vere's excited mental state after the killing, which has been compared by critics to that of Claggart,[46] raises doubts in the surgeon's mind about his sanity, and prompts the narrator to reflect upon the difficulty of defining the border between sanity and insanity (p. 379). It is not my purpose to offer a psychoanalytical reading of *Billy Budd*, but to suggest that Melville's text instantiates the contemporary uncertainty over criminal responsibility by locating the constituents of the action at the borders of normative discourse. Further, this proto-modernistic psychology is only one part of the narrative's explanatory strategies. Brook Thomas has noted how Melville assigns no single cause to the central event, Claggart's death. He links the inclusiveness of the narration, its digressions into history, philosophy and theology, its triple ending, its search for the sources of action in character, its chance juxtapositions and accidental outcomes, to the attack on the legal doctrine of the single, objective cause by nineteenth-century pragmatists.[47] The desire to tell what Melville calls an "inside narrative," an account of the situational complexity of a momentary deed which has lasting consequences for characters who are regarded with sympathetic understanding, is shared by the next novel to be studied, Conrad's *Lord Jim*, in which the objective story constructed by the law and the intersubjective experience reported by Marlow are pointedly contrasted.

Although I have argued that Vere supplants the process of understanding by an act of judgment, it does not follow that these two approaches are incompatible. For the possibility of judgment is recognized in the same chapter that posits the blurred boundary between sanity and insanity. While Barbara Johnson argues that legal judgment postulates a "difference between two knowable entities" and thereby "does violence to the irreducible ambiguities that subvert" such entities,[48] the narrator's question, "Who in the rainbow can draw the line between where the violet tint ends and the orange tint begins? . . . So with sanity and insanity" (p. 379), does not impeach the validity of all judgments, but acknowledges the difficulty created by borderline cases: "In pronounced cases there is no question about them." What is particularly striking about the question posed as to Vere's sanity is that the narrator both invites and suspends judgment: "Whether Captain Vere, as the surgeon professionally and privately surmised, was really the sudden victim of any degree of aberration, everyone must determine for himself by such light as this narrative may afford." Here, as Lawrence Douglas notes, "the narrator specifically abjures the role of judge, and instead places the yoke of the juridical function on the reader."[49] What has hitherto been a strongly monological fiction, dominated by the "voice" of the reflective and digressive narrator and containing little reported speech, becomes at this point dialogical in the wide sense proposed by Bakhtin. As Hayford and Sealts demonstrated through their genetic text, Melville's late revisions to *Billy Budd* had the effect of dramatizing Vere's conduct during the trial scene, and of throwing doubt on the rightness of his decisions and on the narrator's attitude to him.[50] The articulation of the issues becomes the responsibility of Vere, rather than of the narrator, and the surgeon and the members of the drumhead court are given the role of raising questions and doubts. The narrator introduces his conclusion by defining himself as a witness, as the author of a true deposition: "How it fared with the Handsome Sailor during the year of the Great Mutiny has been faithfully given" (p. 405). The problematics of the event, the discursive fullness of Vere's rhetoric, complete with inconsistencies and opportunism, and the misgivings of the characters over the "necessary" execution of Billy ensure that this judgment will itself be judged, as it has been in this chapter and from other perspectives, by the reader.[51] In this respect *Billy Budd* offers through its form a mimesis of judgment at law; and by locating its action where the colours of guilt and innocence blend into each other, it forces a reconnection between the social action of judgment and the complex task of understanding.

IV

Where the plots of *The Heart of Midlothian* and *Bleak House* offer a pattern of progress towards social harmony and improvement, that of *Billy Budd* presents a more pessimistic view of legal history. Melville's examination of the dawn of the modern *nomos* is a story of the victory of violence and the eclipse of Enlightenment values. While the earlier novels achieve a point of normative anchorage, the war between Vere's prescriptive truths and the revolutionary assertion of universal human rights yields no decisive result, no sanctuary in the "sea of faith." *Billy Budd* is imbued by both its epoch of production and its epoch of representation with a sense of inescapable change and conflict, of normative fluidity. What Vere calls "measured forms" are shown to be factitious rather than natural, but capable of intersecting fatally with

the unpredictabilities and the "ragged edges" of existence. The narrator's understanding of the events of the story is manifest, but it
figures as a burden that he would rather not bear. For the plot centres
on death, and on the failure of understanding to avert the perceived
necessity of violent death. The tragic outcome of the plot induces a
philosophical pessimism. The narrator attempts to disclaim any pre-
tension to completeness by appending three sequels to his narration,
two of them by other authors, forswearing imaginary finality and
expressing his sense of the "ragged edges" of truth. One of these is
the antithetical "News from the Mediterranean," a grotesque fabrica-
tion constructed partly out of rumour, but principally dictated by the
presuppositions of the Articles of War and the customary attitudes of
the naval authorities. Against this interpretation, and this record, the
"inside narrative" has been written. The other sequels corroborate the
emphases of the novella, the last words of Captain Vere already noted,
and the sailor's poem, "Billy in the Darbies." Although printed as a
ballad, this work is generically closer to a lyric monologue, for it imaginatively recounts the inner life of Billy the evening before his death.
When it merges his present physical discomfort with his dream of
peaceful death,

> . . . Sentry, are you there?
> Just ease these darbies at the wrist,
> And roll me over fair!
> I am sleepy, and the oozy weeds about me twist
>                                    (p. 409)

the poem reasserts the value of empathy in the death-grip of martial
law, extending the claims of the spirit against the degradation of the
body. The "tarry hand" of the poet, which expands the sentiments
implicit in the primitive murmur of the crew following the hanging,
therefore supplies a final image for the writer of this "inside narrative"
who sets the dignity of the fallible human subject against the "brutal
claim" of a "bloody code."

## CHAPTER SEVEN

# From sympathetic criminal to imperial law-giver –
# Lord Jim

*Lord Jim* was published in book form in 1900, the penultimate year of Queen Victoria's reign and the threshold of a new century.[1] This pivotal date provides the historical clue which dispels any initial surprise that Joseph Conrad should be a subject of this study of novelistic representations of law. For, in the first place, Victoria ruled not only Britain but an Empire "beyond the seas," and British law provided one framework for both the colonies and the maritime service which connected them with "home." As Conrad derived much of his novelistic material from his own experience in the British Merchant Marine and from stories he heard during his years at sea, it is understandable that law should figure in some of his novels. Second, Richard Weisberg has argued that the modern period is characterized by the emergence of law as the dominant discourse of value and that the modern novel is deeply and critically engaged by legalism and the lawyer-figure.[2] Conrad's modernism is a well established proposition of literary history, and in *Lord Jim* the legal process is examined in the context of modernist normative instability and metaphysical uncertainty.[3] The juxtaposition of these two influences, Victorian and modern, creates a tension between fidelity to tradition, to the claims of an inherited *nomos*, and simultaneously, a radical attack upon that *nomos*.[4]

Such ambivalence has been identified as a feature of the modernist outlook: Franz Kuna argues that what Nietzsche labelled "the Janus-face, at once Dionysiac and Apollonian," in which "whatever exists is both just and unjust, and is equally justified in both," finds its clearest embodiment in the novels of Conrad.[5] It will be recalled that the image of Janus was used in chapter five of this study to describe Trollope's combination of conservatism and liberal radicalism. That conjunction consists, however, of two variants within a single system of politics. What is envisaged in the modernist adoption of Janus is the paradoxical co-existence of opposites. It will be suggested then that Conrad's

ambivalence in representing the law is more far-reaching and fundamental than that encountered in earlier novelists. Nonetheless, the
discovery of such compound attitudes – of attraction and repulsion,
sympathy and judgment, affiliation and ironic detachment – towards
law and its operation throughout the nineteenth-century novel is one
of the chief results of this study. Trollope's complex response is preceded by Scott's promotion of law and fascination with violence, and
by Dickens's deployment of the very discourse of equity in his denunciation of Chancery. Throughout the period since the breakdown of
"the republic of letters" a measure of ambivalence is inherent in the
representation of law in the novel, but this is increased in the context
of modernism.

I

To examine this development in more detail I turn to one recurrent
motif in these novels, the "sympathetic criminal." One of the functions
of all the stories told in the novels here studied is to reclaim for sympathetic attention characters who have been legally or morally condemned
by those in authority over them, including parents and step-parents,
courts and commanding officers. Thus, the pathos of Effie Deans is a
vehicle for criticizing the punitive morality which has condemned her
to death; the final happiness of Esther Summerson acts as a rebuff to
those who condemn the victim for even being born; Lady Mason is
perhaps the classic sympathetic criminal, for her cause is explicitly
adopted by the advocate-narrator; and Billy Budd, in what is the most
extreme case, is tragically killed at the end of a plot that sets moral
innocence against legalistic fervour. In all of these instances the novel
tells a more comprehensive story and therefore arrives at a juster
estimate of the individual than that reached by the court or authority-
figure. In only one of these cases however, *Billy Budd*, is the corollary of
this presentation pursued and the society which produced these total
condemnations on partial grounds itself condemned. In the Dickens
novel the establishment of "Esther Woodcourt" in a new Bleak House
signifies the integration of the outcast in a society undergoing reform.
Even less equivocally, Effie Deans is marginalized as the narrative
turns to tell of her sister's virtuous heroism; and Lady Mason, though
acquitted at law, conforms to community morality, gives up Orley
Farm and goes into exile. The effect of this pattern is to accept implicitly the fundamental justice (or capacity for justice) of the society in

question, with the express qualification of the case presented, for which a solution is found and a warning against complacency offered. With some adjustments, then, the community is reintegrated at the conclusion of these narratives and the banished criminal's absence is scarcely felt. It is at precisely this point that the different narrative and normative stance of *Lord Jim* is most clearly marked, for Conrad's novel takes the condemned man for its eponymous hero and follows him into self-chosen exile, leaving the Barchester-like vicarage of his family home as a faint but still traceable influence on the margin of the novel's world. By virtue of such redistribution of narrative attention, and in other ways which this chapter will explore, Conrad is able to focus directly on the complex relationship between Jim the outcast and his society of origin, on the extension of the *nomos* into new geographic domains, and the crises of belief which these experiences produce.

Underlying the concept of the "sympathetic criminal" is an assumption that the character of an individual may not be conclusively revealed by a criminal action he or she has committed. Involvement in a crime may be "out of character" for the person in question, and the reprehension which is the normal response to crime is in such cases overridden by a sense of understanding of and concern for the person. This process, with its associated ideology, is not only a phenomenon of post-Romantic literature, but is also traceable in modern penal policy. Martin Wiener notes the emergence in the 1890s of the concept of adolescence as a developmental stage, and relates it to two important trends in criminal law, "the tendency to attribute ever less responsibility to juveniles," and a gathering doubt as to the effectiveness of imprisonment as a response to youth crime. The Probation of First Offenders Act 1887 established a new alternative in sentencing, and required courts "to have regard to 'the youth, character, and antecedents of the offender, to the trivial nature of the offence and to any extenuating circumstances under which it was committed.'"[6] This new penal policy was only fully implemented after World War One, but the dialogical form of *Lord Jim* enables the various positions taken in this debate, from the meting out of punishment and responsibility to the quest for understanding and the provision of another chance, to be incorporated in the text.

In this connection, Eloise Knapp Hay's claim that "Conrad was often arrested by accounts of actual villainies, which 'sprang to life' for him when his mind sought extenuating circumstances for [the] renegades who had committed them" is crucial.[7] William Roughead, a

Scottish barrister and historian of *Causes Célèbres of Caledonia* who corresponded with Conrad, also attests to this. His own book on the trial of Burke and Hare, the mass-murderers who sold their victims' corpses to the Edinburgh anatomist Dr. Robert Knox, did not reveal any such extenuation. Conrad commented: "The callousness of these wretches is so completely perfect that it reduces the psychological interest to vanishing point." As Roughead concludes, some possibility of complex and sympathetic individuality is a precondition for the imaginative transformation of a criminal act into a Conradian plot.[8] Hay notes that actual crimes provided Conrad with source material for "Gasper Ruiz," *Under Western Eyes*, *Nostromo*, and *Lord Jim*. Others could be listed. In one of the shorter tales, "The Secret Sharer," a story inspired by a murder committed aboard the *Cutty Sark*, the narrator conceals a murderer and assists him to escape, out of sympathy and a private judgment that he is not "a murdering brute."[9] Beyond this, the story is notable for its exploration of empathy, its presentation of the murderer and the narrator as "doubles," implying that "it was quite possible for an ordinary, decent, conscientious person to kill someone."[10] Conventional judgment as embodied in the probable verdict of a judge and "twelve respectable tradesmen" (p. 688) is disparaged, but the criminal is still doomed to be "driven off the face of the earth." "The Secret Sharer" was written ten years after *Lord Jim*, and may be viewed as a reprise of the representation of the sympathetic criminal undertaken in the amplitude of the novel.

The hero of *Lord Jim* is not convicted of a crime in the technical sense of the word. He is not charged with an offence, tried by a jury or penalized by imprisonment or fine. Jim appears before a marine court composed of a magistrate and two nautical assessors, and his punishment relates to his profession (the cancellation of his certificate). Nevertheless, the *Patna* affair is spoken of as a crime, and the court's judgment prompts Marlow to reflect on Jim and his action: "The real significance of crime is in its being a breach of faith with the community of mankind" (p. 157). The desertion of a ship carrying passengers by its officers ranks as such a breach among the nautical community. The case on which the *Patna* story is based, that of the pilgrim ship *Jeddah*, also involved only professional penalties: criminal proceedings were considered, but owing to the disappearance or departure of all witnesses except one, were not instituted.[11] The officer who remained in Singapore was the Chief Mate, Augustine Podmore Williams, on whom the character of Jim is based. The son of a parson, Williams chose to face out the scandal in Singapore, working as a water-clerk. Norman Sherry suggests that this aspect of "facing it out" and thereby displaying what Marlow calls "a kind of courage" was what attracted Conrad to the story.[12] In the "Author's Note" to *Lord Jim* Conrad describes seeing Williams "on an Eastern roadstead" and remarks on the writer's need to gather "all the sympathy of which I was capable, to seek fit words for his meaning."

Marlow's definition of "the real significance of crime" is followed by a disjunctive pair of subordinate clauses: ". . . from that point of view he was no mean traitor, but his execution was a hole-and-corner affair" (p. 157). In its completeness, this sentence captures concisely the mingled notes of judgment of the deed and sympathy for the man. *Lord Jim* is in its early sections propelled forward by the dialectical interplay of the "fact" of the crime and Marlow's sense of Jim's personal claims. The certainty of which Novalis speaks in the epigraph to *Lord Jim*, "It is certain any conviction gains infinitely the moment another soul will believe in it," is subject to fluctuation throughout the novel. Marlow is the other "soul" who listens to and believes in Jim's claims of honour, but neither of them is undeviating in his "conviction."

The conflict is signalled in the opening chapter when the omniscient narrator comments on the significance and the failure of Jim's "incognito" (his dispensing with a surname): "His incognito, which had as many holes as a sieve, was not meant to hide a personality but a fact" (p. 4). It is a measure of the novel's sympathy towards Jim's sensitivity over reminders of the past that neither Marlow nor the omniscient narrator reveals the surname: the incognito is preserved though the ambition of the story is to understand and to reveal Jim as fully as possible. Jim seeks to hide his defection from the *Patna* so that others may respond to him as to a man untainted by guilt. Jim believes that his "personality" is unaffected by his crime and that the crime is irrelevant to the evaluation of him as a man. This theory is never properly tested – the good impression Jim makes as an unknown water-clerk is never given the chance to outweigh the news of his past crime – because he flees at first mention of the *Patna*. The usual function of an incognito is to hide an identity if not a personality, especially in the case of a so-called "fugitive from justice." In a novel constructed on repeated instances of flight, the figure of the fugitive serves as a virtual motif. Its larger significance will be discussed below, but Jim's claims to sympathetic interest depend on the fact that unlike his skipper he did not attempt to evade the justice of the community. In the end, his carefully constructed world is smashed by another fugitive, Gentleman Brown, who greets him as a fellow absconder. Is Jim a fugitive, from the truth about himself, if not from justice? By this stage, as the honorific "Tuan" or "Lord" added to his name suggests, the second chance which is the sympathetic criminal's hope and reward appears to have been mightily successful. On Patusan Jim finds a role that gives him "the certitude of rehabilitation" (p. 248). Trying later to evaluate Jim's death, however, Marlow reverts to the flight motif: "He goes away from a living woman to celebrate a pitiless wedding with a shadowy ideal of conduct. . . . He is gone" (p. 416).

The importance of questions about Jim's character and actions, and the tentativeness – even absence – of answers, gives to the narration a discursive quality. While acts are the basic stratum of the novel, the *causa sine qua non* perhaps, the reflections prompted by the mystery of those acts provide the immediate *causa causans*, the motivation for and the major concern of the narrative. Marlow's narration acquires a hermeneutic quality, not only because Jim is presented as an enigma to be decoded,[13] but because the process of understanding itself becomes an object of reflection and comment. The general tenor is of a negative or sceptical hermeneutic:

"I don't pretend I understood him. The views he let me have of himself were like those rents in a thick fog – bits of vivid and vanishing detail, giving no connected idea of the general aspect of a country. They fed one's curiosity without satisfying it." (p. 76)

Marlow's sense of incomprehension is most often registered through such imagery of mist or (as also in *Heart of Darkness*) of light and dark. For example, his long talks with Jim during the trial yield the reflection, " 'It is when we try to grapple with another man's intimate need that we perceive how incomprehensible, wavering and misty are the beings that share with us the sight of the stars' " (p. 180); and Marlow's last sight of Jim is of his white uniform gradually fading in the distance and the twilight, and seeming " 'to stand at the heart of a vast enigma' " (p. 336). This concentration on the effects of light and shadow parallels the techniques and assumptions of impressionistic art, in which intense perception is accompanied by the dissolution of conceptual distinctions:[14]

"The truth seems to be that it is impossible to lay the ghost of a fact. You can face it or shirk it – and I have come across a man or two who could wink at their familiar shades. Obviously Jim was not of the winking sort; but what I

could never make up my mind about was whether his line of conduct amounted to shirking his ghost or facing him out.
I strained my mental eyesight only to discover that, as with the complexion of all our actions, the shade of difference was so delicate that it was impossible to say. It might have been flight or it might have been a mode of combat." (p. 197)

Jim's case produces in Marlow an epistemological and normative crisis. The wish to register ever finer distinctions, to acquire precision of statement, is met by a sense of the loss of certainty. A direct pronouncement of a principle derived from experience ("The truth seems to be . . .") proves unhelpful when it is applied in connection with Jim (". . . it is impossible to say"). This realization necessitates in turn a suspension of judgment, as the norms invoked come to seem reductive. When it is impossible to tell whether Jim is "facing" or "shirking," the urge to condemn recedes in favour of the urge to understand. Marlow's recognition of the importance of gradations and shades grows through his relationship with Jim. His stance in chapter XIX, from which these quotations are taken and which treats his acceptance that Jim needs an opportunity to do more than earn his bread, contrasts completely with that adopted during their early discussions. In chapter XI Marlow uses irony to condemn as quibbling Jim's references to "the thickness of a sheet of paper" and "the breadth of a hair" between right and wrong or truth and falsehood (pp. 130–1). Here, Marlow's irony is presented as the means of a commonsense rebuttal of Jim's self-serving, self-deluding statement, and as beyond Jim's comprehension.

However, Marlow has his own "ghost" to lay, and his gibes are defensive utterances designed to repel the terror of "doubt." Addressing his own motivation for "grubbing into the deplorable details," Marlow first identifies his normative community: "an obscure body of men held together by a community of inglorious toil and by fidelity to a certain standard of conduct," that is, the profession of merchant seamen (p. 50). His unconscious hope is to vindicate this standard by finding "some merciful explanation, some convincing shadow of an excuse" for the desertion of the *Patna* by its officers. Yet Marlow's belief in the absoluteness of this standard is already qualified by doubt: "the doubt of the sovereign power enthroned in a fixed standard of conduct" is identified as "the most obstinate ghost of man's creation," and must be exorcised for Marlow's normative security. In effect, the rule of the seamen's code needs to be reinforced because it is already being undermined. Although Marlow's discourse is abstract

and metaphysical, an underlying psycho-moral anxiety is admitted
in his retrospection. For the knowledge of Jim's weakness, when set
against the promise of his appearance, prompts a fearful identification: having shared the same dreams and the same education in youth,
is "a destructive fate ready" for Marlow and the whole community of
officers? The reverse of Marlow's nagging and elastic question about
Jim, "Is he one of us?" is, "Are we the same as him?"[15]

Marlow's fear seems exaggerated, unless the encounter with Jim is
itself taken as the agent of destruction. Marlow finds that the urge to
condemn Jim in accordance with the fixed standards of the professional community is in conflict with the growing desire to assist in his
rehabilitation, to provide the conditions for the re-emergence of his
potential and the restoration of his privileges as a member of some
community. It is apparent that the community of mariners remains
closed to him: the conversations in bars and chandlers' shops in various ports show that the *Patna* episode is neither forgotten nor forgiven.
The conflict between fixed standards and individual evaluation is displaced from within Marlow's consciousness to between Marlow and
more conventionally-minded officers. Jim's chance to forge new normative bonds occurs inland. Marlow returns home, and the audience
to which he tells his story, complete with doubts, questions and self-
justifications, is more heterodox than the traditionally uniform society
of seamen. While Marlow does not lose contact with the sea and its
men, the magic circle of unreflective affiliation is broken. Marlow's
fate, if not destructive, is to tell of this breach and to attempt to chart
a new formation.

II

One consequence of the normative crisis by which Jim's claims to
sympathy are put in issue is the need to argue his case, to attempt to
persuade the reader, just as Marlow has become persuaded, that Jim
merits another chance. The narrative is therefore discursive in a more
fundamental sense than that discussed above: not only does Marlow
digressively relate events to ideas, but the bulk of his narration is
presented as discourse, as speech to a group of after-dinner talkers and
listeners. Walter Benjamin's account of the "storyteller" emphasizes
the possibility of constituting a community through sharing both stories and their normative significance, but also insists that the storyteller
as the traditional repository of wisdom is a relic of preindustrial society

and only functions in a few exceptional modern communities, including seamen.[16] Marlow is a prime example of such a storyteller, extending the traditions and lore of his profession, but conscious that they may be inadequate to the changed conditions of the modern age. Marlow therefore adopts the function of the storyteller, being convinced of the significance of Jim for an understanding of the modern metaphysic, but the story he tells is freighted with incertitude, both in the lack of definition as to Jim's significance and in his uncertainty of the story's reception.[17] Marlow's discourse includes some rhetorical strategies of a mingled aggressive-defensive kind, aimed at unsettling and reordering his audience's preconceptions, and by extension, any resistance felt by readers of the novel. Indeed, the major function of Marlow's narration may be described as an attempt to defend Jim and his own interest in Jim: the new community Marlow and also Conrad hope to build through telling this story must go beyond, must be argued out of, reflex denunciation as an assessment of and response to Jim's case.

Marlow's narrative may profitably be located in the tradition of forensic rhetoric. Although this term refers to the oratory of the law courts, and particularly to the need to persuade a judge or jury, it may be applied to Marlow because he is primarily concerned with obtaining justice for Jim.[18] In this project he examines witnesses and presents their evidence. Like the advocate-narrator of *Orley Farm*, he urges the reader-listener to view the accused in a sympathetic light. He is, however, not simply a partisan advocate, but the vehicle for reaching a valid judgment. Several critics, including Dorothy Van Ghent, have adopted the advocate metaphor to describe Marlow's role: "Marlow is unofficial attorney both for the defense and the prosecution. He selects, objectifies and humanizes the evidence on both sides . . . ."[19] This formulation is legally impossible in an adversary system like the common law, but as a rhetorical shorthand, as an oxymoron, it captures well the combination of conflicting interests which engage Marlow, his wish to uphold the code and his sympathy for Jim.

Moreover, Marlow's function of advocate is coeval with his presence as narrator, which actually emerges out of the court inquiry into the abandonment of the *Patna*. As Van Ghent notes, the early chapters are narrated by an omniscient narrator, but "Marlow takes over" when "the processes of judgment have to begin." Before considering the implications of this transfer of narration, the mechanism may be examined. Chapter IV, where the report of the trial begins, opens with Jim in the dock. The proceedings are focalized through Jim. His perception emphasizes their narrowness and tired formality. Amid the vacuous irrelevance he distinguishes Marlow and meets his eyes: "The glance directed at him was not the fascinated stare of the others. It was an act of intelligent volition" (pp. 32–3). From this exchange Jim infers Marlow's sympathetic understanding. Thereupon, the focus pivots around to Marlow, anticipating his retelling of the story in after years, and converting him from a spectator at the trial into a prospective narrator of, and participant in, Jim's story.[20] The chapter ends here, as did the earlier magazine instalment; the next chapter opens with Marlow beginning his account of Jim's trial. This narrative is, however, a retrospective one which fulfils the promise of understanding implicit in Marlow's glance and includes much more than the legal proceedings.[21]

One result of this transition in point of view is to reduce the importance of the *Patna* inquiry as a narrative subject and to devalue the hermeneutic authority of its verdict. In the first case *Lord Jim* contains nothing like the chronological reports of trial proceedings which are integral to *The Heart of Midlothian* and *Orley Farm*. Instead, Conrad's novel proceeds achronologically, juxtaposing the mysterious collision with Jim's evidence and then introducing Marlow. Thereafter, the narrative continues to intercut fragments of the trial with accounts of Marlow's long conversations with Jim and of the other information and opinions Marlow has discovered about the case. What emerges from this cross-cutting of past, present and future events is, in Jacques Berthoud's words, "almost . . . a collage of verdicts" on Jim's jump from the *Patna*.[22] The effect is to relegate the court judgment from a position of eminence as the single and final pronouncement to one among a number of attempts to comprehend Jim's act and Jim himself. Marlow functions as the conduit for all these, the court's, the French officer's, Brierly's private opinion and others. He assesses the assessors, detecting the moral hollowness of Brierly's desire for automatic professional rigour, and commending the Frenchman's courage while recognizing the rigidity that old age has produced. On this basis Berthoud argues that Conrad employs Marlow to conduct an "unofficial Inquiry" in order to supplement that of the court.[23] The official inquiry determines the facts, but Marlow's task is to ponder the meaning of Jim's betrayal, to ask questions "beyond the competency of the court."[24] The primary focus is on the man rather than the facts. Using a formulation similar to that of the "sympathetic criminal," Berthoud suggests that "the second inquiry is concerned with . . . whether anything survives the verdict of the facts."[25] The judgments collected by Marlow are inseparable from the men who propound them, so the "collage" also consists of character portraits: not only Jim, the Frenchman and Brierly, but Cannibal Robinson, Jones, and the "New South Wales German." The effect is to present a normative spectrum in which shades of courage, of degradation, of honour, of other virtues and venalities are revealed so that the assessment of Jim may be conducted on more subtle grounds than a simplistic contrast between law-abiders and law-breakers. Consequently, a moral dimension is added to the meaning of "one of us" – a consciousness of human imperfection which mitigates any impulse to condemn.

Marlow's representation of the official inquiry is limited to the helmsmen's evidence and the verdict, virtually the "edited highlights" of the trial. Even the facts of the case, then, are presented through the private conversation of Marlow and Jim, or Marlow and the Frenchman, rather than the public forum. This structure minimizes the official contribution to the reader's understanding as the bulk of the evidence is presented by Marlow. What is more important, though, is the contrast between the two inquiries' modes of adducing evidence: the court prescribes what information it will hear; Marlow, as Van Ghent observes, lets the evidence "speak for itself."[26] The former is oriented towards excluding material, and demands submission to its rules; the latter is inclusivist, and confers narrative freedom on witnesses. The court's insistence that Jim confine himself to "facts" leads to the frustration of his desire to speak the truth, to the view that "speech was of no use to him" (p. 33). In one of many ironic foreshadowings in this highly patterned novel, the first "opportunity" that Marlow affords Jim is to enable him to speak, to listen to his story, thereby restoring the privilege of communication and the possibility of friendship. The result is Jim's confession, which achieves through its emotional intensity a vivid representation of the abandonment of the ship and, in the dramatic present, a revelation of the unconscious strategies adopted by Jim to cope with his failure. Narrative freedom does not license self-validation: Jim's story forces Marlow to respond with impatience, irony, and grudging respect; it provides the basis for judgment.

The self-deceptions and evasions revealed through Jim's confession cast a retrospectively ironic shadow over his belief that "he remembered everything" and could tell the whole truth about the matter (p. 31). This confidence, revealed by means of *style indirect libre* during the scene of his evidence to the court, induces him to expatiate, to seek

a "meticulous precision of statement" about both the tangible facts
and the "directing spirit of perdition" present within events. The latter speculations are an integral, though problematic part of the story
of Jim, and by rejecting them as irrelevant the court critically adopts
a narrower focus than Marlow. However, despite this limitation, its
insistence on facts does not merit the scorn with which Jim greets it:
"They demanded facts from him, as if facts could explain anything!"
(p. 29). What Jim's eventual narration and subsequent actions show is
that his denigration of facts is in part motivated by his difficulty in
facing one particular fact. Nonetheless, Jim correctly posits a distinction between facts and explanations: facts cannot be ignored, but they
are not self-sufficient. Thus Marlow, seeking to convince Jewel of Jim's
loyalty, reasons from facts: "'it was the only possible conclusion from
the facts of the case'" (p. 309); and again, facing Jim's inability to
formulate a last message to send home, he leaves open one possibility:
"'there shall be no message, unless such as each of us can interpret
from the language of facts, that are so often more enigmatic than the
craftiest arrangement of words'" (p. 340). If the court emphasizes finding
the facts and assumes that the correct interpretation will easily follow,
that the facts virtually speak for themselves, Marlow is more concerned and less confident about the facility of drawing conclusions
from the facts, about the neutrality of conceptual language and standards of evaluation.

The digressive narrative structure of *Lord Jim* confirms this recognition that explanation requires more than bare facts, for it emphasizes
Marlow's search for evidence and for a discourse adequate to the
complexity of the case. The novel heightens the mystery surrounding
the *Patna* by juxtaposing the strange collision with Jim's recollection of
that event at the inquiry. The actions which form the subject of the
court's investigation are withheld from the reader while Jim proceeds
to inveigh against facts. This irony operates partly against Jim, who
frustrates the reader's desire to know "[w]hat had happened?" (p. 26),
but ultimately it is directed against the court's competence to understand the affair in its fullness.[27] Chapter VI opens with a direct narrative comment on the limitations of the inquiry: "Its object was not the
fundamental why, but the superficial how, of this affair" (p. 56). The
focus on the facts ignores the "purely psychological" interest of the
case, "the expectation of some essential disclosure as to the strength,
the power, the horror, of human emotions." This ontological diction
invites comparisons between the *Patna* case and the spectacle of tragedy,

with its mimesis of evil and promise of catharsis.[28] The trial, however, disappoints such hopes. The acknowledgment of fear, the power of circumstances to change suddenly and completely, the possibility that inculcated principles might under pressure be thrown aside are some of the issues awaiting those who hear or read the story of the *Patna*, but not in the court record.

According to Peter Goodrich, the law excludes the operation of chance and the irrational from human social behaviour by enforcing rules and requiring reasoned intentions of actors.[29] The court's insistence on facts is therefore a metonym for rationalist and positivist analysis of conduct and situation. The novel places this demand for facts into a precisely-registered affective context: Jim hears the loudness of his own voice, and feels "the wind of great punkahs that made you shiver, the shame that made you burn, the attentive eyes whose glance stabbed" (p. 28). A broad window under the ceiling illuminates only the heads and shoulders of the tribunal members while the audience are "staring shadows" (p. 29). The light therefore functions as an analogue for the law's positivism. This association is strengthened because Jim's conversations with Marlow take place at night during the trial, and their final meeting ends at nightfall. Some aspects of the important strand of twilight imagery have already been discussed, while the specific claims of nineteenth-century European imperialism to be bringing the light of progress to Asia and Africa will be examined below. Light is the setting for Jim's condemnation, while twilight provides through Stein his opportunity to restore lost honour. Marlow is only half attracted to the "impalpable poesy" with which Stein invests the world: "the great plain on which men wander amongst graves and pitfalls remained very desolate under the impalpable poesy of its crepuscular light" (p. 214); but he can no longer give his complete allegiance to the *nomos* signified by light. The image of twilight is historically important in the *fin-de-siècle*, when Conrad was writing this novel. The twilight of the nineteenth century saw scepticism about inherited norms and systems of thought which led to radically new approaches to jurisprudence as well as to other areas of philosophy and art.[30] Conrad's impressionistic attention to the interplay of light and shade enables a physical symbolization of the uncertainties in the normative world.

This critique of the Court of Marine Inquiry, though far-reaching in its implications, does not entail the relegation of law to the margins of the story. Marlow evokes the evening before judgment by alluding to the sword of Damocles: "'The respectable sword of his country's law

was suspended over his head'" (p. 151). In an unobtrusive foreshadowing of Jim's eventual manner of death, he imagines how the court
would in the morning "'take up the awful weapon and smite his bowed
neck'" (p. 152). Marlow is tempted to thwart the law by telling Jim of
Brierly's offer of escape money. Jim's refusal is consistent with his
decision to face trial and reinforces law's central position in the novel.
Apart from being his most important means of reclaiming honour
from the case, it also implies his acceptance of the court's authority to
penalize him. Jim's submission to its jurisdiction suggests that in leap-
ing from the *Patna* he did not utterly discard his attachment to the
ideals of the seamen's code or to his duties under its legal expression,
the *Merchant Shipping Acts*. A normative contrast between Jim and such
actual fugitives as his skipper and Gentleman Brown is thereby proposed: while the skipper is ready to spit on his certificate (p. 42), Jim
takes the pronouncement of his guilt and stripping of his status to
heart. This response is scoffed at by the pragmatic West Australian,
Chester, who boasts of his partner, Cannibal Robinson, and their
appropriate joint venture in guano collection. In a most pointed
juxtaposition the Court's judgment and Jim's shame are set against
Robinson's unpunished, unabashed cannibalism. Marlow's definition
of crime as "a breach of faith with the community of mankind" (p. 157)
here finds its most primitive expression.[31] Paradoxically, then, Jim's
normative commitment emerges in the shadow of his condemnation
for "'abandoning in the moment of danger the lives and property
confided to [his] charge'" (p. 160). Both elements of this paradox –
commitment and dereliction – are further revealed on Patusan. There
Jim is presented as the creator and defender of a *nomos*; and the terms
of the judgment are fulfilled in his death.

Legal discourse therefore remains important in both the *Patna* and
Patusan sections of the novel. In this respect at least, *Lord Jim* is not
"broken-backed" as many critics have tended to argue.[32] In addition
to its focus on the interplay between the normative and other impulses
in Jim's career, Marlow's narration is notable for occasional and un-
embarrassed usage of legal idioms. Sometimes these are consciously
adopted to highlight the quasi-judicial tenor of his interviews with Jim:
"it behoved me to make no sign lest by a gesture or a word I should be
drawn into a fatal admission about myself which would have some
bearing on the case" (p. 106). When Marlow constructs a narrative out
of the fragmentary information he has gleaned on Jim's last days, he
invokes with respect a legal standard of proof: "I put it down for you

here as though I had been an eyewitness" (p. 343). The adoption of such language suggests that law's place in the formation of Marlow's consciousness was strong and continuing.

These expressions are derived from the very procedural law criticized elsewhere in the novel. They underline the shared concern of novel and law for evidence, an acceptance of the need to prove or demonstrate whatever is asserted as truth. The motif of trial therefore radiates throughout Conrad's novel from the central point of the legal proceedings. That Jim is on trial for his cowardice and that his pretensions to heroism are likewise on trial is suggested in a letter Conrad wrote to William Blackwood about the serialization of *Lord Jim* in *Blackwood's Magazine*. Conrad's work followed a novel actually called *On Trial* by "Zack" (pseudonym of Gwendoline Keats). Conrad's comment to Blackwood, "Isn't it a coincidence me following Zack on essentially the same subject?" directs us to the omnipresence of this motif in *Lord Jim*.[33]

It is traceable not only in Marlow's inquiry but in the Quixotic structure of the story wherein Jim's private cultivation of a heroic self-image is subjected to the test of experience: "he had been preparing himself for all the difficulties that can beset one on land and water. . . . Can you fancy it? A succession of adventures, so much glory . . ." (p. 95). His failure aboard the apparently sinking *Patna* produces more resentment than self-knowledge. He blames the cosmos, nature, the ship, and his colleagues: "He had been taken unawares . . . Everything had betrayed him!" For Jim and eventually for Marlow, the prime obstacle on the former's heroic quest is a "malevolent providence" (p. 159). The bitter results of Jim's trial by "the unconceivable" simply reinforce his agonistic understanding of the universe. Jim submits to his trial by law, but treats other aspersions on his honour with retreat or belligerence. His core of romantic idealism remains intact. He views Marlow's arrangements as offering him the chance to "begin with a clean slate" and as tests: "'I'll show yet . . .'" (p. 185). He is a successor to Don Quixote, for the world is his adversary. The twin conditions of success, retreat and glorious opportunity, are provided on Patusan. Jim proves himself the virtuous hero of romance in every trial until once again the unimaginable presents itself, complete dishonour personified by the outlaw Brown.[34] Then Jim's elevated position in the community magnifies the nature and consequences of the trials created by the actual malevolence of the intruder. Before discussing the ending of the novel, however, it is necessary to examine Jim's relationship

with the people of Patusan and the kind of normative world he has
created there.

## III

One of the mainsprings for the Quixotic hero's idealistic deeds is the
encounter with injustice.[35] On Patusan, however, Jim's quest for justice
is most successful: until his fatal decision to trust Gentleman Brown to
leave, his actions in pursuit of right lose their Quixotic impracticality.
Under the completely new set of conditions of his life, the heroic
imagination finds fruitful expression, and Jim himself is transformed
from an outcast penitent into someone revered as a protector of the
people.

Jim's transformation follows his decisive intervention in Patusan
politics, which itself is the outcome of his immersion in the communal
life of the Bugis under Doramin.[36] As Conrad presents it, Jim arrives at
a time of virtual anarchy, with Doramin openly contesting the authority of the governor, Rajah Allang, to control all trade, and the Rajah
employing increasingly arbitrary force in support of his claim: he "pretended to be the only trader in the country, and the penalty for the
breach of his monopoly was death; but his idea of trading was indis-
tinguishable from the commonest forms of robbery" (p. 257). Super-
imposed on this, both physically and conceptually, is the hillside fort of
the Dyaks, led by the bandit, Sherif Ali, who threatened everyone in
Patusan. The daring raid on the fort led by Jim and Dain Waris lays
the foundation for peace and for Jim's accession to the title of "Tuan."
Credit for this plan and its execution attaches solely to the "white
lord" and not to Dain Waris. By defeating the Dyaks and by demonstrating the capacity of the Bugis to Rajah Allang whilst dissuading
them from attacking him, Jim engineers a new political order. His
interests lie, however, beyond the mere acquisition of power, in its
just exercise and in the defence of right. The physical courage and
strategic insight demonstrated by Jim in the raid are perceived by the
islanders as signs of normative authority. As Marlow rhapsodizes, he
fills the land "with the fame of his virtues" (p. 243).

The "moral effect of his victory in war" (p. 268) is such that Jim becomes, in Fleishman's words, "the unofficial judge in the community":

He arbitrates cases of civil law, such as the affair of the brass pots . . . ; he
defends such groups as the coastal fishing villages from the Rajah's exactions
(still using the terms of the work ethic, Jim condemns the robbery of their

produce as an infringement of the right to work); and he abolishes the Rajah's system of feudalism, which is described as personal slavery.[37]

Jim's motivation as judge is paideic: with the affair of the pots he remains dissatisfied, worrying that he did not discover the truth, despite the fact that his process and judgment please all parties. As a judge, Jim is concerned with equity and justice, not with the forms of law: "'The trouble was to get at the truth of anything. Was not sure to this day whether he had been fair to all parties'" (p. 269). The paideic in Cover's theory of *nomos* is, we recall, the world-creating function, and Jim's judicial work has normative construction, in effect, the renewal of a viable legal system on Patusan, as its aim. Moreover, there is an explicit link between the recognition of justice and the achievement of peace: "'Got the infernal pots back of course – and pacified all hands.'" Berthoud acknowledges this connection in his description of Jim as "pacifier and justicer of an entire community."[38] The archaism "justicer" invests this work with heroic connotations and highlights the normative basis of Jim's success. What he accomplishes is the reconstitution of Patusan from a state of chaos to one of *nomos*. Though nominally operating under the leadership of Doramin and as agent for Stein's interests, Jim is both inspiration and executant in transforming Patusan, temporarily at least, from anarchy into a peaceful community.

Great as Jim's achievements are, they are outstripped by his reputation among some islanders. Marlow reports how the coastal fishermen tell that the tide turned two hours early to carry him up-river on the day he arrived; and among outlying villagers Jim is reputed to have borne the cannon that pounded Sherif Ali's fort uphill on his own shoulders. While these examples elicit patronizing laughter from Jim, as the absurdities of a credulous people, they have their roots in the very "fame of his virtues." Jim himself feels "immense" satisfaction in what he has achieved (p. 271), while Marlow's account of his meeting with Jim in Patusan employs a reverential tone when treating of his greatness: "his word was the one truth of every passing day" (p. 272). Marlow is clearly captivated by the legends surrounding his former protégé, for they fulfil his claims to honour and realize the dreams of his imagination. Visiting the Rajah with Jim, Marlow compares the two leaders: "Jim appeared like a creature not only of another kind but of another essence. Had they not seen him come up in a canoe, they might have thought he had descended upon them from the clouds" (p. 229). Marlow's willingness to attribute supernatural explanations to the Malays when he himself resorts to an image akin to the "superman"

image suggests that the local legends and his own narrative both convert Jim into an object of belief. Though Marlow is sceptical about
"this amazing Jim-myth" (p. 280), his own narration registers the process of myth-making, both Malay and Western.

The elevation of Jim for two cultures is possible because he is a
"charismatic" leader and as such can appeal to "primitive" and modern societies: for the former, the charismatic leader "restores . . . magic
to the conduct of affairs"; while for the latter, the charisma lies in
"exceptional individuality."[39] Whatever the basis of his authority, Jim's
normative transformations, both personal and communal, demand to
be explored and remembered through narrative. In many ancient
cultures, the bringing of the law and the identity of the law-giver are
preserved through myth. Marlow describes Patusan as having been
bypassed by the "stream of civilization" (p. 226). There, the "old mankind" still lives, and the old myths may be expected to flourish. The
function of "the Jim-myth" is to celebrate and explain the renewal of
the *nomos* on Patusan; it is a version of the stories of Moses, Manu and
other myths of the foundation of normative worlds.[40]

Conrad's construction of this myth emerges from a confluence of
nineteenth-century developments in intellectual and political history.
The study of anthropology, of comparative mythology, and even of
legal evolution was facilitated by the availability of different races
and cultures who became the "subject peoples" of the empires and the
disciplines. In the field of legal history, for example, the historian of
early legal institutions, Sir Henry Maine, was appointed Legal Member of the Viceroy's Indian Council in 1862.[41] He was able to study the
legal system founded by Manu whilst putting into effect the new Law
of Succession drafted in Whitehall. Maine's belief in legal evolution led
him to compare the Hindu with the ancient Roman and Greek legal
systems and ultimately to posit an Indo-European family tree of legal
development. This attitude was beneficent insofar as it promoted the
discovery of common elements in the systems of conqueror and conquered rather than the imposition of a completely alien set of laws.
However, it also depended on Social Darwinist assumptions, labelling
the Hindu system as archaic and primitive, and working towards its
replacement by the dominant and therefore better-adapted English
system.

Something of this combination of idealism and cultural domination
is traceable in Conrad's representation of the law-giver. The content
of Tuan Jim's law is nowhere set out in detail. His account of the case

of the three pots emphasizes the goals of truth and fairness, but omits whatever rules of property or principles of redress underlay the judgment. This dependence on abstract ideals, on a vague discourse of "right" is repeated in Marlow's rhapsody on Jim's justice. By its generality it assumes universally-shared norms in a context which otherwise emphasizes intercultural rivalry and social breakdown. This disjunction suggests that Jim's normative conquest is a utopian fantasy. However, the fantasy is formulated out of the facts of English imperialism. The one case in which Jim's reasons are explained is when he protects the coastal fishing village from the Rajah's confiscation of their produce. Here the cultural origin of his idealism is made plain. Jim "enlarges on the text that no man should be prevented from getting his food and his children's food honestly" (p. 250). Taken at face value, this principle seems so unexceptional as to amount to a law of nature. However, as Fleishman points out, this is the language of the Protestant work ethic.[42] Moreover, in the context of the dispute it is a formulation deriving from *laissez-faire* liberalism of the right to work for oneself and to trade freely, a right necessary to Jim's prime function as Stein's agent.

The historical source for the introduction of this particular legal rule into "the archipelago" (p. 219) is specifically connected to a major imperialist enterprise. One of the eight laws promulgated by James Brooke in 1843, after he had ended the insurrection on Sarawak and been appointed Governor, permitted all men "to trade or labour according to their pleasure, and to enjoy their gains."[43] These provisions for "freedom of traffic and commerce" were included along with those stipulating the punishment for murder, robbery and "other heinous crimes." For his success as "pacifier and justicer" Brooke and his heirs were appointed Rajahs of Sarawak by the Sultan of Brunei. Conrad wrote to a member of the family confessing his great admiration for the first "white rajah" – and the portrayal of Jim as law-giver has long been recognized to derive from the Brooke legend.[44] The latter is the modern, imperialist counterpart to the "amazing Jim-myth." As mythology it depends not only on the laws actually instituted, but on the supersession of perceived lawlessness. The standard text on legal development in the archipelago grounds its discussion of imperial rule and subsequent laws on "the prevailing state of lawlessness and piracy in its coasts."[45] However, a letter from Sultan Abdul Momin to the Governor of Labuan quoted in the same text sets out "Brunei customs which have been handed down from ancient times and which are still

in force." This assertion of the existence of normative traditions conflicts with the British perception of lawlessness.

Conrad appears to share the latter view, according to Lloyd
Fernando: an "air of freebooting hangs like a pall over Conrad's more
precise narratives," that is, those that depict the complexities of local
politics, including *Lord Jim*.[46] Fernando proceeds to argue that when
Conrad refers to "lawlessness" he does not mean criminality, but a
"condition where the true laws are hard to discover if they exist at all,"
where armed force presents itself as the solution to conflict.[47] Such is
the condition of Patusan on Jim's arrival. Outlining its history before
Jim leaves for the island, Marlow describes a decline from the wise and
magnificent Sultan who met the seventeenth-century pepper traders
to the imbecilic incumbent which functions as a synecdoche for the
normative and financial collapse of the kingdom (p. 227). Among
the Sultan's extortive uncles is Rajah Allang, whose "frail old body"
(p. 250) is an analogue for his moral degradation, like that of Cannibal
Robinson. The legal system is therefore represented as decadent, a
tradition that is all but lost, in which ancient offices are filled by
decrepit rogues who command force without authority. Jim's ability to
resolve the dissensions and remedy injustices on Patusan is a virtual
function of his commitment to a normative tradition that presumes to
define itself exclusively as civilized and progressive.

An important consequence of this analysis of the *nomos* created by
Jim is an unequivocal correspondence between his assumptions and
discourse and those of English imperialism. This conclusion is not
surprising given the imaginative captivation of late Victorian England
with its empire. The imperial idea was "the energizing myth" of the
society and was embodied in manifold cultural forms, including the
novel.[48] Yet, as Fernando and others have insisted, Conrad does not
simply repeat the clichés of imperialism.[49] On the one hand, he incorporates such attitudes through the voice of Marlow's privileged auditor,
who believes that "'giving your life up to them . . . was like selling your
soul to a brute'" (p. 339). The rhetoric of sacrifice is grounded on
cultural monism and an evolutionary faith: "the truth of ideas racially
our own, in whose name are established the order, the morality of an
ethical progress." On the other hand, the novel also finds space for the
expression of a less idealist, more compromised view through Marlow's
"light (and even electric light) [which] had been carried into the archipelago for the sake of better morality and – and – well – the greater
profit too" (p. 219). The ideal and the pragmatic operate dialectically

in Marlow's effort to comprehend Jim. He comes to personify the faith
and the fear engendered in Marlow by imperialism. In a passage that
images both enlightenment and the hierarchy of cultures Marlow sits
with Jim on the hill where he defeated Sherif Ali:

He dominated the forest, the secular gloom, the old mankind. He was like a
figure set up on a pedestal, to represent in his youth the power, and perhaps
the virtues, of races that never grow old, that have emerged from the gloom.
(p. 265)

Jim inspires belief, like the heroes of mythology, both in himself and in
the nation he represents. However, "like a shadow in the light," the
memory of the *Patna* returns to cast doubt on the superiority of the
man and the faith he bears. Marlow's desire to mythologize Jim, to
convert him into a subject of piety and eloquence "up on a pedestal,"
is qualified by his scepticism which denies complete assent to Jim and
to the imperial claims: "the power and *perhaps* the virtues . . ." (my
emphasis).

Fernando argues that such loss of certainty is the product of
expatriatism; yet it is the repatriated Marlow, rather than the Jim
who can never return home, who experiences the undermining of
values that accompanies the espousal of cultural relativism. A clear
example occurs in Marlow's statement at the beginning of his epistol-
ary account of Jim's last days, "I affirm nothing" (p. 339). This refusal
to articulate the significance of the ending follows many assertions
of Jim's greatness during the oral narration of the trip to Patusan.
The experience on the island is not the source of incertitude, because
it is, with the exception to be discussed shortly, mediated by Jim's
success in transplanting elements of the English *nomos*. What produces
Marlow's loss of faith is something that occurs at home, the news of
Jim's failure and the collapse of his *nomos*. In her otherwise balanced
and searching study of the attitude to imperialism in *Lord Jim*, Benita
Parry reads Marlow's encomium to the "spirit of the land" as entail-
ing a static authorial commitment to the national values.[50] Home, however, becomes the locus of disenchantment for Marlow. The defensive
appeals to his listeners, which are interspersed throughout the story,
urging them to use their residual imaginations, and culminating in his
quotation of the imperialist slogans of his privileged auditor, are signs
that Jim's fate has created a deep disaffection for the assumptions of
his fellows.

The nihilism of the late chapters is foreshadowed on Patusan only
by Marlow's encounter with Jewel. Conrad has been criticized for the

one-dimensionality of his female characters. Jewel's name and the use of the story of the stolen emerald to image her relationship with Jim lend support to this criticism. However, the scene with Marlow in which her "craving for incertitude, [and] clinging to fear" over Jim's faithfulness is made the centre of intense conflict cannot be so criticized. Its dialogic articulation of the fears of both European and Eurasian is precise and prophetic. By questioning the reasons for coming and the irresponsible departures of Europeans, both individual and collective, she becomes the voice of anguished protest against their presence and the harbinger of her own future unhappiness. Marlow's impatient shouting that neither Jim nor anyone is "good enough" for the outside world has been interpreted as an outrage that destroys his narrative authority.[51] More damning, perhaps, in the present context, is his surprise "that she had a voice at all" (p. 315). Marlow functions as a reliable narrator, despite his fallibility, precisely because he focalizes the novelist's mapping of the limits of knowledge. When Jewel tells him of her mother's miserable death, and utters her own fearful hope, "'I didn't want to die weeping'" (p. 313), what he calls "the passive, irremediable horror of the scene" momentarily drives him "out of [his] conception of existence." In its place he glimpses "a world that seemed a vast and dismal aspect of disorder." The sense of pity and fear felt here and the vision of a world negated are apprehensions usually associated with tragedy. The waste of life already experienced and the spectre of a second defection by Jim so profoundly disturb Marlow that everything he knows is briefly wiped out by an intimation of cosmic anomie: "I seemed to have lost all my words in the chaos of dark thoughts I had contemplated for a second or two beyond the pale."

The image of the "pale" is at this point literally represented in the narrative by Jim's fort, where this scene is set, but it also stands for the normative world usually inhabited by Marlow and created in Patusan by Jim. With its origins in the English conquest of Ireland, this hackneyed expression is revitalized in Conrad's novel by its proliferation in such different guises as the leap from the *Patna* into darkness, the "serried circle of facts" from which Jim longs to free himself (p. 31), the escape from Rajah Allang's inefficient stockade, and Marlow's "sheltering conception of light and order which is our refuge." The various rudimentary forts beside the river in Patusan, standing "at the heart of a vast" wilderness (to adapt Conrad's favourite locution), contrast markedly with such citadels of law as the *Heart of Midlothian*.

Marlow's experience has an important consequence for this study, namely the realization that normative worlds are human constructions: "thanks to our unwearied efforts, it is as sunny an arrangement of small conveniences as the mind of man can conceive." Having glimpsed the abyss, Marlow returns anxiously to his "shelter" as a matter of choice. By following its protagonist into the wilderness, *Lord Jim* reveals the fragility of nomic traditions and the conventionality of norms, but it also insists on the necessity of normative commitment. The novel foregrounds the struggle between *nomos* and anomie, representing both the creation and the destruction of a normative world. Finally, it demonstrates that lawlessness is not an aspect of location or part of "the spirit of the land": Jim and Gentleman Brown are both emissaries of "the outside world."

Brown is indeed the personification of lawlessness. Marlow uses the inflated diction of cosmic determinism to present his meeting with Jim as a modernist morality play: "running his appointed course, he sails into Jim's history, a blind accomplice of the Dark Powers" (p. 354). If Jim is the agent of a beneficent imperialism in which trading interests are accompanied by an idealistic commitment to the Bugis and others, then Brown is the image of rapacious conquest. When the two meet, they stand on opposite sides of a creek and "on opposite poles of that conception of existence which includes all mankind" (p. 381). The patterning of the final events in accordance with this opposition is clear: Jim overrides the community's wish to use force against Brown, and Brown massacres Dain Waris's party; Jim trusts that the bargain of a "clear road" (p. 388) will be honoured, but his obvious rectitude inspires a "rage of Caliban" in Cornelius and Brown. However, the sphere in which the conflict takes place is not simply individual and moral. Brown revenges himself against Jim and simultaneously against the world of law from which he is a fugitive and which he so conspicuously finds embodied in Jim. The conflict between *nomos* and anomie is most explicitly formulated in Brown's establishment in the remains of Sherif Ali's fort. The unprovoked killing of a villager by Brown's sniper immediately intimidates the populace, but its larger effect is to recall the old chaos: "The social fabric of orderly, peaceful life, when every man was sure of to-morrow, seemed on that evening ready to collapse into a ruin reeking with blood" (p. 373).

When the "edifice" does collapse, Jim submits to retributive death at the hands of Doramin. The ambiguity of Jim's sacrifice – the acceptance of community justice or the fulfilment of the ego's dreams of

heroism; disloyalty to Jewel or fidelity to his promise never to leave
Patusan – has already been touched upon. The question that remains
is whether this ending, and the collapse of the *nomos*, implies that all
refuges of "light and order" are doomed to fail when tested against
chaotic tendencies. Is the paideic an illusory and unsustainable ideal
which ought to be abandoned in favour of more realistic goals? The
ambiguity of Jim's death does not signal a descent into meaningless
darkness, but the coexistence of many meanings, the possibility of
many "shelters." While the novel concludes on an elegiac note, in
penumbral and diminished tones rather than the glare of "light and
order," it should be remembered that shadows are the ambience of
dream as well as of doubt. Throughout *Lord Jim*, idealism and scepticism run side by side, demanding commitment and rejecting abandonment. The creation of *nomos* entails pursuing the dream as well as
"seeing things as they are" (p. 162). Marlow expresses this faith in the
cautious introduction to his written narrative: "Yet is not mankind
driven by a dream of its greatness and its power upon the dark paths
of excessive cruelty and excessive devotion?" (pp. 349–50). Underlying
the novel's exposure of the limits of legal rationalism and of the hor-
rors of normative chaos, then, is a recognition of the desire for a world
of justice and the need to choose actively to build it.[52]

## CHAPTER EIGHT

# *Freedom, uncertainty and diversity – the critique of imperialist law in* A Passage to India

English law and English literature were closely, yet variously connected during Britain's imperial domination of India. Anglo-Indians – the English who lived and worked in India – have been enrolled in the "configuration of law and letters" traced throughout this study: the first English judge at Calcutta was the poet and Oriental linguist, Sir William Jones; the nineteenth-century administrator, Sir Alfred Lyall, was a poet and critic. Both men were admired by E. M. Forster, not only for their literary avocations, but for their interest in Indian culture, a rare combination in Anglo-India:

after two hundred years of political connexion with India, we in England know next to nothing about the Indian cultures . . . We have sent our soldiers and administrators . . . but few scholars and fewer artists . . . It is unwise to suppose that culture is unimportant . . . What attempt has been made by our rulers to promote Oriental scholarship and to carry on the tradition of Sir William Jones?[1]

Forster's question challenges a century-old policy of "Anglicization" that was most forcefully expounded by another literary lawyer, Thomas Babington Macaulay, in his "Minute on Indian Education." Macaulay's assertion of "the intrinsic superiority of . . . Western literature" underlay an Anglocentric education policy that, by producing "a class of persons, Indian in blood and colour, but English in taste, in opinions, in morals and in intellect," would ensure cultural domination. "Though the sceptre may pass away from us," Macaulay told the House of Commons on 10 July 1833, "the imperishable empire of our arts and our morals, our literature and our laws," would survive.[2] This normative conception of literature and law, and the cultural monism on which it rests are undermined by *A Passage to India*, a canonical work of "Western literature" that offers an eloquent and moving critique of both British rule and Western rationalism.

Forster participates in and extends the tradition of English "Orientalist" writing. He not only read widely among English writers on India and translations of Oriental literature before visiting India, but he wrote journalism, memoirs, reviews and his last novel, *A Passage to India*, on the basis of his Indian experiences. Forster's writings are motivated by a Jonesian attempt to understand and translate Indian culture, and to advance intercultural understanding; and to interrogate the Macaulayan project of building a British hegemony. Forster's "orientalism," I would argue, is not of the kind criticized by Edward W. Said, a Western discourse imposed on an Other called "the East" and often inseparable from political domination.[3] Forster often juxtaposes Indian and English norms with the effect of destabilizing the latter. Moreover, in the penultimate chapter of *A Passage to India* Doctor Aziz is endowed with the politically-charged insight that this "pose of 'seeing India' which had seduced him to Miss Quested at Chandrapore was only a form of ruling India."[4] This quote leads Benita Parry to propose that Forster's approach to India is "libertarian" in that it seeks knowledge without power.[5]

The English novels which have emerged from India in the twentieth century display a consistent interest in legal action. Law could not be called the dominant trope of such fiction: interracial romance, the occult, Anglo-Indian manners and the 1857 Mutiny all receive separate attention in Bhupal Singh's *Survey of Anglo-Indian Fiction*, but these plots can incorporate or be opposed by a legal plot.[6] Leonard Woolf's *The Village in the Jungle* (1913, and actually set in Ceylon) tells the story of a primitive hunter-gatherer caught up in a trial for robbery and later for murder. The Western legal system is manipulated against him, and his alienation is expressed in his comment, "'I do not understand,'" which becomes a refrain directed against the normative validity of the proceedings.[7] The experience of incomprehension is reversed in *A Passage to India* as the Englishwoman invokes the law in a fruitless attempt to order the alien and fearful experience of the Marabar Caves. Paul Scott's *The Jewel in the Crown* (1966) shows the same racist assumptions being made by officers of the law about the sexual attack on Daphne Manners. Once again the trial must be aborted and the charge provokes an outbreak of anti-British violence. The failure of English law in these stories is matched only by the vigour of its application. As I argued in the last chapter, the figure of the law-giver was an essential element in the justification of imperial rule. In *Burmese Days* (1934) George Orwell allows his Burmese doctor, Veraswami, to articulate this belief in Macaulayan fashion, "'at least you have brought us law and order. The unswerving British Justice and the Pax Britannica,'" but only to enable the disillusioned retort of Flory, the timber merchant, "'Pox Britannica.'"[8] Despite this, the magistrate remained a potential symbol of the British attempt to govern the empire, and was used by Philip Mason, the Raj historian, in his novel, *Call the Next Witness* (1945). These works are perhaps not sufficiently numerous to form a tradition, but they suggest that the legal action of *A Passage to India* is historically and formally significant. Accordingly, I commence my discussion of this novel with an historical account of the special place given to law in the normative world of British India.

I

James Fitzjames Stephen, the Victorian barrister and critic, who has figured in this study as a kind of prosecuting counsel, condemning Dickens and other novelists for their inaccurate portrayal of legal proceedings, has a central place in this chapter. Stephen wrote the Indian Evidence Act during his service as Legal Member of the Governor-General's Council, but is better known to historians for his articulation of the basis of British rule in India. He argued that it was an "absolute government, founded not on consent but on conquest . . . implying at every point the superiority of the conquering race."[9] This clear formulation provided the most succinct statement of imperial philosophy in the generation after the Indian Mutiny, and its influence was felt until World War One, and as *A Passage to India* shows, many still hankered for its monological simplicity thereafter. Nevertheless, the "absolute government" of the English was distinguished by its officers from the "Oriental despotisms" it sought to replace. The latter were perceived as states of arbitrary if not tyrannical power, in contrast to British India, which enforced "the rule of law." For Stephen, Law was the centre-piece of the English cultural mythology: "Our law is in fact the sum and substance of what we have to teach them . . . the gospel of the English."[10] However, this scripture, like its Christian counterpart, was to be propagated in a society with its own normative and spiritual traditions. Unlike Lord Jim's Patusan, India could not be represented as a wilderness where the light of *nomos* had never shone. As demonstrated in the previous chapter, Sir Henry Maine, who preceded Stephen as Legal Member of the Council, found in India evidences of the most ancient legal institutions, and postulated not only a general theory of

legal evolution, but a common origin for the indigenous and the imported law. Eric Stokes argues that Maine "did much to dispel militant
superiority; and practically tried to curb precipitating Indian society
from status to contract in one bound."¹¹ However, the evolutionary
paradigm did enable Maine to adopt a critical stance in respect of the
Indian law of his time. There were, he wrote, "vast gaps and interspaces
in the Substantive Law of India."¹² These necessitated the introduction
of Western concepts, remedies and institutional structures. English law
functioned, therefore, as the epitome of English civilization and of the
*nomos* of modernity.

Robert Cover's characterization of *nomos* as possessing paideic and
imperial aspects applies neatly to this normative imposition. Although
Cover uses these terms to denote aspects of *nomos* rather than to define
distinct normative worlds, it is possible to view the traditional indigenous legal systems, particularly the Hindu code of Manu which forms
part of the vast Indian epic text, the *Mahabharata*, as essentially "paideic"
in its participation in a local religious and cosmological system; and,
equally, to regard the imported English legal system, with its emphasis
on codification and on rational and known procedure, as of the "imperial" type. The latter attribution conforms to the self-image of the Raj
lawyers: Stephen compared the Indian Empire to the *Pax Romana*, and
this myth was disseminated by Kipling who likened English law in
India to the Roman *imperium*.¹³ Although the explicit function of this
typology is to glorify Britain as an agent of universal civilization, it also
implicitly celebrates power. For the *imperium* was the Roman magistrate's writ, the source and sign of the occupying power's authority.
The enforcement of peace and justice in this situation is inseparable
from the maintenance of imperial power. Ronny Heaslop's defence of
his work as a magistrate slides quickly from the idealism of, "'We're
out here to do justice and keep the peace,'" to the political pragmatics
of, "'I am out here to work, mind, to hold this wretched country by
force'" (p. 69).

Cover's distinction can usefully be applied to expound Forster's normative commitments. As a Hellenophile, his shrewd understanding of
the "imperial" model is likely to be exceeded by his admiration of the
Greek ideal of the "paideia." Forster's hatred of physical force, his
humanistic belief in dialogue, tolerance and personal relationships,
and his enthusiasm for cultural understanding all suggest that his ideal
*nomos* might well be imaged by the Athenian notion of civic formation
through personal education. It is significant that the Englishman whose

conduct throughout the Aziz case is exemplary in its loyalty and its reasonableness is the college principal, Fielding. In standing by his friend and deserting "the club," Fielding enacts a version of the famous politico-moral choice posed by Forster in "What I Believe" (1938): "if I had to choose between betraying my country and betraying my friend, I hope I should have the guts to betray my country."[14] It is against the background of his recognition that "Love and loyalty to an individual can run counter to the claims of the state" that Forster defines his ideal polity, his secular City of God: "'Love, the Beloved Republic, which feeds upon Freedom and lives.'" He refuses to identify the Beloved Republic with the English liberal democratic *nomos*. He praises the admission of variety and criticism in Democracy, and believes it to be "less hateful than other contemporary forms of government." Forster mounts a two-fold argument concerning force: "all society rests upon force. But all the great creative actions, all the decent human relations, occur during the intervals when force has not managed to come to the front."[15] These are unequivocally paideic sentiments, not least because of their utopian awareness that the Beloved Republic is a dream of fiction. The ending of *A Passage to India* registers this otherworldly, visionary desire in the impaired friendship of Aziz and Fielding: "not there, . . . not yet."

The difficult course of this friendship, with its misunderstandings and rebuffs, its jocularity and awkward intimacy, its essential contingency, becomes a vehicle for exploring the problems caused by the normative plurality of India, or what Malcolm Bradbury has called the "multiverse."[16] By representing India as "the hundred and the one," and by going beyond this conventional paradox in his detailed accounts of landscapes, religions, and social mores at Chandrapore, Marabar, and Mau, Forster is able to incorporate and to valorize Indian norms as well as English ones. By contrast, a later publication, the standard legal history, *The British Commonwealth: The Development of its Laws and Constitutions* invokes in relation to India an iron law of historical evolution to justify its exclusive concentration on the "reception of English law" into India.[17] It overlooks the continuing presence of what anthropologists call "non-State legal systems" or customary law in the country,[18] and offers a single and reductive version of the narrative of the Indian *nomos*.

This univocal history may be contrasted with Forster's complex and "multi-legal" normative fables in his series, "Adrift in India." One, "Advance, India!" offers a modernized Muslim wedding as a synecdoche for the nomic confusion of a country caught between the demands of tradition and modernity. "Crash into the devotions of the orthodox birred the gramophone, 'I'd sooner be busy with my little Lizzie' and . . . we had entered the unlovely chaos that lies between obedience and freedom."[19] On the following morning the bridegroom's brother exhorts the narrator to "'publish some account of it in an English newspaper. It is a great step forward against superstition . . .'" In another, "The Suppliant," a London-trained barrister returns to India, and fulfils the obligation of hospitality when supplicated by a poor old man. The latter installs himself in the lawyer's house under the pretence of working as his clerk, then steals money. When chided by the narrator, the barrister replies, "'You are English and have other customs. I should not have behaved like this in England myself.'" To an Indian friend, however, he remonstrates, "'I am ashamed of you. . . . you have forgotten our traditions of hospitality. You have forgotten the East . . .'"[20] Though small in scale, these stories record Forster's awareness of the normative multiplicity of Indian society, and of the difficult choices forced on Indians by their encounter with the West. A third essay, "Jodhpur," describes that rare achievement, a community in which the English "loved the city and the people living in it," and shared the same club as the Indians. "[U]nder its gracious roof, the 'racial question' had been solved,"[21] achieving that elision of the interpersonal and the political sought in the clubs of *A Passage to India* and *Burmese Days*. Forster ascribes this mutual sympathy to the *genius loci* of this beautiful place, and proceeds to an account of the majestic landscape. This city set on a mountain is rendered fabulous in both its physical and its normative aspect. What all these stories demonstrate is Forster's preoccupation with the heterogeneous features of the Indian *nomos*, and with the mercurial potential for tragicomedy created by the introduction of the English.

It would be wrong to suggest either that the British sought to obliterate or ignore local laws, or that the imported system brought no benefit to Indian society. Alan Gledhill, in his *British Commonwealth* volume relating to India, notes that Hindus and Muslims were able to enforce their personal laws in the courts established by the British, and argues that redress was otherwise haphazard and inefficient.[22] His view is supported by S. P. Sen, who argues that the rule of law "had become so firmly implanted in the Indian mind by the middle of the nineteenth century that people could hardly conceive of any other principle of social organization."[23]

There was, however, a major conflict over Indian legal policy
between those who adhered to the eighteenth-century desire to pre-
serve the Hindu and Muslim customary laws, such as Warren Hastings
and Sir William Jones, and the Utilitarians who favoured codification,
that is a set of entirely new and complete laws, and who abhorred the
notion of customary law as irrational and obscure. While the English
common lawyers were able to resist the codification of their inherited
customary law, Indians could draw on no such hegemony. As J. W.
Burrow writes, "For British theorists, India provided the battle-ground
for the dispute between the advocates of codified and customary law."[24]
The Utilitarians won, and a succession of Law Commissioners, including Macaulay, Maine and Stephen, drafted new penal and other codes
for the sub-continent. The *Minute on Indian Education* is therefore a
parallel development to this "Anglicization" of law in India, and the
overtness of its ideological discourse and political motivation enables
us to see through the "historical law" of legal evolution to a fiercely
contested normative field. Gledhill himself argues that the 1840 Law
Commission's report recommending the adoption of English law
"was based on expediency rather than on a desire to impose British
culture on India,"[25] but these concerns cannot be so simply distinguished. It was clearly consistent with the British interest in ensuring
their rule that the autonomy and hegemony of Indian cultures be challenged. The "Anglicization" policy also absolved the conquerors from
anything like the "thick description" of indigenous cultures (to use
Clifford Geertz's term). The consequent lack of a truly "local" knowledge probably enabled them to characterize the Indian legal system as
threadbare and full of "gaps." Forster's tolerant and ironic sense of the
difficult marriages to be contracted in the developing "constitution" of
a united and independent India exposes the prescriptive Eurocentrism
of Macaulay's maxim: "uniformity where you can have it, diversity
where you must have it, but in all cases certainty."[26] I shall discuss
in a subsequent section the radical refusal of certainty in *A Passage
to India*. Forster's valuation of diversity above uniformity implies his
liberal respect for Indians' right to cultural autonomy and his critical
recognition of the force entailed in uniformity with England.

In opposing such uniformity with toleration and pluralism, however,
Forster draws more on Western than Indian traditions. Part Three
of *A Passage to India* registers the novelist's admiration for the Hindu
embracement of the whole of life, but this co-exists in productive affinity with the earlier influence of liberalism and humanism. Liberalism is

a notoriously ambiguous term, but Forster's collected essays and speeches, particularly those from the 1930s, when he publicly articulated and defended his political faith, provide a clear indication of how *he* defined it. We have already noted Forster's insistence on the primacy of personal relationships. The other major article of his creed was the freedom of individuals. In 1935 Forster spoke on "Liberty in England" to the predominantly-communist International Congress of Writers in Paris. "The applause at the end of his speech was barely polite," which signified to Katherine Anne Porter in the audience the contemporary rejection of liberalism.[27] Despite its initial reception, the speech provides important insights into Forster's sense of the liberal *nomos*, and will be examined at some length.

One of the derived meanings of *nomos* is "tradition," and Forster begins by arguing that "[i]n England, our traditions and our liberties are closely connected, and so it should be possible to treat the two at once."[28] He urges writers to carry on the tradition of asserting the claims of freedom as Milton, Shelley and Dickens did in their centuries. He proceeds to acknowledge the limits of English freedom. Of particular relevance is his recognition that it is "race-bound": "It means freedom for the Englishman but not for the subject peoples of his Empire." Forster's view may be contrasted with a comment by Stephen that India was "the best corrective in existence for the fundamental fallacies of liberalism."[29] Presumably one such fallacy is the democratic ideal that governments should be chosen by popular "consent" rather than imposed by "conquest." Elsewhere, Stephen argued that power preceded liberty and that liberty was therefore dependent on power.[30] The failure of the British to accord political liberties to Indians is tied to the primacy of force in imperial policy. As Stokes remarks, "Mentally [India] reacted upon the English middle class by infusing an authoritarian counter-current into the main tide of liberal opinion, so that serious-minded men from Chatham onwards wondered whether the possession of a despotically-ruled empire might not prove fatal to the cause of liberty in England."[31] Colonization therefore entailed not only the imposition of the English *nomos*, but also the negation of what Forster regarded as its liberal heart.

In "Liberty in England" Forster describes his political position with characteristic self-deprecation: "I am actually what my age and my upbringing have made me – a bourgeois who adheres to the British constitution, adheres to it rather than supports it. . . ."[32] The distinction between "adhere" and "support" is rather fine, but the former suggests an attachment to something outside oneself, while the latter suggests the provision of assistance or qualified endorsement. Forster, as the style as well as the substance of this quote shows, was a constitutional qualifier. His awareness of the limits and the fragility of English freedom made him place value upon "the *forms* of government and the *forms* of justice, [which] need watching so zealously."[33] The speech then identifies a "more insidious" danger, "the dictator-spirit working quietly away behind the facade of constitutional forms, passing a little law (like the Sedition Act) here, endorsing a departmental tyranny there, emphasizing the national need of secrecy elsewhere. . . ." To define this tyrant further, Forster quotes one of the great mythographers of Anglo-India, Rudyard Kipling:

He shall mark our goings, question whence we came,
Set his guards about us, as in Freedom's name.

Forster presents in this speech a complex and possibly surprising persona, the libertarian defender of the rule of law. The "forms" are valued as obstacles to arbitrary power, but they are not self-sufficient. Their application must be inspired by the paideic "spirit of the law," the belief in freedom. These sentiments were uttered in 1935, not an auspicious time for liberty. Their combination of qualification and reiteration of principle may be seen, however, as a response not only to contemporary pressures, but to an earlier denigration of liberty encountered by Forster in India. The legal action of *A Passage to India*, it is argued, offers the possibility of a many-sided critique of Anglo-India from within its most cherished bastion, the law.

II

It is a measure of the contemporary significance of the trial scene in *A Passage to India* that it drew both high praise and severe censure from its initial reviewers. The anonymous review in the *Observer* called it "an amazing piece of descriptive writing."[34] Sylvia Lind in *Time and Tide* elaborated on this reaction by comparing the trial to the pilgrim ship scene in *Lord Jim*: "It does not cease to be grotesquely funny because it is sternly serious."[35] The reaction among Anglo-Indian reviewers, however, was scathing. The Calcutta *Statesman* called the account of the Doctor's trial "a serious blemish . . . so full of technical error – indeed so preposterous, that it cannot even be called a travesty."[36] (I shall discuss the question of travesty below.) In the Calcutta *Englishman*

"C. W. G." discussed the novel under the title, "Unfair Fiction," and listed the inaccuracies of the trial scene: witnesses not removed from the court; the Police Superintendent conducts the prosecution in person; leading questions which are not objected to.[37] An interesting attempt was made to bridge this critical divide: S. K. Ratcliffe, a former editor of the Calcutta *Statesman*, wrote to the *New Statesman* in London, suggesting that *A Passage to India* was "an event of imperial significance" as well as a piece of imaginative writing.[38] He acknowledges that the courtroom scene is "brilliantly written," but exasperating in its inaccuracy: "And yet it will not do. British officials could not have behaved in court as Mr. Forster makes his behave."[39] As with the criticism of the trial of Lady Mason in *Orley Farm*, what is alleged here is the impossibility of misconduct, rather than technical misrepresentation. Forster knew that his knowledge of legal procedure was slight, but insisted that, misconduct or not, most of what he depicted had a basis in fact.[40] However, Ratcliffe proceeds to argue that "the unreality of the Anglo-Indian background" is not conclusive. The "externals" may be wrong, but his officials "are true in the essentials of character and attitude." He concludes that Forster's novel is highly important both to English and Anglo-Indian readers: "for all its mistakes and misreadings, it presents a society, a relation, and a system, which are in the long run impossible."

Despite its contradictions, this complex mimesis is instructive. It underlines the need to revalue a general argument mounted by many critics that while the speeches and essays place Forster in the "public sphere," the novels evoke and belong to private worlds. Virginia Woolf, for example, contended: "He has not great interest in institutions. He has not the wide social curiosity of Mr. Wells. The divorce law and the poor law come in for little of his attention. His concern is with the private life; his message is addressed to the soul."[41] In his 1962 interview with K. Natwar-Singh Forster "welcomed" the political influence achieved by *A Passage to India*, but said that it had not been intended.[42] The contrast between him and such avowedly reformist novelists as Dickens and Wells rests on inferences of intention drawn on the basis of whether institutions are figured in the foreground or the background of the narrative. On such a test Chancery is undoubtedly foregrounded; but the Anglo-Indian imperial apparatus is far more than a "frieze" against which the private lives of Adela and Aziz are explored. The personal sphere is shaped by, and infiltrated by, the institutional framework. This realization forms part of the donnée of the story: Adela cannot decide whether to marry Ronny until she has seen him at work in India. The novel closes as it opens, on the question of whether it is possible for Indians and the English to be friends. Every such relationship attempted is "coloured" by the parties' consciousness of political inequality: Adela and Mrs. Moore are informed that they are "superior to all" the Indian ladies at the Bridge Party; the multiple disasters of the expedition to the Marabar Caves bring to an apparent end the friendship between Mrs. Moore and Aziz, and plummet both Adela and Aziz into an imperial drama where they are assigned roles as "a young girl fresh from England" and "the prisoner," or "the victim" and "the defendant." Fielding realizes that the Aziz case requires him to "take sides" and that he will be labelled "anti-British" because of his loyalty to his friend (p. 183). The effect is, in Ronny's words to his mother, that "Nothing's private in India" (p. 54).

Although this phrase has broad implications for the sense of self that it is possible to construct in Anglo-India, it cannot be taken as an epigraph for the novel in its entirety. The soul's apprehensions of infinity and nothingness felt by Mrs. Moore, and the pain of personal invasion, followed by weeks of introspection, experienced by Adela, testify that the novel retains an interest in individual consciousness and its transformations. Indeed in its exploration of the malleability, the grievances, the impetuous self-dramatizing, of Aziz, the novel enacts the liberal belief in both the attention due to the individual and the equality of all individuals. It therefore offers a corrective to the imperial desire to categorize and control Indians *en masse*. What Woolf calls "the soul" therefore cannot be left out of this account of *A Passage to India*. Among the soul's relations, however, must be included those straitening bonds of the institutions of empire.

The treatment of individuals under the law, by other individuals who have been appointed officials, is one of the major motifs of the legal novel. However, it acquires peculiar force in the colonial setting because of the diminished legal status of the conquered peoples. Forster registers the "race-bound" quality of freedom in India at a number of points in the plot and in different modes. An early, comic example occurs when Aziz observes to Fielding that Indians of his class wear a collar "to pass the police" (p. 83). Another is the passionate, vengeful outburst of Mrs. Turton in the ante-room at the court-house:

"You're weak, weak, weak, weak. Why, they ought to crawl from here to the caves on their hands and knees whenever an Englishwoman's in sight, they oughtn't to be spoken to, they ought to be spat at, they ought to be ground

into the dust, we've been far too kind with our Bridge Parties and the rest."
(p. 220)

The authoritarianism of this statement by the wife of the "Burra
Sahib" is emphasized by its juxtaposition with the actual trial. Its
irrationality and extreme punitiveness provide less a contrast with
than a denial of the English claims to juridical reason, impartiality
and objectivity.

G. K. Das has demonstrated that this small passage not only condenses an attitude, but alludes to an actual punishment imposed after
the Amritsar massacre of 1919. A "crawling-order" was enforced in the
Amritsar street where an English woman missionary was assaulted:
every Indian entering the street was required to crawl its length. Moreover, suspects were publicly flogged; and a "salaaming-order" was
imposed requiring all Indians to "salaam" or respectfully salute English civil and military officers.[43] These repressive orders arose partly
from a policy of severe curtailment of Indians' rights, but that general
approach was tightened by a local atmosphere of hysterical fear. The
policy led to the "show of force" in which hundreds of unarmed dem-
onstrators were killed by troops. Das argues that Forster draws from
this event the assault on "a young girl fresh from England," the outbreak of panic among the English community, and the violently reactionary feelings of Mrs. Turton, Callendar and the Collector himself.
Just as important as the historical plausibility of the Aziz fiasco is
the "eruption of reality" created by the pressure of these events.[44]
Mrs. Turton's violence is the violence of Anglo-India made plain, and
the degradations imposed on Nureddin, Aziz and others manifest the
dehumanizing cruelty of the conquerors.

The officials themselves lack this insight. McBryde, who is re-
putedly the most philosophical of them, tells Fielding that "the Mutiny
Records rather than the Bhagavad-Gita should be your bible in this
country," but his succeeding question, "Am I being beastly?" is rhetorical and idiomatic rather than self-searching. Beastliness is projected
onto Indians in the criminology of the Raj. The 1857 Mutiny revealed
this quality once and for all and became enshrined as the decisive
event in Anglo-Indian history, the figura and antitype of every subsequent act of resistance or crime. The incident in the Marabar Caves
is not simply a case to be tried in the Chandrapore police court, but a
"case-study" in Indian perfidy, a demonstration of something already
known. The narrator evokes the majority view at the Club through
*style indirect libre*: "The crime was even worse than they had supposed –

the unspeakable limit of cynicism, untouched since 1857" (p. 194). The British place the case of Aziz and Adela in a narrative context that is partly historical and partly mythical. The latter dimension arises because the Club members begin to live in the Mutiny story, viewing themselves as besieged and playing out symbolic roles. The fretful Mrs. Blakiston, with her babe in arms and her husband away, "with her abundant figure and masses of corngold hair, . . . symbolized all that is worth fighting and dying for" (p. 188). Mrs. Turton becomes her protector, her "Pallas Athene." Individual stories are subsumed into the communal myth. Adela, too, is received into the Turton household, "but it was her position not her character that moved them" (p. 215). In consequence, her own story and especially her doubts are overlooked. She sits unregarded during Mrs. Turton's tirade: "The issues Miss Quested raised were so much more important than she was herself that people inevitably forgot her" (p. 220).

Fielding alone resists this magnification of the Marabar incident into a myth of imperial martyrdom. He assiduously keeps "the lantern of reason" alight (p. 175), and coolly analyses the processes by which the authorities convert a mystery into a conspiracy. He notes the emotional "rallying-cry" intended in characterizing Adela as "a young girl fresh from England." Despite being its butt, he refuses to react to the escalating anger in the Club, and combines detachment with moral discernment in recognizing that "evil was propagating" through Major Callendar's rumour-bearing. At the first opportunity he asks McBryde, "'What is the charge, precisely?'" (p. 176) and receives a periphrastic reply, "that he followed her into the cave and made insulting advances".[45] Most importantly, he believes that Adela's story is partly constructed by its Anglo-Indian audience and wishes to question her himself:

"... I want someone who believes in him to ask her."
"What difference does that make?"
"She is among people who disbelieve in Indians."
"Well, she tells her own story, doesn't she?"
"Yes, but she tells it to you." (p. 179)

The point is lost on McBryde, but its importance is proved in the conversation between Ronny and Adela in chapter XXII, when he dismisses her statement that Aziz is innocent. The gaps in Adela's story are readily filled by the community which rallies round her, while her own doubts are silenced. In effect, the narrative presented by the prosecution at the subsequent trial is a collective one. Chapter XXII foreshadows the trial in three respects: when Adela articulates her belief in Aziz's innocence, her "echo" briefly dies away; Mrs. Moore also pronounces him innocent, and Adela intuits this belief before it is actually spoken, just as the crowd's chant outside the court, "Esmiss Esmoor," fortifies her in the witness box; and finally, Ronny's reaction to his mother's statement, "'She can think, and Fielding too, but there's such a thing as evidence, I suppose,'" ironically anticipates the *lack* of evidence in support of the charge. The significance of this deficiency will be more fully treated below. Here the point to be underlined is that the failure of the prosecution bears out Fielding's rational and interpersonal commitments, and therefore functions metonymically as a refutation of the authoritarian narrative that Indians cannot be trusted and must be kept in check by force.

In keeping with the legal fiction that the charge is a personal complaint by Adela against Aziz, it is she who takes responsibility for the erroneous narrative put before the court: "'I'm afraid I have made a mistake'" (p. 231). The formulation of the charge does depend on her personal experience, and on her initial interpretation of the mysterious occurrence in the cave. Many critics, however, treat the prosecution solely as the product of temporary neurotic or other dysfunctional behaviour by Adela, rather than as a harmonizing between her personal cry and long-standing communal fears and hatreds. Edwin Thumboo offers one of the best psychoanalytic readings of Adela's passage "from caves to court," using Jung's "personality transformation" theory.[46] Arguing that the caves are intrinsically neither good nor evil, that they amplify the visitors' own thoughts and feelings, he suggests that Adela's shocked recognition that she does not love Ronny, yet is to marry him, induces what Jung calls a personality breakdown. In this condition old patterns of life are unavailing and new centres of being must be discovered. The requisite transformation is completed by Adela in the witness box where her lucid account of the expedition, and the courage and honesty of her admission that Dr. Aziz did not follow her into the cave lead to spiritual growth. Between these poles is an "interregnum" in which she is detached from the world, under the dominance of the echo in her head and, I would argue, of the Anglo-Indian myth. Thumboo's argument is important for its insistence that the caves cannot be understood without reference to their place in the story, and for its recognition of the narrative significance of the court scene. The scene invites a Jungian reading, not only because of the archetypal figure of the punkah-wallah, but because of Adela's sudden endowment with "double vision." When giving evidence, she transcends normal perceptual limits by retracing her own entry into the cave and omnisciently watching outside for Aziz to follow her in. This re-presentation to herself and to the court of the events preliminary to the alleged "insult" carries the same dramatic intensity, epistemological weight and moral seriousness as Jim's narrative to Marlow about the *Patna*. Thumboo concludes that Adela's testimony becomes a means of recovering the truth and achieving spiritual growth. The latter element of this personal harvest is undoubtedly true, but the former is only partly so. The truth revealed is limited to the terms of the charge: her evidence amounts to a declaration of Aziz's innocence, but wider questions of whether she was assaulted and by whom remain unexplored. The trial offers only limited satisfaction to the readers' – and the various Chandrapore communities' – interest in knowing what happened in the cave. To account for this continuing gap in the story, this apparent exaltation of the mystery and secrecy of the caves, we need to look beyond Adela's psyche.

Before examining what the novel does not reveal, the fact that within its limits the trial does produce a just verdict deserves acknowledgment. Aziz is proven innocent and "released without one stain on his character" (p. 232). The official verdict, "not guilty," is an instance of what Gillian Beer calls the novel's preference for "negation." She minimizes its significance, arguing that this "act of proof creates nothing fresh."[47] While the reader already knows that Aziz went into a cave by himself to recover from Adela's discomposing question about polygamy and therefore infers his innocence from the outset, proof remains relevant in the novel's *histoire* if not its *discours*. What is newly proved is that the Anglo-Indians' story and their power to impose it on Chandrapore need not triumph, that Aziz does regain his freedom.[48]

Can the outcome of the trial be read as a vindication of the rule of law, a sign that it has taken root in India and may be used against state oppression as well as indigenous crime? S. P. Sen's historical thesis to this effect was based partly on the fact that law was the first profession open to Indians.[49] The presence of Indian barristers and an Indian magistrate lends support to the argument, but both prosecution and defence view the trial as a political contest. Ronny's faith in his "old Das" is ironically undercut: "he cherished 'illusions' about his own subordinates" (p. 219). The English are cynically confident that Das will not make a finding adverse to his superiors. The episode of the seats is partly a descent into *opera bouffe*, as the proceedings are interrupted first, by the movement of the entire English contingent onto the platform and second, by their return after an interval to the body of the court. However, the effect is not of simple farce, but of travesty of judicial ritual, as the English attempt to put themselves on the same level with the magistrate. The narrator's comment underlines the breach of legal norm: "they had not so much disturbed the trial as taken charge of it" (p. 223). Das asserts his authority with some trepidation, but effectively, both in this incident and in asking McBryde to withdraw the charge after Adela admits her mistake. Despite the pressures, he ironically fulfils Ronny's prediction by adhering to the tradition of judicial independence. Das's final order is barely audible in the tumult, but the "forms of law" are followed to a resolution according to the evidence. "He had controlled the case, just controlled it. He had shown that an Indian could preside." The sense of contingency in Forster's narrative means that it lies somewhere between the historical and mythical variants of Cover's "tales of jurisdiction." As such, the Aziz case produces relief at rather than belief in the working of the imported system. The *nomos* is imaged as a temporary shelter, not the citadel of Jodhpur: "then the flimsy framework of the court broke up" (p. 232).

What remains "on the scene of the fantasy" is "the beautiful naked god," the punkah-wallah. He is the final actor on the stage, and the first figure noticed by Adela in the court. Being first and last he serves to frame the proceedings and to rival Mr. Das for normative dominance. Despite his humble status, "he sat on a raised platform near the back, . . . and he seemed to control the proceedings" (p. 220). His aloofness and beauty, combined with his primitive unselfconsciousness, cause Adela to question "her particular brand of opinions and the suburban Jehovah who sanctified them – by what right did they claim so much importance in the world, and assume the title of civilization?" Though he is silent, the punkah-wallah functions to reduce the univocalism of the court and to Indianize the normative world. He represents the India which has escaped the "net" thrown by Great Britain (p. 39). Jenny Sharpe focuses closely on his role in the final stage of Adela's "transformation": "What causes Adela to question the racial hierarchy of colonialism is her rejection of a *caste* stereotype. Instead of associating the untouchable with filth and pollution, she sees him as a vision of perfection and beauty. Upon noticing the silent dignity of the punkah puller, she begins to unlearn the lessons of colonialism."[50]

Forster's own discourse becomes polyglot at this point as he invokes Greek mythology, likening the pulling of the punkah rope to the weaving of the Fates. The possibility that divine machinery rather than human representations will govern the trial is raised. The deity enters in the surprising form of Mrs. Moore. Though absent, her name acts as a mantra, and she enters the thoughts of everyone present. Her memory has already been invoked by Adela in connection with the questions raised by the punkah-wallah. Now, "travestied into a Hindu goddess, Esmiss Esmoor" (p. 228), she becomes a totem of friendship to the Indians, a prod to the consciences of the English. As her individual life ends, she is woven into the Indian *nomos*. The trial process may be conducted along "imperial" lines, but the result affirms Mrs. Moore's faith in and sympathetic understanding of her friend. "Esmiss Esmoor" becomes a comic *dea ex machina*, drawn despite herself into the "machinery" of Indian law, religion and justice. Her fateful prophecy, "'She has started the machinery. It will work to its end'" (p. 211), remains largely unfulfilled, as the outcome of the trial sees Aziz freed, Adela cured of her echo, and Indians of all creeds temporarily united in celebration of their victory over the British. However, her transformation of the metaphor of "machinery" from Ronny's sense of the working of official procedure into something beyond human agency, requiring a "rapt bardic style" to evoke its prophetic significance,[51] anticipates the novel's own movement beyond the regulated world of English law into the mysteries of Hindu ritual and Jain cave. The "rapt" attention conferred on the oblivious punkah-wallah by Adela and the narrator operates to reverse the conventional invisibility of Indians in English eyes and to embody the strange silence heard behind the clamour of the court and elsewhere.

From the perspective of the British the legal narrative mounted in this case also ends in silence. With the sudden reversal of Adela's evidence and the withdrawal of the charge, the story being told through the trial is curtailed. The consolations of closure, the attainment of a complete understanding of the action and of a resolution which enables the parties to look forward and the file to be closed, are denied them. Even the Indians, whose own story of non-involvement is affirmed by the "negative" ending, are not immediately satisfied, as their demand for compensation shows. The narrator predicts that Raj officials will shake their heads over Adela even in retirement. She herself wishes to rehearse the story with Fielding at the first opportunity after the trial, unhappy with the impression she created in the box. His partisan reluctance to hear her is overcome by a positivist interest in explaining how the case arose. He proposes four alternatives: that Aziz is guilty, that Adela invented the charge out of malice, that she experienced an "hallucination," or that the guard or someone else attacked her (pp. 240–2). Adela's admission that she had been living "at half pressure" before the trip to the caves makes the hallucination possibility attractive, but the difficulty of defining this state of mind leads to inconclusiveness ("'we aren't really sure that it was an hallucination'") and to the fourth explanation, the guard. Hamidullah arrives and expostulates about their willingness to blame Indians, a valid point in that the result of their analysis coincides with the racial presumptions of Anglo-India.

The mystery remains, but in their final talk the search for explanation leads into theological discussion, an area closed to them because of their agnostic materialism. The bridge in both conversations is Mrs. Moore. Adela feels that Mrs. Moore knew what happened in the cave, but in answer to Fielding's sceptical question, "'How could she have known what we don't?'" can only reply, "'Telepathy, possibly.'" As this explanation is inadmissible to the two rationalists, the guard provides a helpful substitute. Though no longer profoundly troubled by their inability to account for the episode in the cave, the two sense that they have discovered the limitations of what they can know. That these are not absolute boundaries, but the consequences of their world-view, is underlined by the narrator's question, "Were there worlds beyond which they could never touch, or did all that is possible enter their consciousness?" Although this question is posed in the alternative, the reader's choice is guided by the narrator's manipulation of omniscient viewpoint. By comparing Adela and Fielding to dwarfs who had "seen their own gestures from an immense height," the narrative discourse imagines a transcendental macrocosm reacting to the human microcosm. This enlargement of perspective ought to increase the stature of the protagonists as it endows them with self-knowledge. However, not only are they diminished in size, but their statements are exposed as inauthentic, ignoring "the shadow of the shadow of a dream [which] fell over their clear-cut interests." The narrative here travesties what might have been an important liberal-humanist image, the handshake of former opponents, in order to register the "wistfulness" of their agnosticism, the sense that India might have offered them a different view of reality.

With this translation into religious rhetoric, the narrator abandons interest in the facts of the Marabar incident. The imagined omniscience of the narrator is confined to an exploration of the characters' minds in the dramatic present, and upon that psychologically realist base no definitive representation of what actually happened can be furnished. The action remains as dark and enclosed as the interior of the cave itself, as capable of reducing all explanations to a meaningless "ou-boum" as the echo in the cave. It remains ambiguous. As Forster wrote to Goldsworthy Lowes Dickinson, "In the cave it is *either* a man or the supernatural *or* an illusion. . . . I will it to remain a blur, and to be uncertain, as I am of many of the facts of daily life."[52] He proceeds to argue that this is a specific strategy to express the pervasive "mystery or muddle" of India. Sara Suleri criticizes this representation of India as "disappointing emptiness," arguing that "India" thereby becomes a vacant space which the narrator, "the only locus of rationality in an area of engulfing unreliability," fills with metaphor or metaphysical posture.[53] I have argued that the experience of the caves moves the narrator to question rationalism and to accept ambiguity, in contrast to Adela and Fielding. These characters, it must be noted, are the sites of the experience of darkness and uncertainty, which is not simply projected onto the landscape. What is far more determinedly imposed on India is the rape story and its attendant assumptions. To condemn Forster as a cartographer of the amorphous and to ignore the grid or net which the English have sought to impose on India, as Suleri does, seems to me a criticism too narrowly focused.

In the course of showing Forster's debt to the Romantics, John Beer links the net image in *A Passage to India* to Blake's image of the net of Urizen: "Urizen imposed a mathematical grid over the universe which then turned into a net in which humanity struggled."[54] Forster's own reading of this story has Urizen "applying laws to the universe."[55] The net-like streets of the Civil Station at Chandrapore can serve, then, as a figure for the imposition of law on Indian society, and specifically for the new, comprehensive and rationalist codes. The perceived "gaps and interspaces," the blocked entrances and indecipherable echoes of Indian law provided the Law Commissioners with a justification for treating India as a normative "vacant space" on which a new edifice could be built.

Among these codes was Stephen's Indian Evidence Act. As Alexander Welsh has shown, this fundamental law is unique in the Anglo-American tradition as it positively defines what evidence is, rather than operating through a set of exclusions. Welsh argues that its simplicity and directness derive not only from a Benthamite premise of beginning from first principles, but also from a perception that the Indian context required special clarity and explicitness.[56] The Act, which is still in force, states that evidence may be given of a fact in issue, or of a fact relevant thereto; it defines a "fact" as a thing, a state of things, or a relation of things, perceivable by the senses, or a mental condition; and it defines a "fact in issue" as a fact necessary to establish the right in issue.[57]

The positivist assumptions of this legislation, particularly the belief that individuals can testify to the facts of their own experience, or that the relevance of facts to rights in issue may be determined without prejudice or self-interest, or even the confidence that facts will be available, are put in question by the Marabar case. Sensory perceptions are distorted in the cave, and, deprived of this basis of knowledge, the foreign visitors are assailed by latent fears and repressed doubts.[58] Facts become elusive, impressions unreliable, and the best evidence seems to come through telepathy. The Evidence Act is intended as an epistemological manual, a vehicle for the production of Macaulay's ideal, "in all cases, certainty," but the Marabar case narrative casts doubt on the validity, in India at least, of an exclusively rationalist theory of mind. Ultimately *A Passage to India* bears a double relation to the topic of evidence: it depends on human witnesses for its revelation of action, and criticizes the prosecution's reliance on prejudice rather than fact; but it turns the inductive basis of Stephen's code against itself by using the failure of evidence in this case to generalize about the residual mystery of India and the cosmos.

Most of the novels examined in this study emplot the long but usually successful struggle to rectify the false narrative proclaimed by a court. *A Passage to India* mounts a more extensive critique of legal epistemology, foreshortening the prosecution's story, and expanding interim uncertainty into a proclamation of abiding doubt. The order of the Chandrapore court is just and, within the limits of its enquiry, true. As a verdict on the English system, however, this success is outweighed by the failures implicit in the withdrawal of the charge: the goals of objectivity and certainty, the myths of nomic superiority and necessary force, are all questioned. The Aziz case is indeed a test case, but the result undermines the Anglo-Indian *nomos*.

### III

For both prosecution and defence the Marabar incident possesses broader significance than the facts in issue before the court. The failure of the charge represents a crisis in the explanatory frameworks available to the Chandrapore station. The visit of the Lieutenant-Governor promises new and enlightened policies, and staff transfers imply a recognition of the need for change. Despite these signs the Indians find that "British officialism remained" (p. 258). They want to follow up their legal victory with political change, "to develop an offensive," and to expand the local breach into a permanent division between the emerging nation of India and England. These terms, "breach," "crisis," and "division," are borrowed from Victor Turner's theory of "social drama." It offers an illuminating approach to Part Three and, especially to the relationship between the Hindu festival and the secular ritual of the trial. Some readers have felt such illumination to be necessary: for example, Arnold Bennett wrote in his Journal that the life of the Indian Native State "is beautifully done; but it doesn't seem to relate itself directly to the problem of the previous part of the book."[59]

An anthropologist, Turner argues that social drama is "an experiential matrix from which the many genres of cultural performance, beginning with redressive ritual and juridical procedures and eventually including oral and literary narrative, have been generated."[60] The matrix contains four stages, breach, crisis, redress, and reintegration or consolidation of division. The interest of this theory lies less in step-by-step parallelism with the Marabar case than in its general identification of legal process, ritual and narrative as related cultural genres by virtue of their common origin in social drama. The social drama is a means of dealing with conflict, of bringing it on for resolution, of recognizing its stages. While the Indian Empire was perhaps a site of perennial conflict, of constant breaches, the presumed assault on Adela undoubtedly precipitates a crisis. The trial is offered as a neutral forum for redress, but its verdict perpetuates the schism between Anglo-India and its indigenous subjects. As a genre of cultural performance, *A Passage to India* narrates the plot of a social drama which reveals to the reading public in the imperial centre the crisis and the lack of a reintegrative resolution. It undermines the myth of a harmonious and benevolent relationship between rulers and ruled.

Turner argues not only that social drama provides the plot or content of the later-developed narrative genres, but that "redressive procedures" provide their form. He emphasizes that the third stage, redress, entails procedures for "assigning meanings to events and relationships in reflexive narratives." More than its representation of irredeemable cultural conflict, then, *A Passage to India* reproduces in its form the quest for understanding pursued by Adela, Fielding, Mrs. Moore, Stella and Ralph, and (within their traditions) Aziz and Godbole. Having reached the narrative impasse of the trial, the narrator must look beyond the English "gospel" of law, and hence outside Anglo-India in order to find a point of closure, a higher stage of understanding. The caves, with their implications of indeterminacy, remain the dominant image of Part Two, unchallenged by the court. "Ritual and legal procedures mediate between the formed and the indeterminate," according to Turner. Between the grid of English law and the normative amorphousness of the caves, no mediation is possible. Part Two ends in a series of disengagements: the departures of Adela and Fielding; the estrangement between Aziz and Fielding over compensation and scandal; the ethnocentrism of Fielding's praise of Venice. Such an ending expresses retreat from India. A new passage is demanded if the narrative is not to dissolve in cognitive and affective failure.

Accordingly, the third part opens on a note of bold translation, of passage achieved: "Some hundreds of miles westward of the Marabar Hills, and two years later in time, Professor Narayan Godbole stands in the presence of God" (p. 281). The incongruity of divine presence in such a precise spatio-temporal setting creates a comic-sublime effect, which is sustained throughout the following chapters by a dual focus on manners and myth. By viewing the Hindu ritual of the birth of Krishna through the eyes of Aziz, Ralph, Stella and Fielding, interested outsiders, the plenitude of meaning endowed by Hinduism on Indian life is evoked for the desacralized West. While Krishna refused to come to Godbole at Fielding's party, here in the annual ritual he comes, is revealed processionally, and his image is thrown away on the flooding waters. The narrator is alert to the contradictions of the festival, to the underlying belief that God cannot be thrown away, to the substitution of the venerated Krishna symbol with another disposable one.

Notwithstanding such ironic detachment, the process is respected as a form for apprehending the absolute, as a negation of the "undying worm" in the cave (p. 212). Turner himself uses this phrase to describe the indeterminacy or irresolution against which the social drama is deployed. Biblical in origin, the undying worm is one of Isaiah's images for those punished by the Lord: "for their worm shall not die, neither shall their fire be quenched; and they shall be an abhorring unto all flesh."[61] Against this image of stasis and despair, Forster presents the Gokul-Ashtami festival as a rite of passage, to the Otherworld of communion with infinite love, of intercultural understanding and international friendship. The God is thrown with "emblems of passage; a passage not easy, not now, not here, not to be apprehended except when it is unattainable: the God to be thrown was an emblem of that" (p. 309). In addition to its anticipation of the last paragraph of the novel, this quote recalls the sense of loss and defeat generated by the Marabar incident, the intensified desire for knowledge denied, the pain of affection soured. Turner argues that "ritual transforms," and while this applies to participants rather than observers, the festival catalyses the reconciliation of Aziz and Fielding and restores to the plot the hope of change.

The relationship between this scene and that of the trial is under-scored by the appearance of the "servitor" – naked, impassive, im-mersed in his duty, "the Indian body again triumphant" (p. 309). Like the punkah-wallah, he seems blind to the interruptions of the English, and performs his more meaningful task despite them. Yet the collision of the boats so close to the servitor does disrupt the ritual, in an allegory of sacred tradition versus secular tourism. The comic world of muddle, accident, and human failure reasserts itself against the novel's venture into the meditative sublime. Having reaffirmed the value of transformative vision, *A Passage to India* cannot commit itself entirely to the mythic realm by sacrificing its sense of historical contingency. The linguistic equivalent of ritual, says Turner, is the subjunctive mood, the vehicle of "'wish, desire, possibility, or hypothesis,'" the world of "as if."[62] Forster acknowledges the wish for union, but having done so, returns to the indicative mood of realism, to the inevitable rocks which sunder Fielding and Aziz on their last ride. Thrust up by the earth, these rocks remind us of the Marabar Hills, but now they are only one detail in a landscape thick with signs: "the temples, the tank, the jail, the palace, the birds, the carrion, the Guest House" (p. 316). Though international friendship and understanding are deferred, the inclusive-ness of this list declares the novel's debt to the Hindu vision of tran-scending conventional opposites.

The ending therefore contrives to combine both the paideic dream and the current obstacles to its achievement. "Love, the beloved republic," remains Forster's ideal polity: the passage to this state lies through the channel of personal relationships. In refusing to overlook the difficulties faced by Aziz and Fielding in their friendship, Forster proves himself an unillusioned liberal. Despite his awareness of the fragility of liberalism, the possibility of international friendship remained

Forster's faith and hope. It is incorporated into the ending through the mysterious, intuitive sympathy between Aziz and Ralph Moore. Upon an impulse of love, Aziz casts away the protective reserve he has worn since the cave, and offers to show Ralph his country. "Was the cycle beginning again? His heart was too full to draw back"(p. 307). Though Aziz describes the cycle as "mosque, caves, mosque, caves," the temple is not simply a reprise of Part One, but a new, inclusive passage born out of the experiences of both previous sections.

If the qualified vision of the conclusion is to be criticized, it cannot be for failure to imagine an emblem of hope or a possible transformation.[63] Though the reiteration of "didn't want it" apparently negates the subjunctive realm of desire, the finality of this refusal of possibility is undercut by the narrative style of the final sentence. Encompassing the whole paragraph, it invokes all the named features of the Mau landscape, which "said in their hundred voices, 'No, not yet,' and the sky said, 'No, not there.'" The total effect of syntactical and imaginative unboundedness suggests a world metamorphosing as the narrative withdraws from its scene. If anything, the ending is too fictive, for the denial of union is attributed to nature, rather than to what Pascal called "second nature," custom or *nomos*.[64] Forster's self-consciously figurative language may be distinguished, however, from the literalism and loose naturalism of the Anglo-Indians' racial and climatic theories. His anthropomorphic chorus is prospective and unisonic. Its fusion of scene and voice has aesthetic and normative implications. For it expresses the hope with which Forster concluded *Aspects of the Novel*, namely that the development of the form "implied the development of humanity."[65]

## CHAPTER NINE

# *Settling out of court*

One of the witnesses in the trial of Phineas Finn, in Trollope's *Phineas Redux*, is a novelist, Mr. Bouncer. The surly Chaffanbrass does not cross-examine him on his evidence, but tests the prosecution case according to the canons of fiction! After conducting him through murders in Shakespeare, Scott and Bulwer, Chaffanbrass suggests to Bouncer, "'You would not dare so to violate probability in a novel, as to produce a murderer . . . who should contrive a secret hidden murder, – contrive it and execute it, all within a quarter of an hour?'"[1] This episode inverts the novel's usual fascination with the law by making the law attend to fiction. It represents the obverse of the demand for authentication addressed by Walter Hartright in *The Woman in White*. This fantasy is Trollope's last hurrah against the lawyers,[2] and a jocular assertion of fiction's claim to rival the law as an authoritative interpreter of reality. The effect of adducing literary evidence in a legal trial in a novel is an unpretentiously comic, but nonetheless watertight, imbrication of novel and law.

While Trollope's claim to authoritative representation is based on writers being "masters of human nature," the novelists here studied have characteristically challenged the cultural forms through which human nature has been required to express itself. The cases of Effie Deans, Esther Summerson, Billy Budd and Doctor Aziz tell of the various fates awaiting those victimized by restrictive conceptions of the human and the natural. Juxtaposed against these are alternative forms, pastoral co-operation, familial love, democracy, Hindu mythology, which dialogize the dominant notions enforced through law. The novel, then, becomes an alternative forum, a second normative space, in which the narrator appears as witness, or as advocate, or as victim.

As supplements, these novels occupy, in shifting ways, the speaking positions offered by legal discourse. Whether it be the faithful deponent of *Billy Budd* or Marlow or Lady Mason's defender, the narrators exploit the probative possibilities and cultural authority of the Anglo-American system of law, drawing on aspects of this *nomos* in both their speech and their writing. However, whilst recognizing the value of this tradition, they push these forms beyond lawful bounds and incorporate the inadmissible, the scandalous, the heterodox: the history of Effie's child, Esther's narrative, Marlow's anecdotes of suicide and cannibalism, or "Billy in the Darbies." By opening what was closed, and by eclectic juxtaposition, these texts enact a re-formation of legal discourse. In this respect, they undoubtedly draw on – and advance – that "spirit of reform" which was the dominant narrative of law, defining its sense of tradition and challenge, in the nineteenth century.

If there is one area where this reformist effect is especially noticed, it is in the representation of subjectivity. From Scott to Forster novelists demonstrate a developing interest in reclaiming characters marginalized by the criminal or civil law. *Bleak House* brings within the order of discourse those whose speech is legally proscribed: Jo, the crossing sweeper; Gridley, of whose existence "the Chancellor . . . is legally ignorant after making it desolate for a quarter of a century," but whose story is collected by Esther and John Jarndyce; and Esther herself, prematurely adjudged " 'not related to any party in the cause.' " Billy Budd, having faltered at the threshold of speech, becomes the subject of a fictional appeal. The inclusion of new speakers entails a questioning of authorized voices and established forms. Parody is an important resource in the recurrent critique of legal formalism, from Bartoline Saddletree and Conversation Kenge to Ronny Heaslop. On the other side of the bar, characters who have committed a crime are represented with increasing sympathy. In *The Heart of Midlothian* and *Billy Budd* the novel invites a reconsideration of the prisoner's case, questioning the justice of the death penalty in the light of all the circumstances. Effie Deans's pardon is conditional on her banishment, an outcome which the novel implicitly endorses through its concentration on Jeanie. In the later works, however, the narrative centres on the criminal both before and after trial, and social exclusion is not reproduced in fictional structure. Psychological analysis infiltrates normative application in the stories of Lady Mason, Billy Budd and Lord Jim, thus confirming Alexander Pettit's argument that a trope of sympathetic criminality emerges in the novel from the mid-Victorian period, assisting the emergence of social dissatisfaction with an exclusively moral discourse of crime that would result in a new criminology from the 1880s.

Concomitant with this reformation of the subject is a refiguring of the space of law. From the invasion of the Tolbooth to the noisy crowd pressing on the "flimsy framework of the court" in Chandrapore, the institutional site of justice is described in detail, and then destabilized. In these novels, as in legal usage, the court is both a place and a jurisdiction. Consequently, the space functions as a metonym of the law it administers. If the citadel of law is not always literally breached, it is nonetheless undermined and supplemented: whether it is the rocking of the ship as Captain Vere paces his state room in *Billy Budd*, the doubling of the fog-bound Court of Chancery with Krook's Rag-and-Bone shop, or the tedious and shadowy court-room of *Lord Jim*, the vulnerability of judicial space is a means of suggesting the distortions of the law. This expressionistic tendency in fiction contrasts with the deployment of architectual imagery in legal writing. Blackstone's comparison of the common law with a "noble pile" is confidently extended by legalists well into the twentieth century. Sir Frederick Pollock, addressing law students at Oxford in 1886, made perhaps the highest claims for English law as a cultural monument: "So venerable, so majestic, is this living temple of justice, this immemorial and yet freshly growing fabric of the Common Law, that the least of us is happy who hereafter may point to so much as one stone thereof and say, The work of my hands is there."[3] Pollock's Palladian image of the temple harks back to Blackstone's century, setting at nought the challenges of the reformers and novelists. Nor is any trace of instability admitted by Learned Hand in 1939: "The customary law of English-speaking peoples stands, a structure indubitably made by the hands of generations of judges, each professing to be a pupil, yet each in fact a builder who has contributed his few bricks and his little mortar."[4] The possibility that this structure is not completely made of bricks and mortar is recognized in a long, but complacent, restatement of this image by Francis Cowper:

The English legal world, like so many other English institutions, is like an old house which has been altered, adapted, extended, refurnished across the generations, sometimes for convenience, sometimes for necessity, sometimes even for fun, but which has never been pulled down and rebuilt from the foundations. No Justinian, no Napoleon, has ever made *tabula rasa* of all that has gone before to start afresh with a code of his own devising. So in the rambling old house of our law there are tortuous passages, dark corners, even some accumulations of antiquated rubbish, but there are also splendid lofty halls full of light and air and majesty. It is a house that is lived in, and the Englishman feels that it is his home, for it fits the way of life to which he is accustomed, a way of life that is easy-fitting and not too rigid. If there is some junk in the attic, there is good wine in the cellars; there are many fine portraits on the walls, and the windows look out on a wide landscape of ancient freedom, even though there have been times when those windows needed cleaning and polishing afresh.[5]

In this passage the "rambling old house of our law" is at once Bleak House and the "noble pile" of Blackstone's apologetics. If this rhetoric illustrates the New Historicist insight that a dominant discourse may absorb and contain any attempted critique, it also differs from Conversation Kenge's panegyrics by acknowledging an occasional need for reform. The emphasis on habitation, rather than on building, in Cowper's formulation connects with Cover's image of law as a normative environment. However, the repeated emphasis on the ease of this space, the absence of felt restraint, distinguishes this picture from those of the novelists or Cover. What the comparison of Cowper's language and Dickens's shows with startling clarity is the unconscious class blindness of the legal mythographer. In this utopian fantasy the "noble pile" is literally a stately home, replete with old wines and portraits, set in a landscape where the workers are invisible, and the only juridical subject is the lord of the manor (who is probably also a justice of the peace). In the courts of Scott, Dickens, Trollope, Conrad and Forster, the people, as well as the profession, are present in crowds, and the tension between their noisy activity and the desired solemnity of the legal officials is central to the representation of law as social action. Without quite desecrating the temple, the novelists consistently refuse the static tableaux of authority. Moreover, the fictional court never becomes a space of actual justice, a theatre of effective action. Rather, it is a place of injustice, or inaction, or incompletion; and when a just outcome is obtained, in *A Passage to India*, it puts at risk the authority of the system.

Effective and meaningful outcomes, where they occur, take place outside the court. Jeanie and the Duke of Argyle are the agents of justice in *The Heart of Midlothian*, as are Esther and Jarndyce in *Bleak House*. Lady Mason's confession and surrender of Orley Farm are performed in the private sphere. Alternative worlds are presented, in which different norms are established. The novel functions as a vehicle for what Cover calls "jurisgenesis," and the "radical relativization of law" is instantiated not only by the critique of the legal system, but through the proposal of other ideals.

In these three novels a successful legal hermeneutic is theoretically possible upon the reform of attitudes and processes. However, in the later novels, some element in the plot proves irrecoverable in such a way as to cast doubt on the very process of rational investigation. Adela Quested is assaulted in the Marabar cave, but by whom or what? The *Patna* strikes a submerged object, and begins to take in water, but does not sink, despite its officers' fears. Billy Budd is accused wrongfully, and inexplicably, of mutiny. In all three plots, legal processes are invoked less by an event than a chimera: not a positive act, not a demonstrable falsity, but a perception affirmed and yet denied, an unfounded allegation that develops its own momentum; not a fact, but the ghost of a fact. From the late nineteenth century, fiction registers the physical destabilization of legal space as the mark, not only of normative and political challenge, but of an epistemological crisis. These ghosts can never be exorcised, and the characters' immediate responses to them have lasting consequences. Radical scepticism or tragic irony in these novels denies both the romance plot and the confident testimonial discourse of Scott, and confounds the law's desire for certainty and its promise of justice. While they continue to employ the authenticating rhetoric of evidence, their plots set severe limits to its availability and its efficacy.

The novelists' interest in legal alternity, already strong in Scott and Dickens, is an urgent imperative for Melville, Conrad and Forster. Billy Budd's conscription from the *Rights-of-Man* to the *Bellipotent* serves to juxtapose the unreformed English *nomos* with its revolutionary alternative; in addition to which the reader is invited to compare the represented past with subsequent history, the time of production and the reading present. The ship at sea is a source of contrasting normative tropes for Conrad too. Marlow's idealization of the ethos of the English merchant marine is both exalted and undermined by Jim's failure among the hybridized community on the *Patna*. Professional commitment, idealism and marine commerce support Marlow's world, and they underpin the *nomos* that Jim establishes on Patusan. Conrad invests in this imperialist fantasy of benign domination, but his scepticism prevents him succumbing to the temptations of a normative romance. With the failure of this tradition against the rapacious Brown, Conrad seems, through Marlow's final isolation, to privilege the individual mind over the social body as the only authentic location of meaning and value. However, as the English novel deepens its engagement with law in the imperial context, the existence of other normative worlds and the possibility of interpersonal friendship despite the imperialist distortions provide new imaginings for *nomos* that are social in

character. Forster supplements the deficiencies of English law and
Anglo-Indian manners with a recognition of the appeal and power of
the various Indian belief systems, while also resorting to the private
sphere to dream of cross-cultural personal relationships.

Throughout the hundred years of this study, the novel's consistent
dissatisfaction with the resolutions of the law and search for alternatives causes it to "settle out of court" in its narrative resolutions. This
metaphor suggests, in addition to the spatial representation of alternity,
the desire for a new consensus. As our period draws to its close, the
destructive effects of legal verdicts are registered in fiction precisely
through a preference for settlement over trial. In Galsworthy's *The
Country House* (1907) George Pendyce falls in love with Helen Bellew,
and is cited as co-respondent in her husband's divorce suit. His father
threatens to disinherit him, but his mother, who is dissatisfied with her
own marriage, leaves home to travel to London and her son. She finds
that Helen has broken off the affair, and in an interview with the
husband, Jasper, persuades him to withdraw the action. Comparing
her own marital relationship with these others, she reassesses its quality, and returns to her "country house" happy. The conventionality
and contradictions of this plot have been subtly analysed by Frank
Kermode, but its linkage of settlement and succession allegorizes
the struggle for normative preservation at a time of social change.[6]
The various personal and social interests in succession and its settlement are given an extended and agonized treatment in Ford Madox
Ford's *The Marsden Case* (1923). Here the plot concerns the quest by
George Heimann and his sister, Marie Elizabeth, to prove that they
are the legitimate son and daughter of Earl Marsden. Set in the last
days before the Great War, it rehearses Ford's theme of the conflict
between the aristocratic ethos and modern vulgarity and self-interest.
In this emerging society, literature and law are not equals, as the
barrister-narrator finds: "But when I said I did not practise, was not
the legal adviser of Marie Elizabeth, and was by occupation a novelist,
his distress almost touched me."[7] In the narrator's imaginative world,
however, the court is an object of travesty: "I don't know why a
Court of Law always reminds me of a shallow soap-dish."[8] While
social conflict escalates into war, the legal conflict between the presumptive heir and George is an intra-familial affair and must be settled
out of court. George demands of his supporters, "'either our case is
silently demonstrable by passing papers across a table or it does not
exist. Contentious litigation about it is impossible in the nature of the

case.'"⁹ The documents necessary to fulfil this wish are discovered, albeit only with the aid of lawyers and vulgarians. In both these novels, the area of consensus established by the settlement of disputes at law is small, and under threat from larger social conflicts.

Galsworthy and Ford employ, as Dickens and Trollope did before them, the inheritance plot in ways that question whether the country house of law and its landscape of ancient freedom can be maintained or defended for transmission to succeeding generations. In all the novels we have examined, it is not simply a matter of cleaning the windows, as Cowper would have it, but of opening the gates that prevent Esther Summerson or Jo from gaining shelter, or overcoming the wastes of a prodigal heir, or repairing dry rot, or installing hot water. By contrast, the problems of estate management in the "house of fiction" *are* confined to windows. For Henry James writing in 1908,

The house of fiction has in short not one window, but a million – a number of possible windows not to be reckoned rather; every one of which has been pierced or is still pierceable, in its vast front, by the need of the individual vision and the pressure of the individual will. These apertures, of dissimilar shape and size, hang so, all together, over the human scene that we might have expected of them a greater sameness of report than we find.¹⁰

James's house metaphor arises, like Blackstone's, out of an attempt at systematic historical commentary on centuries-old cultural practice. His mission to present the novel as a total structure with its own architecture, invites readers to consider not only its internal form, but its solid presence in the social landscape. James describes the novelists' inheritance as a structure of immense variety, complexity and social significance. As an estate of increasing symbolic capital, the house of fiction develops from Scott onwards the necessary "effrontery" to critique its venerable neighbour. It reconnects the beautiful but depopulated fields of legal doctrine with "the human scene," and it reveals how few and uniform are the windows in the palladium of justice. The emphasis on individual vision in James's analogy highlights the growing acknowledgment of the subjectivism of perception traceable in Melville, Conrad and Forster, and, more than that, the plurality of values inscribed in all these novels of *nomos*. At least some of the windows in the house of fiction, however, are copied from law. It is through such openness to the variety of cultural influences that the novel accomplishes its "radical relativization of law."

The value of the novel to *nomos* continues to lie not, as Chaffanbrass wishes, in the assessment of probability, but in the adumbration of possibility. I refer not only to such utopian speculations as John Fowles's _A Maggot_ (1985), in which testimonial form is yoked to a fantasy ending, but to the many novels which invite us to "unthink the impossible." In the era of the rule of law, the works discussed show that a person can be wrongly convicted of murder, that barristers like Chaffanbrass regularly breach the norms of their profession, and that a fragile hold on power reveals the authoritarian in officials and the Machiavellian in jurists. By their very contiguity to known societies and events, such novels force a re-examination of the mythology of liberty and legality. Two hundred years ago, during the sedition trials, Godwin's Caleb Williams told a tale of "Things As They Are," and challenged the country to "do justice" to him and his oppressor. If novelists have become more equivocal in their formulations of _nomos_, the historical need and the paideic desire still animate their work. My concluding illustration is from another writer penalized for freedom of expression, Salman Rushdie. When in _Midnight's Children_ Saleem Sinai reached Dacca with the invading army, he "saw many things which were not true, which were not possible, because our boys would not could not have behaved so badly."[11] Saleem finds the abandoned office of a notary public. The "stamps and seals which had made him an arbiter of what was true and what was not" remain. The scene offers scope for further ironic play with the authoritative forms of the law, but the comic inversion that follows is accompanied by regret: "I could not ask him to verify what was happening, I could not give a deposition under oath." By invoking, however unavailingly, the role of witness, the narrator challenges the conventional rhetoric of denial and impossibility, and provides us with a final emblem of _nomos_ under threat and a final "proof" that normative concern continues to express itself in fictional narrative.

# Notes

## I NARRATIVE FORMS AND NORMATIVE WORLDS

1 Wilkie Collins, *The Woman in White* (1860; Harmondsworth: Penguin, 1974), p. 33.
2 Ian Watt, *The Rise of the Novel* (London: Chatto and Windus, 1957), p. 31.
3 M. M. Bakhtin, "Forms of Time and Chronotope in the Novel," in *The Dialogic Imagination*, Michael Holquist (ed.), Caryl Emerson and Michael Holquist (trans.) (Austin: University of Texas Press, 1981), p. 124.
4 Ibid., p. 84 (subtitle of "Forms of Time").
5 R. Howard Bloch, *Medieval French Literature and the Law* (Berkeley: University of California Press, 1977), p. 1. See also John A. Alford, "Literature and Law in Medieval England," *PMLA*, 92 (1977), pp. 941–51.
6 See chap. 3 on page 46.
7 Robert A. Ferguson, *Law and Letters in American Culture* (Cambridge: Harvard University Press, 1984), pp. 10–11.
8 Brook Thomas, *Cross-examinations of Law and Literature* (New York: Cambridge University Press, 1987).
9 Ibid., pp. 5ff.
10 Theodore Ziolkowski, *German Romanticism and its Institutions* (Princeton University Press, 1990), p. 80.
11 John Sutherland, "The Victorian Novelists: Who Were They?" in his *Victorian Fiction: Writers, Publishers, Readers* (Basingstoke: Macmillan, 1995), p. 162.
12 Ibid., p. 163.
13 Alexander Welsh, *Strong Representations* (Baltimore: Johns Hopkins University Press, 1992), p. 48. Sutherland argues that Collins's interest in circumstantial evidence, sparked by the Palmer poisoning trial of 1856, is demonstrated in the character and actions of Fosco in *The Woman in White*. See Sutherland, *Victorian Fiction*, pp. 34–42.
14 Lennard J. Davis, *Factual Fictions: The Origins of the English Novel* (New York: Columbia University Press, 1983).
15 John Bender, *Imagining the Penitentiary: Fiction and the Architecture of Mind in Eighteenth-Century England* (University of Chicago Press, 1987), p. 7.

16 John P. Zomchick, *Family and the Law in Eighteenth-Century Fiction* (London: Cambridge University Press, 1993), pp. 2, 18.

17 David Punter, "Fictional Representations of Law in the Eighteenth Century," *Eighteenth-Century Studies*, 16 (1982–3), p. 47.

18 Ibid., p. 73.

19 Ibid., p. 74.

20 D. A. Miller, *The Novel and the Police* (Berkeley: University of California Press, 1988); Marie-Christine Leps, *Apprehending the Criminal: The Production of Deviance in Nineteenth-Century Discourse* (Durham: Duke University Press, 1992); Martin A. Kayman, *From Bow Street to Baker Street: Mystery, Detection and Narrative* (Basingstoke: Macmillan, 1992).

21 See John R. Reed, *Dickens and Thackeray: Punishment and Forgiveness* (Athens: Ohio University Press, 1995) and Alexander Pettit, "Sympathetic Criminality in the Mid-Victorian Novel," *Dickens Studies Annual*, 19 (1990), pp. 281–300.

22 Walter Benn Michaels, "Romance and Real Estate," in *The New Historicism Reader*, H. Aram Veeser (ed.) (London: Routledge, 1994), pp. 186–205; Brook Thomas, "The Construction of Privacy in and around *The Bostonians*," in *New Historicism Reader*, Veeser (ed.), pp. 161–85.

23 Welsh, *Strong Representations*; Roslyn Jolly, "The Unreliable Reader: The Problem of Circumstantial Evidence in Nineteenth-Century Narrative," *Australian Journal of Law and Society*, 9 (1993), pp. 81–8.

24 Franco Moretti, *The Way of the World* (London: Verso, 1987), chap. 4.

25 For an overview of this process, see Jeffrey N. Cox and Larry J. Reynolds, "The Historicist Enterprise," in *New Historical Literary Study: Essays on Reproducing Texts, Representing History*," Cox and Reynolds (eds) (Princeton University Press), pp. 4–10.

26 For an early feminist example, see Françoise Basch, *Relative Creatures: Victorian Women in Society and the Novel*, Anthony Rudolf (trans.) (London: Allen Lane, 1974). Among postcolonial critics, see Gary Boire, "*Rationes Officii*: Representing Law in Postcolonial Literatures," *Mosaic*, 27 (1994), pp. 199–214.

27 Richard H. Weisberg and Jean-Pierre Barricelli, "Literature and the Law," in *Interrelations of Literature*, Joseph Gibaldi and Jean-Pierre Barricelli (eds) (New York: MLA, 1982), p. 150.

28 See especially James Boyd White, "Reading Law and Reading Literature: Law as Language," in his *Heracles' Bow: Essays on the Rhetoric and Poetics of the Law* (Madison: University of Wisconsin Press, 1985), pp. 78–9.

29 Richard H. Weisberg, *Poethics and other Strategies of Law and Literature* (New York: Columbia University Press, 1992).

30 Gary Minda, *Postmodern Legal Movements: Jurisprudence at Century's End* (New York University Press, 1996), chap. eight, "Law and Literature," p. 158.

31 Ian Ward, *Law and Literature: Possibilities and Perspectives* (Cambridge University Press, 1995), pp. 22–6.

32 For a powerful demonstration of gender discourses at work in legal judgments and attack on the gender blindness of Law and Literature courses,

see Carolyn Heilbrun and Judith Resnik, "Convergences: Law, Literature and Feminism," *Yale Law Journal*, 99 (1990), pp. 1913–53.

33 See Kim Lane Scheppele, "Foreword: Telling Stories," *Michigan Law Review*, 87 (1989), pp. 2073–98, introducing papers on "legal narrative and its 'counter-hegemonic' power" (p. 2075). Peter Brooks, "Illicit Stories," *Diacritics*, 25 (1995), p. 51, questions whether story-telling is necessarily a vehicle of liberation.

34 Simon Petch, "Law as Literature?" *Sydney Studies in English*, 16 (1990–91), p. 129.

35 See especially Peter Goodrich, *Reading the Law* (Oxford: Blackwell, 1986), *passim*. The conjunction of social linguistics and political critique is well illustrated in Terry Threadgold, "Re-Writing Law as Postmodern Fiction: the Poetics of Child Abuse," in *The Happy Couple: Law and Literature*, J. Neville Turner and Pamela Williams (eds) (Annandale, NSW: Federation Press, 1994), pp. 322–41.

36 Richard H. Weisberg, *The Failure of the Word* (New Haven: Yale University Press, 1984) and *Poethics*, chap. five.

37 Robert M. Cover, "Violence and the Word," *Yale Law Journal*, 95 (1986), p. 1609.

38 See Michel Foucault, *Discipline and Punish: The Birth of the Prison*, Alan Sheridan (trans.) (1977; London: Penguin, 1979), pp. 9f.

39 Robert M. Cover, "*Nomos* and Narrative," *Harvard Law Review*, 97 (1983–4), p. 4.

40 The most accessible source for this aspect of narrative theory is *On Narrative*, W. J. T. Mitchell (ed.) (University of Chicago Press, 1981).

41 Clifford Geertz, "Local Knowledge: Fact and Law in Comparative Perspective," in his *Local Knowledge* (New York: Basic Books, 1983), pp. 173, 219; Pierre Bourdieu, "The Force of Law: Toward a Sociology of the Juridical Field," *Hastings Law Journal*, 38 (1987), p. 838.

42 Donald R. Kelley, *The Human Measure: Social Thought in the Western Legal Tradition* (Cambridge: Harvard University Press, 1990), p. 10.

43 Ibid.

44 Cover, "*Nomos*," p. 9.

45 Gerald Prince, *A Dictionary of Narratology* (Lincoln: University of Nebraska Press, 1987), p. 60.

46 Cover, "*Nomos*," p. 4, n. 3.

47 See *Law-Making in Australia*, Eugene Kamenka and Alice Ehr-Soon Tay (eds) (Port Melbourne: Edward Arnold, 1980), p. 5.

48 I am grateful to Professor Rowland McMaster of the University of Alberta for this point and the reference to Virgil's *Aeneid* VI.851–3. See Virgil, *The Aeneid*, Robert Fitzgerald (trans.) (New York: Random House, 1983).

49 Cover, "*Nomos*," p. 14.

50 Scheppele, "Telling Stories," pp. 2073–98.

51 Austin Sarat and Thomas R. Kearns, "Making Peace with Violence: Robert Cover on Law and Legal Theory," in *Law's Violence*, Sarat and Kearns

(eds) (Ann Arbor: University of Michigan Press, 1992), p. 224. This article is a fine critical study of Cover's thought.

52 *Bob Jones University* v. *United States* 1103 S.Ct. 2017 (1983). See Cover, "*Nomos* and Narrative," p. 26.

53 Cover, "*Nomos* and Narrative," p. 28.

54 Ibid., p. 43.

55 Michael Ryan, "Meaning and Alternity," Afterword to *Narrative, Violence and Law*, Martha Minow, Michael Ryan and Austin Sarat (eds) (Ann Arbor: University of Michigan Press, 1992), p. 68.

56 Ibid., p. 66.

57 Bourdieu, "Force of Law," p. 830.

58 Robert Cover, "The Folk-tales of Justice: Tales of Jurisdiction," *Capital University Law Review*, 14 (1986), p. 182.

59 Thomas, *Cross-Examinations*, p. 5.

60 M. M. Bakhtin, "Epic and Novel," in *The Dialogic Imagination*, p. 7.

61 Ibid., p. 11.

62 Lynne Pearce, *Reading Dialogics* (London: Edward Arnold, 1994), p. 60. Cf. Benedict Anderson, *Imagined Communities* (London: Verso, 1983).

63 Cates Baldridge, *The Dialogics of Dissent in the English Novel* (Hanover: University Press of New England, 1994), p. 12.

64 Ibid., p. 111.

65 Bakhtin, "Epic and Novel," p. 39.

66 George Lukács, *The Theory of the Novel*, Anna Bostock (trans.) (1920; London: Merlin Press, 1971), p. 56.

67 *Prospective Review* (30 April 1853); quoted in *Victorian Criticism of the Novel*, Edwin M. Eigner and George J. Worth (eds) (Cambridge University Press, 1985), pp. 85f.

68 Harry Levin, "Society as its own Historian," in *Contexts of Criticism* (Cambridge: Harvard University Press, 1957), p. 187. Levin also records Hegel's description of the novel as "*das burgerliche Epos*" – the epic of the middle classes – and Zola's "the genre *par excellence*" of the nineteenth century: p. 173.

69 Janice Carlisle, *The Sense of an Audience: Dickens, Thackeray and George Eliot at Mid-Century* (Athens: University of Georgia Press, 1981), pp. 15–16.

70 Pettit, "Sympathetic Criminality."

71 Linda K. Hughes and Michael Lund, *The Victorian Serial* (Charlottesville: University Press of Virginia, 1991), pp. 8–9.

72 W. Wolfgang Holdheim, "On the Genealogy of the *Judicial Error*," *Cardozo Studies in Law and Literature*, 7 (1995), p. 126.

## 2 THE MODERN WESTERN *NOMOS*

1 Cover, "*Nomos* and Narrative," *Harvard Law Review*, 97 (1983–4), p. 5, n. 7 (referring to Geertz, *The Interpretation of Cultures* (New York: Basic Books, 1973), p. 5).

2 Dominick LaCapra, *Rethinking Intellectual History* (Ithaca: Cornell University Press, 1983), p. 59.

3 Sir William Blackstone, *Commentaries on the Laws of England*, 1st edn. (1769; rpt. London: Dawsons of Pall Mall, 1966), IV, pp. 435–6.

4 The quoted phrase figures in the long subtitle of his monograph, *The Mysterious Science of the Law* (1941; rpt. Boston: Beacon, 1958).

5 Michael Meehan, "An Anatomy of Australian Law," *The Happy Couple: Law and Literature* (Annandale: Federation Press, 1994), pp. 376–89.

6 Franco Moretti, *The Way of the World* (London: Verso, 1987), chap. IV.

7 Northrop Frye, *The Critical Path* (Bloomington: Indiana University Press, 1971), p. 44.

8 Michael Lobban, *The Common Law and English Jurisprudence 1760–1850* (Oxford: Clarendon, 1991), p. 13.

9 See Jeremy Bentham, *A Comment on the Commentaries and A Fragment on Government*, J. H. Burns and H. L. A. Hart (eds) (London: Athlone Press, 1977), p. 124.

10 Bentham, *Comment on the Commentaries*, p. 508.

11 See pp. 3–4 in this book.

12 Lionel Gossman, "History and Literature: Reproduction or Signification," in *The Writing of History: Narrative Form and Historical Understanding*, Robert H. Canary and Henry Kozicki (eds) (Madison: University of Wisconsin Press, 1978), p. 7.

13 Ross Harrison, *Bentham* (London: Routledge and Kegan Paul, 1983), p. 7.

14 Louis O. Mink, "Narrative Form as a Cognitive Instrument," in *The Writing of History*, Canary and Kozicki (eds), p. 138.

15 Peter Stein, *Legal Evolution* (Cambridge University Press, 1980), p. 15.

16 Ernst Cassirer, *The Philosophy of the Enlightenment*, Fritz C. A. Koelln and James A. Pettagrove (trans.) (Princeton University Press, 1951), pp. 234–52 ("Law, State and Society").

17 See John Barrell, "Imaginary Treason, Imaginary Law: the State Trials of 1794," in his *The Birth of Pandora* (Basingstoke: Macmillan, 1992), pp. 119–43.

18 Robert A. Ferguson, *Law and Letters in American Culture* (Harvard University Press, 1984), pp. 201ff and 266ff.

19 See Robert M. Cover, *Justice Accused* (New Haven: Yale University Press, 1977); Charles Reich, "The Tragedy of Justice in Melville's *Billy Budd*," *Yale Review*, 56 (1967), pp. 368–89.

20 John T. Noonan, *Persons and Masks of the Law* (New York: Farrar, Strauss and Giroux, 1976).

21 Franco Moretti, *Signs Taken For Wonders* (London: Verso, 1988), p. 136, quoting Max Weber, *The Methodology of the Social Sciences* (New York: The Free Press, 1949), p. 169.

22 Martin J. Wiener, *Reconstructing the Criminal: Culture, Law and Policy in England 1830–1914* (Cambridge University Press, 1990).

23 See the symposium on "Romanticism and Criminal Justice," *Wordsworth Circle*, 19 (1988), pp. 65–108.

24 Michel Foucault, *Discipline and Punish*, Alan Sheridan (trans.) (London: Allen Lane, 1977), p. 7.
25 For studies of literature's relations with the criminal law, see Martin A. Kayman, *From Bow Street to Baker Street: Mystery, Detection and Narrative* (London: Macmillan, 1992) and Marie-Christine Leps, *Apprehending the Criminal* (Durham: Duke University Press, 1992), and on particular authors, Bruce Beiderwell, *Power and Punishment in Scott's Novels* (Athens: University of Georgia Press, 1992) and John R. Reed, *Dickens and Thackeray: Punishment and Forgiveness* (Athens: Ohio University Press, 1995).
26 Simon Petch, "Law, Equity and Conscience in Victorian England," *Victorian Literature and Culture*, 25 (1997), pp. 123–39.
27 David Sugarman, "Legal Theory, the Common Law Mind and the Making of the Text-book Tradition," in *Legal Theory and the Common Law*, William Twining (ed.) (Oxford: Blackwell, 1986), p. 54.
28 Morton J. Horwitz, *The Transformation of American Law 1780–1860* (Cambridge: Harvard University Press, 1977) argues that an "instrumental" philosophy of law emerged in America during the nineteenth century.
29 A. W. B. Simpson, "The Survival of the Common Law System," in his *Legal Theory and Legal History* (London: Hambledon, 1987), pp. 383–4.
30 See Patrick Brantlinger, *The Spirit of Reform* (Cambridge: Harvard University Press, 1977), Joseph Kestner, *Protest and Reform* (London: Methuen, 1985), and especially, Catherine Gallagher, *The Industrial Reformation of English Fiction 1832–1867* (University of Chicago Press, 1985).
31 Brantlinger, *Spirit of Reform*, pp. 215f.
32 See P. S. Atiyah, *The Rise and Fall of Freedom of Contract* (Oxford: Clarendon Press, 1979).
33 Atiyah, *Freedom of Contract*, p. 285; Houghton, *The Victorian Frame of Mind* (New Haven: Yale University Press, 1957), p. 145.
34 See Stein, *Legal Evolution*, pp. 99ff.
35 Atiyah, *Freedom of Contract*, pp. 402ff.
36 A brief statement of this disagreement may be found in Walter Michaels, *The Gold Standard and the Logic of American Naturalism* (Berkeley: University of California Press, 1987). Thomas also locates Melville's *Billy Budd* in the context of contemporary developments in the law of associations: see "*Billy Budd* and the Untold Story of the Law," *Cardozo Studies in Law and Literature*, 1 (1990), pp. 49–69; and chap. six below.
37 In a full-length survey of inheritance law in fiction Geoffrey Hogg argues that it persists until the 1880s: "An Examination of the Theme of Inheritance in the English Novel of the Nineteenth Century," thesis, University of Leicester 1981, pp. 8off.
38 E. P. Thompson, *Whigs and Hunters* (London: Allen Lane, 1977), p. 263.
39 Ibid., p. 264.
40 Douglas Hay, "Property, Authority and the Criminal Law," in Hay *et al.*, *Albion's Fatal Tree* (London: Allen Lane, 1975), pp. 17–63.

41 David Sugarman argues that Hay's concept of law allows no scope for change: see "Theory and Practice in Law and History: A Prologue to the Study of the Relationship between Law and Economy from a Socio-Historical Perspective," in *Law, State and Society*, Bob Fryer *et al.* (eds) (London: Croom Helm, 1981), p. 89. And see Thompson, *Whigs and Hunters*, p. 261.

42 Ferguson, *Law and Letters in Early American Culture*, pp. 11, 14–15.

43 Brook Thomas, *Cross-Examinations of Law and Literature* (New York: Cambridge University Press, 1987), pp. 218ff.

44 Quoted from *Introduction to the Study of the Law of the Constitution* by Geoffrey De Q. Walker, *The Rule of Law* (Melbourne University Press, 1988), p. 129.

45 See Sugarman, "Legal Theory, the Common Law Mind and the Making of the Text-book Tradition," pp. 48–9.

46 See Simpson, "Survival of the Common Law System," p. 384.

47 Walker, *The Rule of Law*, p. 2.

48 Sugarman, "Legal Theory, the Common Law Mind and the Making of the Text-book Tradition," p. 54. See also Stefan Collini, *Public Moralists: Political Thought and Intellectual Life in Britain 1850–1930* (Oxford: Clarendon Press, 1991), chap. seven.

49 "Pre-transformations: Victorian Britain," in *Law and Social Control*, Eugene Kamenka and Alice Erh-Soon Tay (eds) (London: Edward Arnold, 1978), p. 118.

50 Robert M. Cover, "The Folk-Tales of Justice," *Capital University Law Rev.*, 14 (1986), pp. 187–9.

51 See chap. three below.

52 See the title page of *Celebrated Trials and Remarkable Cases of Criminal Jurisprudence from the Earliest Records to the Year 1825* (London: Knight and Lacey, 1825), vol. I.

53 Lord Birkenhead, *Famous Trials* (London: Hutchinson, 1926), p. 7.

54 See *In Cold Blood* (London: Hamish Hamilton, 1966), *The Trial of Mrs. Harris* (London: Hamish Hamilton, 1986), and *Evil Angels* (Ringwood, Vic.: Viking, 1985) respectively.

55 *Caleb Williams, or Things as They Are*, Maurice Hindle (ed.) (1794; London: Penguin, 1988), p. 325.

56 Paul Jackson, *Natural Justice*, 2nd edn. (London: Sweet and Maxwell, 1979), pp. 14ff.

57 A summary of this change is given in Graham Parker, "The Prisoner in the Box – The Making of the Criminal Evidence Act, 1898," in *Law and Social Change in British History*, J. A. Guy and H. G. Beale (eds) (London: Royal Historical Society, 1984), pp. 156–75.

58 Christine L. Krueger, "Witnessing Women: Trial Testimony in Novels by Tonna, Gaskell, and Eliot," in *Representing Women: Law, Literature and Feminism*, Susan Sage Heinzelman and Zipporah Batshaw Wiseman (eds) (Durham: Duke University Press, 1994), pp. 337–55.

59 A. V. Dicey, *Lectures on the Relation between Law and Opinion in England during the Nineteenth Century* (2nd edn.; London: Macmillan, 1913), p. xc.

60 Simpson, "Survival of the Common Law System," p. 384.

61 Eugene Kamenka and Alice Erh-Soon Tay, "Social Traditions, Legal Traditions," in *Law and Social Control*, Kamenka and Tay (eds), p. 8.

62 Kamenka and Tay, "Social Traditions, Legal Traditions," p. 19.

63 Other writers who argue that Foucault has prematurely announced the death of law are Gillian Rose, *Dialectic of Nihilism* (Oxford: Blackwell, 1984), pp. 176ff; and François Ewald, "Norms, Discipline and the Law," *Representations*, 30 (Spring 1990), pp. 138–61.

64 For a Durkheimian interpretation of the modern *nomos* which, like Kamenka and Tay, argues for the obsolescence of the nineteenth-century tradition, see Richard Harvey Brown, "From Legalism to Delegitimation: Nineteenth-Century Solutions and Twentieth-Century Crises in Law and Social Change," *NLH*, 17 (1986), pp. 249–53; commenting on, Calvin Woodard, "Dimensions of Legal and Social Change: The Making and Remaking of the Common Law Tradition," *NLH*, 17 (1986), pp. 233–48.

65 Donald R. Kelley, *The Human Measure* (Cambridge: Harvard University Press, 1990), p. 274.

66 "Thus Spake Zarathustra," in *The Portable Nietzsche*, Walter Kauffmann (ed.) (1954; Harmondsworth: Penguin, 1968), p. 308.

67 James Fitzjames Stephen, *A History of the Criminal Law in England* (London: Macmillan, 1883), III, p. 366.

68 Ibid., p. 367.

69 D. H. Lawrence, "Democracy," posthumously published in *Phoenix* (1936); quoted in *The Good Society*, Anthony Arblaster and Steven Lukes (eds) (London: Methuen, 1971), p. 323.

70 Bertrand Russell, *Roads to Freedom: Socialism, Anarchism and Syndicalism* (London: Allen and Unwin, 1918); excerpted in *The Good Society*, p. 291.

71 See Richard H. Weisberg, *The Failure of the Word*, (New Haven: Yale University Press, 1984), pp. 17 and 19, quoting from Nietzsche, *Genealogy* 2.11:207 and 3.14:259 respectively.

72 Cover, "The Folk-Tales of Justice," part II.b.

3   TRUE TESTIMONY AND THE FOUNDATION OF *NOMOS* –
THE HEART OF *MIDLOTHIAN*

1 Quoted by Anand C. Chitnis, *The Scottish Enlightenment: A Social History* (London: Croom Helm, 1976), p. 76.

2 Ina Ferris, *The Space of Literary Authority: Gender, History and the Waverley Novels* (Ithaca: Cornell University Press, 1991), p. 23.

3 See Ian Simpson Ross, *Lord Kames and the Scotland of his Day* (London: Oxford University Press, 1972), p. 289.

4 Kelley, *The Human Measure*, p. 184.

5 Jane Millgate, "Scott and the Law: *The Heart of Midlothian*," in *Rough Justice: Essays on Crime in Literature*, M. L. Friedland (ed.) (University of Toronto Press, 1991), p. 100. This article is instructive on both Scott's legal career and the representation of law in this novel.

6 Duncan Forbes, "The Rationalism of Sir Walter Scott," *Cambridge Journal*, 7 (1953), pp. 25 and 31 respectively.

7 Ross, *Lord Kames and Scotland*, p. 55.

8 Ibid., p. 51.

9 Ibid., p. 55. In his statement of Scott's dual attitude Ross draws on the work of David Daiches, "Scott's Achievement as a Novelist," in *Walter Scott: Modern Judgments*, D. D. Devlin (ed.) (London: Macmillan, 1968), pp. 33–62.

10 Daniel Cottom, "Violence and Law in the Waverley Novels," *Studies in Romanticism*, 20 (1981), p. 80.

11 Alexander Welsh, *The Hero of the Waverley Novels* (New Haven: Yale University Press, 1963), p. 110.

12 See Robert A. Ferguson, *Law and Letters in American Culture* (Cambridge: Harvard University Press, 1984), p. 58.

13 Ibid., p. 68.

14 J. G. Lockhart, *Memoirs of Sir Walter Scott*, vol. i, chap. xv; quoted in David Daiches, *Sir Walter Scott and his World* (London: Thames and Hudson, 1971), p. 69. Graham McMaster considers in detail Scott's responses to Scots law reform proposals, and concludes they were "practical and highly informed," rather than reactionary: see *Scott and Society* (Cambridge University Press, 1981), p. 84.

15 P. H. Scott, *Walter Scott and Scotland* (Edinburgh: William Blackwood, 1981), p. 95, quotes from Lockhart's *Peter's Letters to his Kinfolk*: "the great genius to whom whatever is Scottish in thought, in feeling, or in recollection owes so large a share of its prolonged, or reanimated, or ennobled existence."

16 Henry Cockburn, *Memorials of his Time* (Edinburgh: Adam and Charles Black, 1856; rpt. James Thin, 1971), p. 241; also quoted by P. H. Scott, *Walter Scott and Scotland*, p. 96.

17 Mary Lascelles, *The Story-teller Retrieves the Past* (Oxford: Clarendon Press, 1980), p. 88, closely studies Scott's response to his sources.

18 Sir Walter Scott, *Waverley*, Claire Lamont (ed.) (Oxford: Clarendon Press, 1981), p. 352. See also *Sir Walter Scott: On Novelists and Fiction*, Ioan Williams (ed.) (London: Routledge and Kegan Paul, 1968), p. 413.

19 Avrom Fleishman, *The English Historical Novel* (Baltimore: Johns Hopkins University Press, 1971), p. 52.

20 "Daniel Defoe," in Sir Walter Scott, *The Lives of the Novelists* (1827; rpt. London: Dent, 1910), pp. 361–2.

21 Sir Walter Scott, "Review of *Fleetwood, or the New Man of Feeling*," *Edinburgh Review*, 6 (1805); see Williams (ed.), *Scott on Novelists*, pp. 193–4.

22 Sir Walter Scott, *The Heart of Midlothian*, Claire Lamont (ed.) (1818; rpt. London: Oxford University Press, 1982), chap. i, pp. 21–2. Lamont's text is that of the Magnum Opus edition of 1830. Dual references to chapter and page are given parenthetically in the text.

23 James Kerr, "Fiction against History: *Redgauntlet* and the Power of Romance," *Texas Studies in Literature and Language*, 29 (1987), p. 237.

24 James Fitzjames Stephen, "The Relation of Novels to Life," *Cambridge Essays Contributed By Members of the University*, 1855; rpt. *Victorian Criticism of the Novel*, Edwin M. Eigner and George J. Worth (eds), pp. 100–1.

25 Welsh, *Strong Representations*, p. 153.

26 On this point see also Kerr, "Fiction against History," pp. 246–9.

27 See Scott, *Heart of Midlothian*, p. 544, note 3.

28 The original formulation was that of Daiches: see note 9 above.

29 George Levine, *The Realistic Imagination* (University of Chicago Press, 1981), chap. iv. Levine's argument emphasizes by contrast the prescriptiveness of Cottom's account of the opposition between law and violence, past and present.

30 For a full discussion of *The Heart of Midlothian* as an exploration of the problematic bases of criminal punishment in Enlightenment thought, see Bruce Beiderwell, *Power and Punishment in Scott's Novels* (Athens: University of Georgia Press, 1992), chap. 4.

31 Cf. Bender, *Imagining the Penitentiary* (University of Chicago Press, 1987), p. 32.

32 The quoted phrase is V. S. Pritchett's. See *The Living Novel* (1946; rpt. London: Arrow Books, 1960), p. 65.

33 Scott, *Heart of Midlothian*, p. 528, note 23, "Child Murder."

34 This argument derives from Judith Wilt, *Secret Leaves: The Novels of Sir Walter Scott* (Chicago and London: University of Chicago Press, 1985), pp. 131–4. For a contrary argument, that "there is no perceptible sentiment on Scott's part that the cruel and stupid *law* should be changed," see John Sutherland, *The Life of Sir Walter Scott* (Oxford: Blackwell, 1995), p. 215.

35 Fiona Robertson, *Legitimate Histories: Scott, Gothic and the Authorities of Fiction* (Oxford: Clarendon Press, 1994), p. 149.

36 McMaster, "Realism and Romance in *The Heart of Midlothian*," *Cambridge Quarterly*, 10 (1981/2), pp. 202–18; Kerr, "Scott's Fable of Regeneration: *The Heart of Midlothian*," *ELH*, 53 (1986), pp. 801–20.

37 George Eliot, *Adam Bede* (1859; rpt. London: Zodiac Press, 1952), chap. 17, p. 169. Interestingly, Eliot's novel also narrates a case of child murder.

38 Wilt, *Secret Leaves*, p. 134.

39 See Kelley, *The Human Measure* (Cambridge: Harvard University Press, 1990), p. x.

40 For a discussion of presumptive infanticide which focuses on the women in this and other texts, see Simon Petch, "The Poetics of Infanticide," in *The Happy Couple: Law and Literature* (Annandale: The Federation Press, 1994), pp. 52–61.

41 Kerr, "Scott's Fable of Regeneration," p. 804. Cf. Welsh, *Hero of Waverley Novels*, p. 131.
42 Karl Kroeber, *Romantic Narrative Art* (1960; rpt. Madison: University of Wisconsin Press, 1966), pp. 185–7.
43 Leland Monk, "The Novel as Prison: Scott's *Heart of Midlothian*," *Novel*, 27 (1994), p. 298, argues that the doubling of the name Duncan indicates a symbiotic relationship between law and lawlessness.
44 Margaret Movshin Criscuola, "The Porteous Mob: Fact and Truth in *The Heart of Midlothian*," *ELN*, 22 (1984), pp. 45ff notes Scott's use of univocal crowds to represent national character.
45 P. H. Scott, *Scott and Scotland*, p. 54.
46 Cf. Virginia Woolf's image, "Gas at Abbotsford," *Collected Essays* (London: Hogarth, 1966), pp. 134–9.

4 REFORMIST CRITIQUE IN THE MID-VICTORIAN
"LEGAL NOVEL" – *BLEAK HOUSE*

1 *Athenaeum*, 6 Mar. 1852, rpt. *Bleak House: A Casebook*, A. E. Dyson (ed.) (London: Macmillan, 1969), pp. 49–50.
2 Generations of lawyers have written on these cases from the point of view of legal history. Whilst often neglecting the conventions of fictional discourse, they form a distinctive part of the novels' reception. Some such responses are engaged with below. A good recent example is K. J. A. Asche, "Dickens and the Law," in *The Happy Couple: Law and Literature*, Turner and Williams (eds), pp. 81–93.
3 *Athenaeum*, 17 Sept 1853, rpt. in Dyson (ed.), *Casebook*, p. 55.
4 Lennard Davis, *Factual Fictions: The Origins of the English Novel* (New York: Columbia University Press, 1983), discusses the influence of such narratives on the development of the novel. Compare the "Last Speech etc. of Margaret Murdockson" in *Heart of Midlothian* and the broadside on the death of Billy Budd.
5 For a history of law reporting see J. H. Baker, *An Introduction to English Legal History* (2nd edn., London: Butterworths, 1979), pp. 151–8.
6 Philip Collins, *Dickens and Crime* (1962; rpt. London: Macmillan, 1994), p. 182.
7 *The Speeches of Charles Dickens*, K. J. Fielding (ed.) (Hemel Hempstead: Harvester-Wheatsheaf, 1988), pp. 97–8.
8 Frye points especially to the trial in *Alice in Wonderland* and the inheritance plot in *Wuthering Heights* ("what Satan could do with the law of entail!"). See "Literature and the Law," *Law Society of Upper Canada Gazette*, 4 (1970), pp. 70–7.
9 Samuel Warren, *Ten Thousand A Year* (1841; Edinburgh: Blackwood, 1854), p. 225.
10 On the ideology of "family" see Andrew Blake, *Reading Victorian Fiction* (London: Macmillan, 1989), p. 52. See also Peter Brooks, *Reading for the Plot* (New York: Knopf, 1984), p. 63.

11 *Quarterly Review*, 79 (1846), p. 61. An excerpt from this review containing the reference to the "legal novel" is printed in *A Victorian Art of Fiction*, John Charles Olmstead (ed.) (New York: Garland, 1979), I, pp. 527–30.

12 Review of *Tales by a Barrister*, p. 63.

13 Ibid., p. 68.

14 See Patrick Brantlinger, *The Spirit of Reform*, pp. 215ff.

15 Ibid., p. 1.

16 Another discussion of the use of novels in the advocacy of reform is Joseph Kestner, *Protest and Reform* (London: Methuen, 1985).

17 Letter to Mrs. Cropper, 20 Dec. 1852. See *The Pilgrim Edition of the Letters of Charles Dickens*, VI (1850–2), Graham Storey, Kathleen Tillotson and Nina Burgis (eds) (Oxford: Clarendon, 1988), p. 827.

18 Marjorie Stone, "Dickens, Bentham and the Fictions of the Law: A Victorian Controversy and its Consequences," *Victorian Studies*, 29 (1985), pp. 125–54.

19 The concluding sentence to Dickens's Preface to *Bleak House*. See the authoritative Norton Critical edition of the novel, George Ford and Sylvère Monod (eds) (New York: Norton, 1977), p. 4. All future references will be included parenthetically in the chapter. On pushpin, see Jeremy Bentham, "The Rationale of Reward," *Works*, John Bowring (ed.) (New York: Russell and Russell, 1962), II, p. 253.

20 A. V. Dicey, *Law and Popular Opinion in Nineteenth-Century England* (London: Macmillan, 1905), p. 419, quoting Sir Henry Maine, *Popular Government*, p. 153.

21 Brantlinger, *Spirit of Reform*, p. 41.

22 John Butt and Kathleen Tillotson, "The Topicality of *Bleak House*," in their *Dickens at Work* (London: Methuen, 1957), p. 187; rpt. Dyson (ed.), *Casebook*, p. 116.

23 These quotes are taken from contemporary reviews excerpted in Dyson (ed.), *Casebook*, pp. 62, 56, 82, 69–70, and 87 respectively.

24 Sir Gerald Hurst K. C., "Arising out of *Bleak House*," in his *Lincoln's Inn Essays* (London: Constable, 1949), p. 112.

25 See *Bleak House*, p. 3 and Susan Shatto, *The Companion to Bleak House* (London: Unwin Hyman, 1988), p. 14.

26 Hurst, "Arising out of *Bleak House*," p. 113.

27 See for example, J. Hillis Miller, "Introduction to *Bleak House*," *Bleak House*, Norman Page (ed.) (Harmondsworth: Penguin, 1971), pp. 11–34; Jack Lindsay, *Charles Dickens: A Biographical and Critical Study* (London: Andrew Dakers, 1950); and Mark Spilka, "Religious folly," in Dyson (ed.), *Casebook*, pp. 204–23; as respective examples of these approaches.

28 John R. Reed, *Dickens and Thackeray: Punishment and Forgiveness* (Athens: Ohio University Press, 1995), p. 208.

29 Quoted in W. S. Holdsworth, *A History of English Law*, XIII (London: Methuen, 1952), p. 306.

30 See, e.g., his strictures on "split jurisdiction" in "Justice and Codification Petitions." In Jeremy Bentham, *Works*, John Bowring (ed.), V, pp. 481–4.

31  Q. D. Leavis, "Bleak House: A Chancery World," in F. R. and Q. D. Leavis, *Dickens the Novelist* (London: Chatto and Windus, 1970), p. 123.
32  Many critics have insisted on the dual, social and symbolic, function of Chancery: see, for example, Angus Wilson, *The World of Charles Dickens* (London: Secker and Warburg, 1970), p. 232; and James M. Brown, *Charles Dickens: Novelist in the Marketplace* (London: Macmillan, 1982), p. 10.
33  Quoted by W. S. Holdsworth, *Charles Dickens as a Legal Historian* (New Haven: Yale University Press, 1929), p. 80. For a full account of this case and its influence on *Bleak House* see E. T. Jaques, *Charles Dickens in Chancery* (1914; rpt. New York: Haskell House, 1972).
34  Douglas Hamer, "Dickens and the Old Court of Chancery," *N&Q* [N.S.], 17 (1970), pp. 341–7, argues thus.
35  Quoted by Baker, *Introduction to English Legal History*, p. 90.
36  Ibid., p. 84.
37  Ibid., p. 95.
38  See *Snell's Principles of Equity*, 8th edn. (London: Sweet and Maxwell, 1887), chap. 11.
39  Edgar Johnson, *Charles Dickens: His Tragedy and Triumph* (New York: Simon and Schuster, 1952), 2 vols; 11. p. 771; excerpted in Dyson (ed.), *Casebook*, p. 145. Johnson refers to the case under the name "Jennings" but the correct name appears to be "Jennens": see Hurst, "Arising out of *Bleak House*," pp. 116–17.
40  See Robert A. Donovan, "Structure and Idea in *Bleak House*," *ELH*, 19 (1962), p. 181 for a discussion of the appropriateness of a Chancery suit as a vehicle for Dickens's exploration of the theme of the human responsibility to care for others. On the Chancellor's *parens patriae* jurisdiction see D. M. Kerly, *An Historical Sketch of the Equitable Jurisdiction of the Court of Chancery* (Cambridge University Press, 1890), p. 225; and for a modern discussion see R. E. Megarry and P. V. Baker, *Snell's Principles of Equity*, 25th edn. (London: Sweet and Maxwell, 1960), p. 482.
41  Hamer, "Dickens and Chancery," p. 342.
42  Leigh Hunt, *The Autobiography of Leigh Hunt* (1850; London: Cresset Press, 1949), pp. 267–8. On the question whether Dickens knew Hunt's book, see R. D. Altick, "Harold Skimpole Revisited," in *The Life and Times of Leigh Hunt* (Iowa City: Friends of the University of Iowa Libraries, 1985), pp. 1–15. Altick shows numerous connections between Hunt's circumstances, personal qualities and literary works, and the novels of Dickens.
43  D. A. Miller, *The Novel and the Police* (Berkeley: University of California Press, 1988), p. 90.
44  Irene E. Woods, "On the Significance of Jarndyce and Jarndyce," *Dickens Quarterly*, 1 (1984), pp. 811–17 argues that Dickens derives this trope, through Carlyle, from the German Romantics.
45  J. Hillis Miller, "Introduction," *Bleak House* (Harmondsworth, Penguin, 1971), pp. 11, 17.
46  Ibid., p. 34.

47 This argument by D. A. Miller is further discussed below.
48 Donovan, "Structure and Idea," p. 189, so characterizes the plot of *Bleak House*.
49 Jeremy Hawthorn, *Bleak House* (Basingstoke: Macmillan, 1987), pp. 57–8, insists that the combination of "diegetic" and "extradiegetic" narrators is "a problem."
50 Holdsworth, *Charles Dickens as a Legal Historian*, pp. 92–3.
51 For an important review of this literature, arguing that the novel is "an extension and a critique of the sexual division into separate spheres," see Virginia Blain, "Double Vision and the Double Standard in *Bleak House*," *Literature and History*, 11 (1985), pp. 31–46.
52 For a different interpretation of this aspect of the text, see Anny Sadrin, *Parentage and Inheritance in the Novels of Charles Dickens* (Cambridge University Press, 1994), chap. five.
53 See for example Edgar Johnson, note 39 and Q. D. Leavis, note 31.
54 Holdsworth, *Charles Dickens as a Legal Historian*, pp. 105–7.
55 J. Hillis Miller, "Introduction," *Bleak House*, pp. 11, 29.
56 D. A. Miller, *The Novel and the Police*, p. 92.
57 Ibid.
58 Hurst, "Arising out of *Bleak House*," pp. 118–19.
59 David Suchoff, *Critical Theory and the Novel: Mass Society and Cultural Criticism in Dickens, Melville and Kafka* (Madison: University of Wisconsin Press, 1994), p. 25.
60 Contrast Franco Moretti's argument that the English *Bildungsroman*, shaped by a restorative and not a transformational "culture of justice," is characterized by a plot of loss and recovery in which the ending restores the hero(ine) and so renders much of the plot an aberration: *The Way of the World* (London: Verso, 1987). Michal Peled Ginsburg argues that transformational plots can be traced in Dickens, though less so in *Bleak House* than in *Our Mutual Friend*. See "The Case Against Plot in *Bleak House* and *Our Mutual Friend*," *ELH*, 59 (1992), pp. 175–95.
61 Hillis Miller, Introduction to Penguin *Bleak House*, pp. 14ff.
62 Shatto, *Companion*, p. 35.
63 See Dyson (ed.), *Casebook*, p. 156.
64 Plato, *The Republic*, F. M. Cornford (trans.) (Oxford: Clarendon Press, 1941), chap. XIV (IV.441–4). This allusion is made in a slightly different argument by Judith S. Koffler, "Injustice as Disease: the Homeless in *Bleak House*," Dickens Project – Law and Humanities Institute Conference, Santa Cruz, 6 August 1988.
65 D. A. Miller, *The Novel and the Police*, p. 101. A more general account of the representation of the family in reformist fiction is given by Catherine Gallagher, *The Industrial Reformation of English Fiction*, chap. five.
66 P. J. M. Scott's phrase, from *Reality and Comic Confidence in Charles Dickens* (Fulham: Vision Books, 1979), p. 109, is quoted by Hawthorn, *Bleak House*, p. 32.

67 Hamer, "Dickens and Chancery," p. 361: "The world was full of Gridleys trying to save a few pounds against a brother and finding themselves penniless in the end . . ."

68 See Patricia Hollis (ed.), *Women in Public: Documents of the Victorian Women's Movement* (London: Allen and Unwin, 1979), Part Six, for contemporary accounts of the legal status of women.

69 Note also "the valley of the shadow of the law" (chap. 32) with its echoes of the 23rd Psalm: see Garrett Stewart, "Epitaphic Chapter Titles and the New Mortality of *Bleak House*," in *Charles Dickens's Bleak House*, Harold Bloom (ed.) (New York: Chelsea House, 1987), p. 86.

70 See John O. Jordan, "*Bleak House* and the Crisis of Legitimacy," Dickens Project/Law and Humanities Institute Conference, Santa Cruz, 5 August 1988. For a different reading of Esther's illegitimacy, see Jenny Bourne Taylor, "Representing Illegitimacy in Victorian Culture," in *Victorian Identities*, Ruth Robbins and Julian Wolfreys (eds) (Basingstoke: Macmillan, 1996), p. 138.

71 The significance of will in this latter sense is explored in Timothy Peltason, "Esther's Will," *ELH*, 59 (1992), pp. 671–91.

72 See Hurst, "Arising out of *Bleak House*," p. 117.

5  REPRESENTATION, INHERITANCE AND ANTI-REFORMISM
IN THE "LEGAL NOVEL" − *ORLEY FARM*

1 *Orley Farm*, David Skilton (ed.) (Oxford University Press, 1985), vol. 1, p. 1. All subsequent references are to this edition. Both volume and page number are cited, hereafter, in the body of the chapter. For a good discussion of Trollope's mixture of historical and metafictional narrative rhetoric, see George Levine, *The Realistic Imagination* (University of Chicago Press, 1981), chap. 9.

2 *The Times*, 26 Dec. 1862, p. 5.

3 Asa Briggs, "Trollope, Bagehot and the English Constitution," in *Victorian People* (Harmondsworth: Penguin, 1965), pp. 95–123.

4 Winifred Gregory Gerrould and James Thayer Gerrould, *A Guide to Trollope* (1948; Westport: Greenwood Press, 1970), pp. 54 and 137–9.

5 See in general Stephen Wall, *Trollope and Character* (London: Faber and Faber, 1988) and, in reference to a Trollopian lawyer, Rowland McMaster, *Trollope and the Law* (London: Macmillan, 1986) ,chap. 3, "Mr. Chaffanbrass for the Defence."

6 See McMaster, *Trollope and the Law*, chap. 2: "Sex in the Barrister's Chambers."

7 Wall, *Trollope and Character*, p. 302.

8 An essay of this name by James Fitzjames Stephen appeared in the *Cornhill Magazine*, 3 (1861), pp. 447–59, in the same issue as the final instalment of Trollope's previous novel, *Framley Parsonage*, and before the commencement of *Orley Farm*. McMaster suggests that Trollope must have been

aware of it: see McMaster, *Trollope and the Law*, p. 10. Trollope rehearses many of the arguments that Stephen seeks to counter.

9 "Review of *Orley Farm*," *Saturday Review*, 14 (1862), pp. 444–5.

10 Glynn-Ellen Fisichelli, "The Language of Law and Love: Anthony Trollope's *Orley Farm*," *ELH*, 61 (1994), p. 642. By contrast L. J. Swingle, *Romanticism and Anthony Trollope* (Ann Arbor: University of Michigan Press, 1990), p. 14, emphasizes the "intricate drama of Lady Mason's crime, her subsequent trial in a court of law, and the problems raised thereby concerning accurate judgment upon her innocence or guilt."

11 McMaster, *Trollope and the Law*, p. 60; Wall, *Trollope and Character*, p. 305.

12 Quoted in *Anthony Trollope: The Critical Heritage*, Donald Smalley (ed.) (London: Routledge and Kegan Paul, 1969), p. 147. Smalley speculates that the anonymous reviewer is Richard Holt Hutton.

13 Walter Kendrick's idea of pellucid language (*The Novel-Machine* [Baltimore: Johns Hopkins University Press, 1980], p. 46) is quoted by Fisichelli, "Language of Law and Love," pp. 646–7.

14 See note 2 above. Excerpts of the review appear in Smalley, *The Critical Heritage*, pp. 160–3, but much of the discussion of the law is omitted.

15 Sir Francis Newbolt K. C. "Reg. v Mason," *Nineteenth Century and After*, 95 (1924), pp. 230–1.

16 Sir Owen Dixon, "Sir Roger Scatcherd's Will in Anthony Trollope's *Doctor Thorne*," *Jesting Pilate* (Melbourne: Law Book Co., 1965), p. 71.

17 *Saturday Review*, p. 445. Smalley suggests that this review was written by Sir Henry Maine.

18 See especially Maine in the *Saturday Review*, Newbolt, and Newbolt's critic, Clement Franklin Robinson, "Trollope's Jury Trials," *Nineteenth Century Fiction*, 6 (1952), pp. 247–68.

19 Stephen, "Morality of Advocacy," p. 450.

20 Ibid., p. 458.

21 See Raymond Cocks, *Foundations of the Modern Bar* (London: Sweet and Maxwell, 1983), p. 21.

22 Dallas, *The Times*, p. 5.

23 Coral Lansbury, *The Reasonable Man: Trollope's Legal Fiction* (Princeton University Press, 1981), p. 158.

24 *Anthony Trollope and his Contemporaries* (London: Longman, 1972), p. 26. In the introduction to his edition of *Orley Farm* Skilton argues persuasively that Trollope rejects the suspense of the sensation novel for the demands of realism: see p. x. It is a point worthy of critical attention that the novel promotes some inadvertent suspense through naming a number of minor characters "Johnson." This is Lady Mason's maiden name, and the name of one of the commercial travellers met by Dockwrath in Leeds, a coincidence which led this reader to wonder whether he might turn out to be related to her and the possessor of new evidence. A third Johnson accompanies Furnival to the Birmingham conference! A possible explanation of this slip is Trollope's pace of writing.

25 On the persistent technical emphasis and resistance to theory in legal education, see Cocks, *Foundations of Modern Bar*, chap. 5. Newbolt's article was published in the *Law Journal* and in *Nineteenth Century and After*.

26 Stephen, "Morality of Advocacy," p. 455.

27 This exchange is summarized in Donald Smalley's introduction to *Anthony Trollope: The Critical Heritage*, p. 23. In his study of *Doctor Thorne* in the context of Victorian anthropology, Christopher Herbert describes this insertion as a "stylistic perversity meant to throw into relief the novel's fixation on the decoding of 'norms, rules and systems.'" See Christopher Herbert, *Culture and Anomie: Ethnographic Imagination in the Nineteenth Century* (Chicago: University of Chicago Press, 1991), p. 282.

28 Dixon, *Jesting Pilate*, p. 71.

29 *Phineas Finn* (1867–69; London: Oxford University Press, 1982), I. chap. 29.

30 Kenneth Graham, *English Criticism of the Novel 1865–1900* (Oxford: Clarendon Press, 1965), p. 26. Though it antedates this post-1865 critical context, *Orley Farm* amply illustrates the point made by Graham and may be taken as an early example of the same trend.

31 Quoted by R. C. Terry, *Victorian Popular Fiction* (London: Macmillan, 1983), p. 175 n. 21.

32 Skilton, *Anthony Trollope and his Contemporaries* (London: Longman, 1972), p. 144.

33 Ibid., p. 145.

34 Thomas Pavel, *Fictional Worlds* (Cambridge: Harvard University Press, 1986), p. 106.

35 "Representation," in *Critical Terms for Literary Study*, Frank Lentricchia and Thomas McLaughlin (eds) (University of Chicago Press, 1990), pp. 11–22 at p. 12. See also Hanna Pitkin, *The Concept of Representation* (Berkeley: University of California Press, 1967). For a historical argument linking concepts of political and novelistic representation in the 1860s, see Catherine Gallagher, *The Industrial Reformation of English Fiction* (University of Chicago Press, 1985), chap. nine.

36 Wall, *Trollope and Character*, p. 289. A comparable argument is made by P. D. Edwards, *Anthony Trollope: His Art and Scope* (University of Queensland Press, 1977), pp. 109–10.

37 Lansbury, *The Reasonable Man*, p. 169. Cf. Laura Hapke, "The Lady as Criminal: Contradiction and Resolution in Trollope's *Orley Farm*," *Victorian Newsletter*, 66 (1984), p. 19: ". . . Trollope, himself her advocate, has done everything literarily possible to persuade his jury of readers to the lady's acquittal."

38 See Anthony Trollope, *An Autobiography*, intro. Michael Sadleir (1883; London: Oxford University Press, 1923), p. 152.

39 J. B. White, *Heracles' Bow* (Madison: University of Wisconsin Press, 1985), pp. 174ff.

40 Anthea Trodd discusses Lady Mason's dramatic lifting of her veil as a sign of the private Victorian woman emerging into a public sphere in *Domestic*

*Crime in the Victorian Novel* (London: Macmillan, 1989), chap. six. The veil is a motif in many court scenes involving respectable women, which Trodd traces back to the appearance of the Deans sisters in *Heart of Midlothian*.

41 Brantlinger, *The Spirit of Reform*, p. 215.

42 See the editor's note to *Orley Farm*, p. 105.

43 See Brian Rodgers, "The Social Science Association 1857–86," *Manchester School of Economic and Social Studies*, 20 (1952), pp. 283–310.

44 On this point see Robert Hughes, "'Spontaneous Order' and the Politics of Trollope's Fiction," *Nineteenth Century Fiction*, 41 (1986), pp. 32–48.

45 Levine, *The Realistic Imagination*, p. 188. See also Hughes, "Spontaneous Order," p. 42.

46 Trollope, *Autobiography*, p. 266.

47 See Robert Tracy, "*Lana Medicata Fuco*: Trollope's Classicism," in *Trollope Centenary Essays*, John Halperin (ed.) (London: Macmillan, 1982), pp. 1–23.

48 Ibid., p. 11.

49 For a general account of Maine's significance, see R. C. J. Cocks, *Sir Henry Maine* (Cambridge University Press, 1988). I have taken the phrase "legal evolution" from Peter Stein's monograph of that name.

50 See *A New Dictionary of Sociology*, G. Duncan Mitchell (ed.) (London: Routledge and Kegan Paul, 1979).

51 "Introduction" to *Family and Inheritance*, Jack Goody, Joan Thirsk and E. P. Thompson (eds) (Cambridge University Press, 1976), p. 1.

52 Franco Moretti, *The Way of the World* (London: Verso, 1987), defines this interest in the inheritance of rights as the characteristic of the English *Bildungsroman*.

53 Sir Frederick Pollock and F. W. Maitland quoted by Michael Seidel, *Satiric Inheritance: Rabelais to Sterne* (Princeton University Press, 1979), p. 40.

54 See, e.g., Juliet McMaster, "Trollope's Country Estates," *Trollope Centenary Essays*, Halperin (ed.), p. 79; and Richard C. Burke, "Accommodation and Transcendence: Last Wills in Trollope," *Dickens Studies Annual*, 15 (1986), pp. 297ff. Peter Ingram notes that the representation of property in Trollope is dominated by abstract legal discourse rather than by physical description of places: see Ingram, "Victorian Values: Law and Justice in the Novels of Trollope," in *Tall Stories? Reading Law and Literature*, John Morison and Christine Bell (eds) (Aldershot: Dartmouth, 1996), pp. 228–9.

55 See Skilton's introduction to *Orley Farm*, p. xiii: "The law fails, but the novel sees justice done", for example.

56 As noted in chap. 1, John Sutherland, *Victorian Fiction* (Basingstoke: Macmillan, 1995), p. 163, points to the link between the concept of poetic justice and the attraction of the novel to law and lawyers.

57 See John R. Reed, *Victorian Conventions* (Ohio University Press, 1975), chap. 12 for a general discussion of the inheritance convention. See also Raymond Williams, *The English Novel from Dickens to Lawrence* (London: Chatto and Windus, 1970), p. 86 for a brief discussion of Trollope's use of inheritance in the unquestioning transmission of gentry values.

58 Alexander Pettit, "Sympathetic Criminality in the Mid-Victorian Novel," *Dickens Studies Annual*, 19 (1990), pp. 281–300.

59 Dallas, Review, p. 5.

60 Quoted by J. G. A. Pocock, *Politics, Language and Time* (Cambridge University Press, 1972), p. 212.

61 Ibid.

62 See e.g. Lansbury, *The Reasonable Man*, p. 168; Wall, *Trollope and Character*, p. 304.

## 6 POWER, CHANCE AND THE RULE OF LAW – *BILLY BUDD, SAILOR*

1 *Collected Poems of Herman Melville*, Howard P. Vincent (ed.) (Chicago: Packard, 1947), p. 234.

2 See Kenneth Graham, *Indirections of the Novel: James, Conrad, Forster* (Cambridge University Press, 1988).

3 Darwin's *Voyage of the "Beagle"* appears in the list compiled by Merton R. Sealts, *Melville's Reading* (Madison: University of Wisconsin Press, 1966), as item no. 175.

4 On the place of law in Darwin's thought see George Levine, *Darwin and the Novelists* (Cambridge: Harvard University Press, 1988), pp. 89ff.

5 See generally Weisberg, *The Failure of the Word*; Thomas, *Cross-Examinations of Law and Literature*; Johnson, "Melville's Fist: The Execution of *Billy Budd*," in *The Critical Difference* (Baltimore: Johns Hopkins University Press, 1980), pp. 79–109.

6 Cover, *Justice Accused: Antislavery and the Judicial Process* (New Haven: Yale University Press, 1975), "Prelude: Of Creon and Captain Vere."

7 Cover, "Violence and the Word," *Yale LJ*, 95 (1986), p. 1609.

8 Ferguson, *Law and Letters in American Culture* (Cambridge: Harvard University Press, 1984), p. 288.

9 Herman Melville, *Billy Budd, Sailor and Other Stories*, Harold Beaver (ed.) (Harmondsworth: Penguin, 1967), pp. 387–8. This edition reprints the text of *Billy Budd* established by Harrison Hayford and Merton Sealts. All subsequent references are incorporated parenthetically in the body of the chapter.

10 Thomas, *Cross-Examinations of Law and Literature* (New York: Cambridge University Press, 1987), p. 9.

11 Thomas, "Legal Fictions of Melville and Shaw," *Critical Inquiry*, 11 (1984), p. 24.

12 Thomas, *Cross-Examinations*, p. 212.

13 See for example Charles Robert Anderson, "The Genesis of *Billy Budd*," *American Literature*, 12 (1940), pp. 329–46; Thomas, *Cross-Examinations*, pp. 206–14; and Michael Paul Rogin, "The *Somers Mutiny* and *Billy Budd*: Melville in the Penal Colony," in *Herman Melville: Modern Critical Views*, Harold Bloom (ed.) (New York: Chelsea House, 1986), pp. 197–221.

14 Thomas, *Cross-Examinations*, p. 220.

15 Ibid., p. 222.
16 Foucault, *Discipline and Punish*, Alan Sheridan (trans.) (London: Penguin, 1979), p. 169.
17 See Weisberg, *The Failure of the Word*, pp. 147–59. The following is a summary of the errors listed by Weisberg: (i) only squadron or fleet commanders, not individual ship commanders, were commissioned to conduct court-martial; (ii) no capital offence could be tried or punished without the complaint being referred to the Admiral; (iii) at least five judges were required to constitute a court; (iv) summary proceedings were allowable only for trivial offences; (v) Vere acts as sole witness, prosecutor, and has a commanding influence over the members of the court; (vi) a capital offence could not be executed without review by the admiral; (vii) while hanging is the sole prescribed penalty for Billy's crime, leniency was usually offered and a lesser punishment imposed; and (viii) court-martial should be conducted in the most open part of the ship, and not in secret.
18 Stuart-Smith, "Military Law: Its History, Administration and Practice," *Law Quarterly Review*, 85 (1969), pp. 478–504; Bishop, *Justice Under Fire* (New York: Charterhouse, 1974), p. 8.
19 Warner Berthoff, "The Example of Billy Budd," rpt. in *Twentieth-Century Interpretations of Billy Budd*, Howard P. Vincent (ed.) (Englewood Cliffs: Prentice-Hall, 1971), p. 70.
20 William Domnarski, "Law-Literature Criticism: Charting a Desirable Course with *Billy Budd*," *Journal of Legal Education*, 34 (1984), p. 707.
21 The quoted phrase is from Jack Ledbetter, "The Trial of Billy Budd, Foretopman," *ABA Journal*, 58 (1972), p. 614: Domnarski, "Law-Literature Criticism," p. 706.
22 "Vere's Use of the Forms: Means and Ends in *Billy Budd*," *American Literature*, 47 (1975), p. 43.
23 Ives, "*Billy Budd* and the Articles of War," *American Literature*, 34 (1962), pp. 31–8; Weisberg, pp. 163ff.
24 Ives, "Billy Budd," p. 34.
25 Herman Melville, *Redburn, White-Jacket and Moby-Dick*, G. Thomas Tanselle (ed.) (New York: Library of America, 1983), p. 666.
26 Melville, *White-Jacket*, p. 498.
27 Ibid., p. 662.
28 John P. McWilliams, *Hawthorne, Melville and the American Character* (Cambridge University Press, 1984), p. 223.
29 Weisberg, *Failure of the Word*, pp. 155–7, discusses the two meanings of "martial law," but does not differentiate them historically.
30 Reich, "The Tragedy of Justice in *Billy Budd*," *Yale Review*, 56 (1967), p. 375.
31 Ibid., p. 386.
32 For a study of the contingencies which underpinned the prosecution of the sailors and cast doubt on the "necessity" of Coleridge's conclusion, see A. W. B. Simpson, *Cannibalism and the Common Law* (1984; Harmondsworth: Penguin, 1986).

33 This aspect is central to Berthoff's argument: see note 19 above.
34 For a more positive formulation of the narrator's hypotheses, see Susan Weiner, *Law in Art: Melville's Major Fiction and Nineteenth-Century American Law* (Bern: Peter Lang, 1992), p. 154.
35 Domnarski, "Law-Literature," p. 703.
36 Johnson, "Melville's Fist," p. 94.
37 Ibid., p. 104.
38 Ibid., p. 107.
39 Ibid., p. 83.
40 Ibid., p. 84.
41 Ibid., pp. 85–6.
42 Martin J. Wiener, "Some Images of Man and their Relation to the Administration of the Criminal Law in Britain," in *Legal Record and Historical Reality*, Thomas G. Watkin (ed.) (London: Hambledon Press, 1989), p. 213.
43 Ibid., pp. 206–7.
44 Lawrence Friedman, *A History of American Law* (New York: Simon and Schuster, 1973), p. 514.
45 See Leonard W. Levy, *The Law of the Commonwealth and Chief Justice Shaw* (1957; New York: Harper and Row, 1967), pp. 211–17; and *American Legal History: Cases and Materials*, Kermit L. Hall, William M. Wiecek and Paul Finkelman (eds) (New York: Oxford University Press, 1991), pp. 290–4.
46 E.g., Weisberg, *Failure of the Word*, p. 166.
47 Thomas, *Cross-Examinations*, p. 234.
48 Johnson, "Melville's Fist," pp. 105–6.
49 Lawrence Douglas, "Discursive Limits: Narrative and Judgment in *Billy Budd*," *Mosaic*, 27 (1994), p. 152.
50 Editors' Introduction to *Billy Budd* (University of Chicago Press, 1962), Part Three: "Perspectives for Criticism."
51 Among the critics who have adopted the function of "judge" are Weisberg, pp. 145ff, "The Framework for Adjudication"; Steven Mailloux, "Judging the Judge: *Billy Budd* and 'Proof to all Sophistries,'" *Cardozo Studies in Law and Literature*, 1 (1989), pp. 83–8; and, most fully, Johnson, "Melville's Fist," p. 102: "it is judging, not murdering, that Melville is asking us to judge," and Brook Thomas, "*Billy Budd* and the Judgment of Silence," *Bucknell Review*, 27, No. 1 (1982), pp. 57–78, a reply to Johnson.

## 7 FROM SYMPATHETIC CRIMINAL TO IMPERIAL LAW-GIVER – *LORD JIM*

1 The novel first appeared as a serial in *Blackwood's Edinburgh Magazine* during 1899–1900. All references to *Lord Jim* in this chapter are to John Batchelor's World Classics edition (Oxford University Press, 1983). This text is based on the Dent Collected Edition of 1946, which is in turn based on the first edition of 1900.
2 See Weisberg, *Failure of the Word*, p. 7.

3 The enrolment of Conrad in the modernist canon is attested by chapters devoted to his work in such standard histories as J. I. M. Stewart, *Eight Modern Writers* (Oxford: Clarendon, 1963), and *Modernism*, Malcolm Bradbury and James McFarlane (eds) (Harmondsworth: Penguin, 1976).

4 For a different interpretation of the significance of the publication date, see Ross C. Murfin, *Lord Jim: After the Truth* (New York: Twayne, 1992), p. 16. Linda K. Hughes and Michael Lund, *The Victorian Serial* (University Press of Virginia, 1991), p. 246, relate the "Victorian audience's diminishing enthusiasm" for the serial of *Lord Jim* in *Blackwood's Magazine* to the introduction of modern elements into this Victorian mode of narrative production.

5 See Franz Kuna, "The Janus-Faced Novel: Conrad, Musil, Kafka, Mann," in *Modernism*, Bradbury and McFarlane (eds), pp. 443–52.

6 Wiener, *Reconstructing the Criminal*, pp. 292–3.

7 Eloise Knapp Hay, "*Lord Jim*: From Sketch to Novel," *Comparative Literature*, 12 (1960), pp. 289–309; rpt. in *Lord Jim: A Norton Critical Edition*, Thomas C. Moser (ed.) (New York: Norton, 1968), pages 418–37 at p. 424n.

8 "Conrad on Crime: A Note in Admiration," *Juridical Review*, 40 (1928), p. 251.

9 Originally published in *Twixt Land and Sea* (1912), "The Secret Sharer" is reprinted in *The Portable Conrad*, Morton Dauwen Zabel (ed.) (New York: Viking, 1952), pp. 648–99. The quoted phrase is on p. 663.

10 Jocelyn Baines, *Joseph Conrad: A Critical Biography* (New York: McGraw-Hill, 1952), p. 356.

11 The fullest exploration of the *Jeddah* case, the character of A. P. Williams and the changes made by Conrad is Norman Sherry, *Conrad's Eastern World* (Cambridge University Press, 1966). See especially p. 59.

12 Ibid., p. 72.

13 Benita Parry, *Conrad and Imperialism* (London: Macmillan, 1983), p. 77.

14 See Ian Watt, *Conrad in the Nineteenth Century* (London: Chatto and Windus, 1980), 4. iv. a.

15 For a wide-ranging reading of the various discourses of affiliation (e.g., race, gender, profession) inscribed in this "elusive and elliptical rhetoric," see Christopher GoGwilt, "Lord Jim and the Invention of the West," *Conradiana*, 27 (1995), p. 49.

16 See Walter Benjamin, *Illuminations*, Hannah Arendt (ed.) (London: Collins, 1973).

17 Marxist-oriented critics have examined Marlow as a Benjaminite storyteller: see especially Mark Conroy, *Modernism and Authority* (Baltimore: Johns Hopkins University Press, 1985), pp. 88ff; Vincent P. Pecora, *Self and Form in Modern Narrative* (Baltimore: Johns Hopkins University Press, 1989), pp. 35–6.

18 For the importance of justice in forensic rhetoric, see Peter Dixon, *Rhetoric* (London: Methuen, 1971), p. 22.

19 See Dorothy van Ghent, "On *Lord Jim*," in *The English Novel: Form and Function* (New York: Rinehart, 1953), p. 237; rpt. in *Lord Jim: A Norton*

*Critical Edition*, pp. 383–4. Cf. Hay, p. 435: "Marlow was there to argue Jim's brief as both Prosecutor and defense attorney."

20 Fredric Jameson compares this scene with Mersault's recognition of his future narrator in *L'Etranger*: see *The Political Unconscious* (Ithaca: Cornell University Press, 1981), p. 224n.

21 Edward W. Said stresses the retrospectivity and discursiveness of Marlow's narration, describing it as "retrospective ruminations." See "Conrad and Nietzsche," in *Joseph Conrad: A Commemoration*, Norman Sherry (ed.) (London: Macmillan, 1976), p. 71.

22 Jacques Berthoud, *Joseph Conrad: The Major Phase* (Cambridge University Press, 1978), p. 66. Likewise, Daniel R. Schwarz argues that "reading *Lord Jim* involves the reader in . . . responding to different judgments of Jim's behaviour": see "Joseph Conrad," in *The Columbia History of the British Novel* (New York: Columbia University Press, 1994), p. 698. However, Schwarz proceeds to privilege the judgment of the omniscient narrator.

23 Berthoud, *Joseph Conrad*, pp. 78–9.

24 Douglas Hewitt, *Joseph Conrad: A Reassessment* (3rd edn.; Totowa: Rowman and Littlefield, 1975), p. 38.

25 Berthoud, *Joseph Conrad*, p. 79.

26 Van Ghent, rpt. *Lord Jim*, Moser (ed.), p. 384.

27 Only first-time readers would be possessed by a sense of mystery or suspense. For a discussion of the different responses likely on first and subsequent readings, see Albert J. Guerard, *Conrad the Novelist* (Cambridge: Harvard University Press, 1958), pp. 129ff; rpt. *Lord Jim*, Moser (ed.), pp. 394ff.

28 Van Ghent examines the similarity between *Lord Jim* and *The Oresteia* and *The Theban Plays*.

29 Goodrich, *Reading the Law* (Oxford: Blackwell, 1986), pp. 209–11.

30 Ibid., pp. 210ff.

31 Allen Boyer uses Conrad's treatment of cannibalism here as the basis for arguing that the novelist rejects defences of necessity in favour of a stance of moral absolutism. Unfortunately Boyer neglects to examine the function of Marlow's doubts and qualifications in the novel: see "Conrad, Cannibalism and *Lord Jim*," *Loyola of Los Angeles Law Review*, 20 (1986), pp. 9–34.

32 See Norman Sherry, *Conrad: The Critical Heritage* (London: Routledge and Kegan Paul, 1973), pp. 122–3 for the original statement of this criticism; and Jameson, *The Political Unconscious*, pp. 206–7; and Watt, *Conrad in the Nineteenth Century*, p. 308 for two modern expressions of this view.

33 See *Conrad's Letters to Blackwood and Meldrum*, William Blackburn (ed.) (Durham: Duke University Press, 1958), pp. 68–70. Blackburn notes that the "theme of both stories is the loss of honour."

34 Jameson categorizes the Patusan section as "a virtual paradigm of romance . . . [which] comes before us as the prototype of various 'degraded' subgenres such as the adventure story": Jameson, *Political Unconscious*, p. 207.

35 See Alexander Welsh, *Reflections on the Hero as Quixote* (Princeton University Press, 1981), chaps. II and III. Welsh refers only in passing to *Lord Jim*.

36 Avrom Fleishman, *Conrad's Politics: Community and Anarchy in the Fiction of Joseph Conrad* (Baltimore: Johns Hopkins University Press, 1967), p. 110, stresses the redemptive function of Jim's rediscovery of community, and links this to Conrad's organicist social philosophy.

37 Ibid., p. 108.

38 Berthoud, *Joseph Conrad*, p. 90.

39 D. G. Macrae, "Charisma," in *A Dictionary of the Social Sciences*, Julius Gould and William L. Kolb (eds) (London: Tavistock, 1964), p. 84.

40 This list of lawgivers from "the mythic beginnings of many national traditions" is derived from Theodore Ziolkowski, *German Romanticism and its Institutions* (Princeton University Press, 1990), p. 65.

41 George Feaver, *From Status to Contract* (London: Longmans, 1969), pp. 62ff.

42 Fleishman, *Conrad's Politics* (Baltimore: Johns Hopkins University Press, 1967), p. 108.

43 Quoted by R. H. Hickling, "The Borneo Territories," in *The British Commonwealth: The Development of its Laws*, vol. IX, *Malaya and Singapore; The Borneo Territories*, L. A. Sheridan (ed.) (London: Stevens, 1961), p. 118.

44 An extract from Conrad's letter to Lady Margaret Brooke, 15 June 1921, is quoted in Martin Green, *Dreams of Adventure, Deeds of Empire* (New York: Basic Books, 1979), p. 304. On Brooke as a source for Jim, see Watt, *Conrad in the Nineteenth Century*, pp. 267–8; and Sherry, *Conrad's Eastern World* (Cambridge University Press, 1966), p. 135.

45 Hickling, "The Borneo Territories," p. 117.

46 Lloyd Fernando, "Conrad's Eastern Expatriates: A New Version of the Outcast," *PMLA*, 91 (1976), p. 81.

47 Ibid., p. 82.

48 Martin Green, *Dreams of Adventure*, p. 1, argues that adventure stories expressed "the energizing myth of English imperialism."

49 Fernando, "Conrad's Eastern Expatriates," p. 80; and John McClure, *Kipling and Conrad* (Cambridge: Harvard University Press, 1981), especially chap. IV.

50 Parry, *Conrad and Imperialism*, pp. 87ff.

51 Daniel R. Schwarz, "Reading *Lord Jim*: Reading Texts, Reading Lives," in *The Transformation of the English Novel 1890–1930* (London: Macmillan, 1989), p. 229.

52 See Zdzislaw Najder's tripartite division of Conrad's attitude to "the breakdown of established moral codes": "Conrad in His Historical Perspective," *English Literature in Transition*, 14 (1971), pp. 157–66.

8 FREEDOM, UNCERTAINTY AND DIVERSITY –
THE CRITIQUE OF IMPERIALIST LAW IN *A PASSAGE TO INDIA*

1 Introduction to K. R. Srinivasa Iyengar, *Literature and Authorship in India* (1943), quoted by G. K. Das, *E. M. Forster's India* (London: Macmillan,

1977), p. 30. Forster's tribute to Lyall, "A Great Anglo-Indian," is reprinted in *Albergo Empedocle and Other Writings*, George H. Thomson (ed.) (New York: Liveright, 1971), pp. 211–15.

2 See "Minute on Indian Education" (1835), rpt. in Thomas Babington Macaulay, *Selected Writings*, John Clive and Thomas Pinney (eds) (University of Chicago Press, 1972), p. 241; and "Government of India," rpt. in *Thomas Babington Macaulay: Life and Works* (Edinburgh: Longmans, Green, 1904), vol. 8: p. 142.

3 See Edward W. Said, *Orientalism* (London: Routledge and Kegan Paul, 1978).

4 Oliver Stallybrass (ed.), *A Passage to India* (London: Penguin, 1979), p. 301. This text is a paperback reprint of the definitive Abinger Edition. All subsequent references are incorporated parenthetically in the body of the chapter.

5 "The Politics of Representation in *A Passage to India*," in *A Passage to India: Essays in Criticism*, John Beer (ed.) (London: Macmillan, 1985), esp. pp. 27 and 43.

6 Bhupal Singh, *A Survey of Anglo-Indian Fiction* (1934; rpt. London: Curzon, 1974), sections 49, 67, 71.

7 Leonard Woolf, *The Village in the Jungle* (1913; rpt. London: Hogarth Press, 1961), p. 204.

8 George Orwell, *Burmese Days* (1934; rpt. London: Secker and Warburg, 1955), p. 41.

9 Letter to *The Times*, 1 March 1883, quoted by Eric Stokes, *The English Utilitarians and India* (Oxford: Clarendon, 1959), p. 288; paraphrased by Benita Parry, *Delusions and Discoveries: Studies on India in the British Imagination 1880–1930* (London: Allen Lane, 1972), pp. 15ff. For an interesting literary-historical account of Stephen's Evidence Act (further discussed below) see Alexander Welsh, "The Evidence of Things Not Seen," *Representations*, 22 (1988), pp. 60–88.

10 Quoted by Stokes, *English Utilitarians*, p. 307.

11 Ibid., p. 313.

12 Quoted by Lipendra Baxi, "People's Law in India: The Hindu Society," in *Asian Indigenous Law*, Masabi Chiba (ed.) (London: KPI, 1986), pp. 216–66 at p. 224.

13 For Stephen see Stokes, *English Utilitarians*, p. 306; for Kipling, see Shamsul Islam, *Chronicles of the Raj* (London: Macmillan, 1979), p. 11.

14 Forster, *Two Cheers for Democracy* (1951; rpt. London: Edward Arnold, 1972), p. 66.

15 Forster, "What I Believe," p. 68.

16 Malcolm Bradbury, "Two Passages to India: Forster as Victorian and Modern," in *A Passage to India: A Casebook*, Malcolm Bradbury (ed.) (London: Macmillan, 1970), p. 230.

17 Alan Gledhill, *The British Commonwealth: The Development of its Laws and Constitutions: Volume Six: India*, 2nd edn. (London: Stevens, 1955), p. 211.

18 The quoted phrase is drawn from Baxi, "People's Law in India," p. 234: "Indian society is *multi-legal*, comprising congeries of non-State legal systems in dynamic interaction with the State legal system."

19 The series is reprinted in Forster, *Abinger Harvest* (1936; London: Edward Arnold, 1953): see p. 302.

20 Ibid., p. 309. This incident happened to a barrister whom Forster met through Syed Ross Masood, the dedicatee of *A Passage to India*, during 1910. The barrister's name, Mahmoud, was to be used in the novel.

21 Ibid., p. 305.

22 Gledhill, *India*, p. 211.

23 S. P. Sen, "Effects on India of British Law and Administration in the Nineteenth Century," *Journal of World History*, 4 (1958), p. 859.

24 J. W. Burrow, *Evolution and Society* (Cambridge University Press, 1966), p. 44.

25 Gledhill, *India*, pp. 218ff.

26 Quoted ibid.

27 P. N. Furbank, *E. M. Forster: A Life* (London: Secker and Warburg, 1978), II, p. 194.

28 Forster, *Abinger Harvest*, p. 62.

29 Burrow, *Evolution and Society*, p. 176.

30 See his *Liberty, Equality and Fraternity* (1873).

31 Stokes, *English Utilitarians*, p. xi.

32 Forster, *Abinger Harvest*, p. 63.

33 Ibid., p. 64 (Forster's italics).

34 *E. M. Forster: The Critical Heritage*, Philip Gardner (ed.) (London: Routledge and Kegan Paul, 1973), p. 211.

35 Ibid., p. 215.

36 Ibid., p. 245.

37 Ibid., pp. 271–2.

38 Ibid., p. 251.

39 Ibid., p. 252, also the source of the next two quotations.

40 Furbank, *Life*, II, p. 127 quotes from a letter to another Anglo-Indian complainant: "when you lay down that certain things can't happen I am reminded from experiences that they can. . . ." Furbank also recounts how Forster, worried by the legal details, sent the typescript to Masood. He replied, "'It is magnificent. Do not alter a word'" (p. 119).

41 Virginia Woolf, "The Novels of E. M. Forster," in *Collected Essays*, I (London: Hogarth Press, 1966), pp. 342–51; rpt. in Gardner, *Critical Heritage* p. 322.

42 Excerpted in Natwar-Singh's "Only Connect: E. M. Forster and India," *Focus on E. M. Forster's "A Passage to India"*; originally published in *Aspects of E. M. Forster* (London: Edward Arnold, 1969).

43 See G. K. Das, *E. M. Forster's India* (London: Macmillan, 1977) generally, and "*A Passage to India*: A Socio-historical Study," in Beer (ed.), *A Passage to India: Essays in Criticism*, pp. 4–8.

44 The quoted phrase is from Martin Price's account of Forster in *Forms of Life* (New Haven: Yale University Press, 1983), p. 297. Cf. Lionel Trilling's argument that the plot "brings to spectacular virulence the latent antagonisms" between the races: *E. M. Forster* (1943; Oxford University Press, 1982), p. 112.

45 On this point see Brenda R. Silver, "Periphrasis, Power, and Rape in *A Passage to India*," *Novel*, 22 (1988), pp. 86–105. Silver rejects the argument that rape symbolizes the colonial experience, quoting Salman Rushdie: "if a rape must be used as the metaphor of Indo-British connection, then surely in the interests of accuracy it should be the rape of an Indian woman by one or more Englishmen" (p. 88).

46 Edwin Thumboo, "*A Passage to India*: From Caves to Court," *Southern Review [Australia]*, 10 (1977), pp. 131ff. For a Jungian analysis of the significance of the caves, see Wilfred Stone, "The Caves of *A Passage to India*," in Beer (ed.), *Passage: Essays in Criticism*, pp. 16–26.

47 Gillian Beer, "Negation in *A Passage to India*," in Beer (ed.), *Passage: Essays in Criticism*, p. 56.

48 Barbara Harlow, "Law and Order in *A Passage to India*," in *A Passage to India*, ed. Tony Davies and Nigel Wood (Buckingham: Open University Press, 1994), pp. 65–89, undervalues these outcomes in interpreting the withdrawal of the charge as a containment strategy, politically and narratively.

49 See note 23 above.

50 Jenny Sharpe, *Allegories of Empire: The Figure of Woman in the Colonial Context* (Minneapolis: University of Minnesota Press, 1993), pp. 121, 133 (italics in original).

51 See E. M. Forster, *Aspects of the Novel* (London: Arnold, 1949), p. 132.

52 Letter of 26 June 1924, quoted by Furbank, *Life*, II, pp. 124–5.

53 Sara Suleri, "The Geography of *A Passage to India*," in *E. M. Forster: Modern Critical Views*, Harold Bloom (ed.) (New York: Chelsea House, 1987), p. 170.

54 John Beer, "*A Passage to India*, the French New Novel and English Romanticism," in Beer (ed.), *Passage: Essays in Criticism*, p. 123.

55 Quoted in Beer, *Passage: Essays in Criticism*, p. 123.

56 Welsh, "Evidence of Things Not Seen," *Representations*, 22 (1988), p. 64.

57 I have drawn this summary from Gledhill, *India*, p. 242.

58 See Parry, *Delusions and Discoveries*, p. 293.

59 Excerpted in Gardner, *Critical Heritage*, pp. 287–8. Cf. Roger Fry's wish that Forster had left the mysticism out of the novel: see ibid., p. 296. See also Trilling, *E. M. Forster*, p. 120: "it is not easy to know what to make of the Hindu section."

60 Victor Turner, "Social Dramas and Stories about Them," in *On Narrative*, W. J. T. Mitchell (ed.) (University of Chicago Press, 1981), p. 158.

61 Isaiah 66:24; cf. Mark 9:44.

62 Turner, "Social Dramas," p. 163, quoting *Webster's Dictionary*.

63 Said, *Orientalism* (London: Routledge and Kegan Paul, 1978), p. 244, misreads the "disappointing conclusion" as evoking a state of "permanent estrangement" between India and the West. Rustom Baruccha reminds us that Aziz and Fielding have reconciled, which suggests that the estrangement is temporary: "Forster's Friends," in Bloom (ed.), *Forster: Modern Critical Views*, pp. 164ff.

64 Quoted by Kelley, *The Human Measure*, p. ix.

65 Forster, *Aspects of the Novel* (London: Edward Arnold, 1949), p. 158.

## 9 SETTLING OUT OF COURT

1 Anthony Trollope, *Phineas Redux* (1873; rpt. London: Oxford University Press, 1983), II, 194–5.

2 See McMaster, *Trollope and the Law* (London: Macmillan, 1986), p. 58.

3 Sir Frederick Pollock, "Oxford Law Studies," in his *Oxford Lectures* (1890; rpt. Buffalo: Wm. S. Hein, 1970), p. 111.

4 Learned Hand, "Mr. Justice Cardozo," quoted in *Quote It! Memorable Legal Quotations*, ed. Eugene C. Gerhart (New York: Clark Boardman, 1969), p. 191.

5 Francis Cowper, "Legal London," in *Quote It! Memorable Legal Quotations*, ed. Gerhart. This quotation is undated, however, Cowper was active as a law reporter during the 1950s.

6 Frank Kermode, "The Novel *circa* 1907," in his *Essays on Fiction 1971–82* (London: Routledge and Kegan Paul, 1983), pp. 45–6.

7 Ford Madox Ford, *The Marsden Case* (London: Duckworth, 1923), p. 169.

8 Ibid., p. 284.

9 Ibid., p. 248.

10 Henry James, Preface to the New York edition of *The Portrait of a Lady* (1908; rpt. New York: Norton, 1975), p. 7.

11 Salman Rushdie, *Midnight's Children* (1981; rpt. London: Pan, 1982), pp. 375–6.

# Index